IMAGES
of America

KEENELAND RACE COURSE

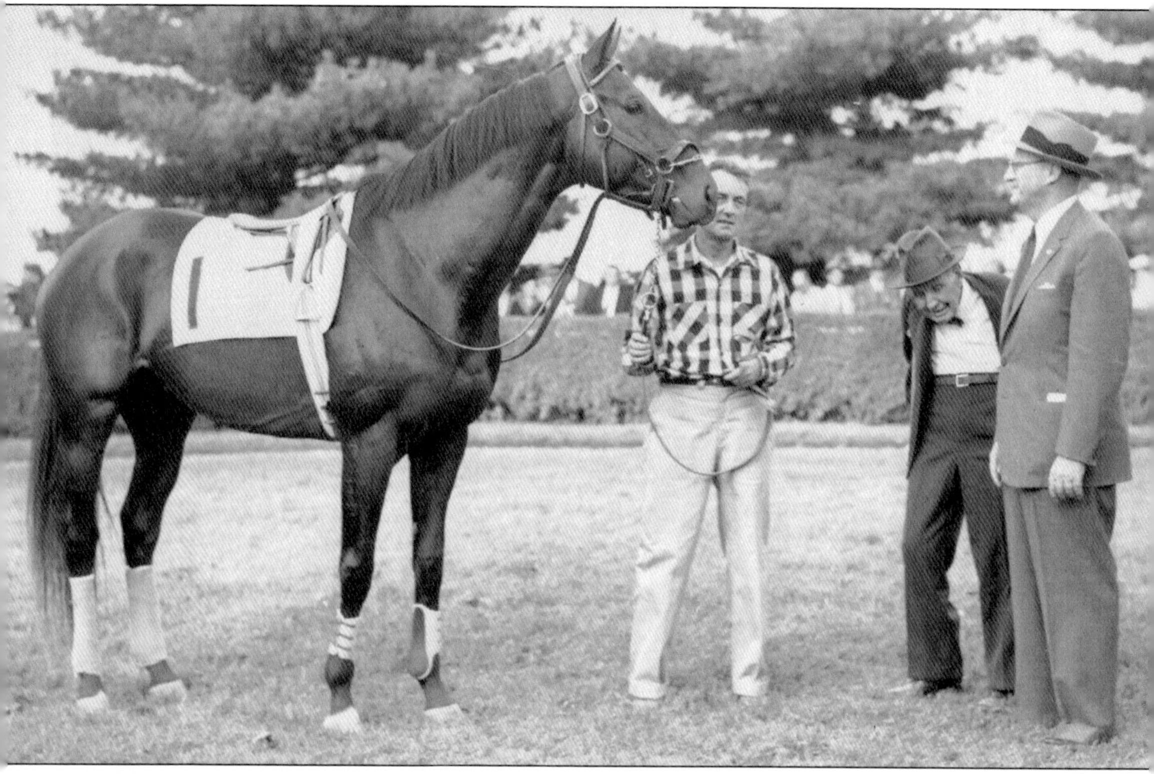

Nashua at Keeneland. In October 1956, Nashua galloped at Keeneland in his last public appearance before retiring to stud at Spendthrift Farm. Nashua was the first Thoroughbred to win more than $1 million and the first to sell for more than $1 million when he was purchased by a syndicate headed by Leslie Combs II in late 1955. Shown here from left to right are Nashua, his groom Al Robertson, trainer "Sunny Jim" Fitzsimmons, and Combs. (Courtesy of the Keeneland Library.)

On the Cover: Patrons got a close look at the horses and jockeys on display during the post parade before the 1951 Thoroughbred Club Dinner Purse race at Keeneland Race Course in Lexington, Kentucky. The complete photograph, along with more information, is on pages 92 and 93. (Courtesy of the Keeneland Library.)

IMAGES
of America

KEENELAND RACE COURSE

Berkeley and Jeanine Scott

ARCADIA
PUBLISHING

ISBN 978-0-7385-8874-2

Published by Arcadia Publishing
Charleston, South Carolina

Printed in the United States of America

Library of Congress Control Number: 2011938981

For all general information, please contact Arcadia Publishing:
Telephone 843-853-2070
Fax 843-853-0044
E-mail sales@arcadiapublishing.com
For customer service and orders:
Toll-Free 1-888-313-2665

Visit us on the Internet at www.arcadiapublishing.com

We dedicate this book, like all our other books, to our wonderful family: sons Sean and Robert, daughter-in-law Rebecca, and grandchildren Noah and Alison.

Contents

Foreword

When the Kentucky Association racetrack closed in 1933, Lexington was without a track for the first time in more than 100 years. To many, that simply was not acceptable in a community that had become so firmly associated with Thoroughbred racing.

Keeneland Race Course opened in 1936 after a group of bold horsemen and community leaders bought Jack Keene's unfinished training track and 147.5 acres a year earlier. But these men didn't plan to build just any track; they had a vision of showcasing racing at its highest level while giving back to the industry and community. It was an audacious vision during the Great Depression.

After 75 years, Keeneland remains true to its founders' vision. Our race meets each spring and fall feature some of the best jockeys, trainers, and Thoroughbreds in the world. Four times a year, we host Thoroughbred auctions that attract buyers from all 50 states and dozens of countries.

Keeneland continues to give back to the industry and the community. We strive to be a leader in innovations that ensure the safety of our human and equine athletes and enhance the fan experience. We take pride in the contributions we have made over the years to dozens of charitable organizations in central Kentucky.

I confess that one of my favorite things to do at Keeneland is peruse old photographs and memorabilia. On many occasions, I have gone to the library to research something in particular, only to look up at the clock and realize I have lost hours wandering through Keeneland's storied past.

I was thrilled to see the collection of photographs chosen for this book, many of which were new to me and our librarians. It is like dusting off the old photograph albums in the attic and taking a journey back to yesteryear. It is fun to look at the different hairstyles, clothes, and cars, as well as fascinating to see how the facility has grown over the years, yet in so many ways has stayed the same.

Keeneland is excited to share its history and photographs. I hope you enjoy your journey back in time as much as I did.

—Nick Nicholson
President and CEO of Keeneland Association

INTRODUCTION

As a landmark, an icon, or industry leader, Keeneland is relatively young. Beginning in 1935, after the century-old Kentucky Association track closed in Lexington two years earlier, a group of Blue Grass sportsmen came together to build a "model racecourse." Since October 15, 1936, when the first race was run, Keeneland has served the Thoroughbred industry, indeed the entire sporting world, as that model for others to strive to equal.

In the years since opening day, many of the sport's most famous horses, jockeys, trainers, and owners have walked on the grounds at Keeneland, a place where so many dreams were found and lost. European royalty, sheiks, industry leaders, and Hollywood stars have all stood in the Kentucky afternoon sun and squinted to see if their favorite won the race. Thousands more race fans and hardworking track workers have cheered and moaned at the results of races run in cold and heat, sunshine, rain, and the occasional snowfall.

As the years passed by, the beautiful trees in the paddock grew larger and grander and so did the reputation and heritage that is so unique to Keeneland. The foundation for that growth took place during the track's first quarter century, beginning in 1935, which is covered by this book.

Fortunately, the people who created the dream of a "model racecourse" had the wisdom to record all of the hard work and exciting times of those first 25 years and of the many years since in photographic scrapbooks preserved at the Keeneland Library. Thousands of photographs taken by a succession of amateur and professional photographers fill extra-large, leather-bound volumes that are carefully preserved.

Those scrapbooks cover almost every aspect of life at Keeneland: from the exercise riders, grooms, trainers, vets, and blacksmiths who care for the horses on the back side to the front side's management, track employees, race patrons, and jockeys.

But first and foremost, the scrapbooks include hundreds of photographs of horses. There are lots of race photographs from start to finish, and in chapter four photographs are used to show the jockey's race day from the controlled chaos of the jock's room before a race to the final weigh-out after the race. Images of some of the most well-known Thoroughbreds that raced from 1935 to 1961—such as Round Table, Whirlaway, Nashua, Bull Lea, and Iron Leige—are featured in this book. Also included are photographs of the less well-known horses that made up the bulk of the approximately 20,000 horses that raced at Keeneland during its first 25 years.

After looking at hundreds of pages of photographs, most accompanied by identifying information, we chose the 182 images in this book. It was a difficult choice and, of course, we could not include every horse or every notable personage, but we hope readers will get a feel for the timeless values that Keeneland stands for and the unique personality of the place.

We were also given the opportunity to look at some of the other treasures at the Keeneland Library. Some of the photographs in the final chapter of the book on the Keeneland Library come from a few of the outstanding photographic collections the library holds. This allowed us to include photographs of Thoroughbred racing stars that never raced at Keeneland, like Man o'War, Citation, and Seabiscuit.

The Keeneland Library contains the horse-racing world's largest collection of information about the Thoroughbred industry and North American racing. The partnership between the Keeneland

Association, the University of Kentucky, and the *Daily Racing Form*, to preserve and index the more than 100-year-old archive of the *Racing Form* and to make it available to all researchers, ensures the Keeneland Library's position at the top of the Thoroughbred researcher's world for the foreseeable future.

Our personal experience with Keeneland goes back nearly 35 years, when we first enjoyed a glorious spring day at the clubhouse and watched magnificent Thoroughbreds in the picturesque paddock and track. We both worked in the Thoroughbred industry and spent hours at races and at the sales, and we still came back and spent more of our own time relaxing and socializing there with friends and family. It was always a special place to us.

But, now that we have learned more about the earliest years of the track and the men and women who fulfilled a dream to build a unique racecourse, creating a heritage that seems destined to last for a very, very long time, we are enjoying the Keeneland experience even more.

Acknowledgments

We would like to especially thank Nick Nicholson, the president and CEO of Keeneland Association, for his support and assistance in this project. We also want to thank the wonderful staff of the Keeneland Library, led by library director Becky Ryder and longtime librarian Cathy Schenck. Without their cheerful assistance, fact-checking, and suggestions, this book would have been much more difficult to do and less accurate. That being said, any errors and opinions in this book are entirely that of the authors. The Keeneland founders and countless people since have backed a real winner when they built and carefully tended the ideal Thoroughbred racecourse in the heart of the Bluegrass country of Kentucky. We hope all of our readers will learn a little more about the tradition and heritage that is part of that experience from our book and will take the time to learn more from other sources, but most importantly, we hope people will take the time to visit and enjoy the Keeneland experience firsthand.

All the images included in this book are from the Keeneland Library Collection.

Other Arcadia Books by the Authors

Bourbon County: 1860–1940
Paris and Bourbon County
The Kentucky Bourbon Trail

One

Off to the Races

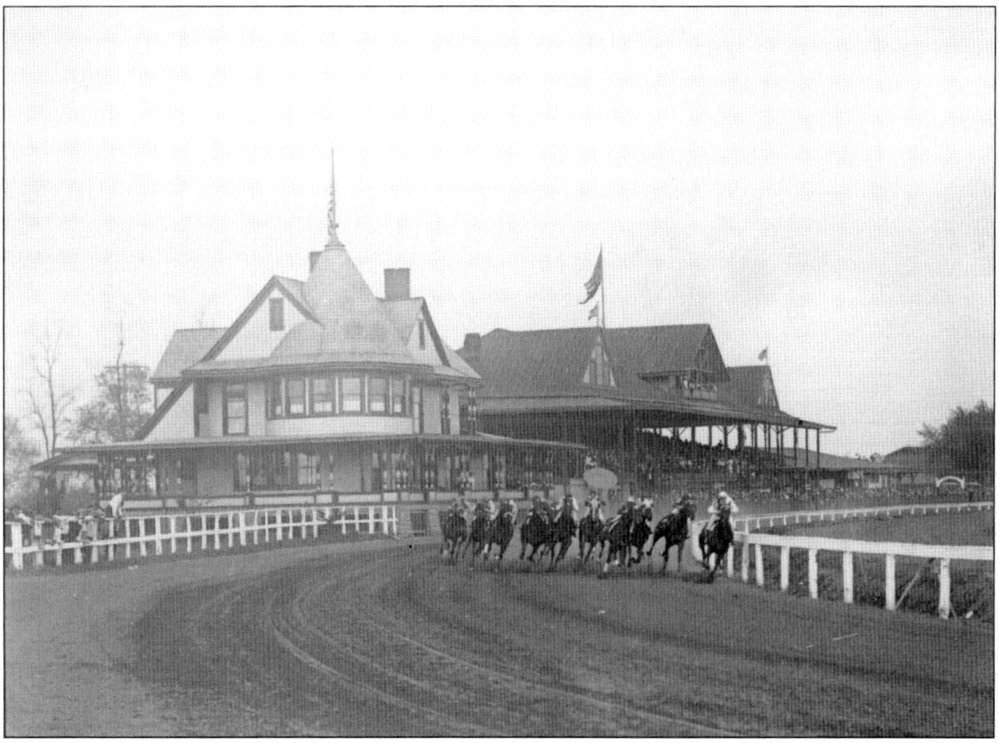

Kentucky Association Track, 1920. Keeneland has roots deep in Kentucky history. In 1826, fifty prominent horsemen, including statesman Henry Clay, formed the Kentucky Association for Improvement of the Breed of Horses, known simply as the Kentucky Association. The group built a one-mile track on the east end of Lexington, Kentucky. The track enjoyed off-and-on success for more than a century until it closed during the midst of the Depression in 1933.

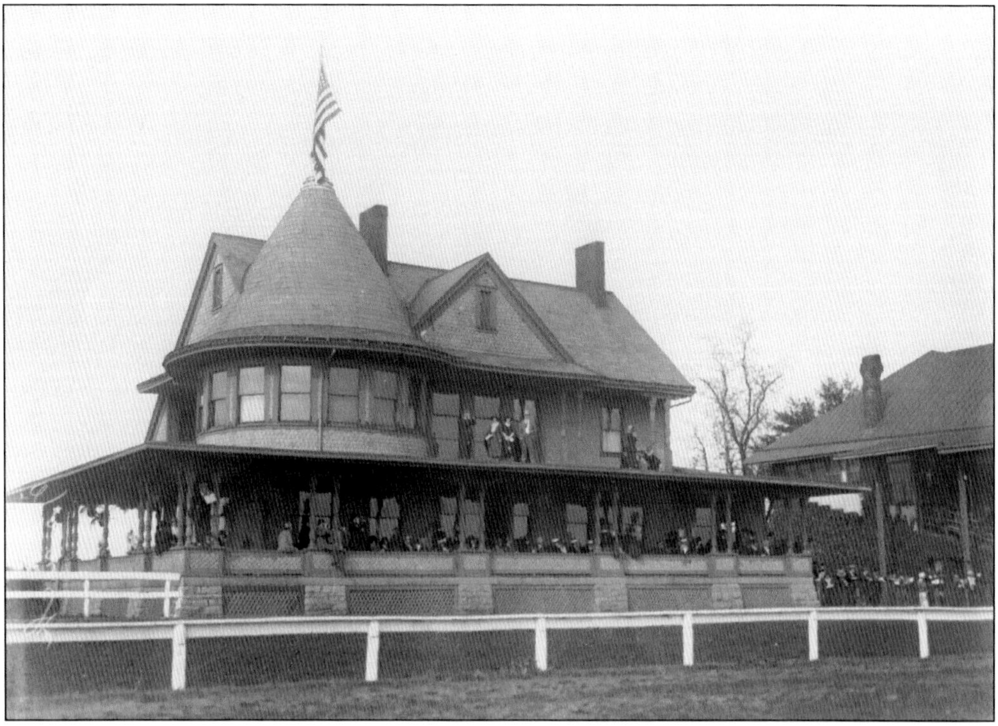

Kentucky Association Clubhouse. For more than 100 years, the Kentucky Association conducted some of the most spirited races among Thoroughbred breeders and owners. The clubhouse, pictured here, was built in the 1870s and was host to many champagne parties and dinners after major stakes races. The Phoenix Hotel Stakes was first raced here in 1831, is still run at Keeneland, and is considered the oldest stakes race in America.

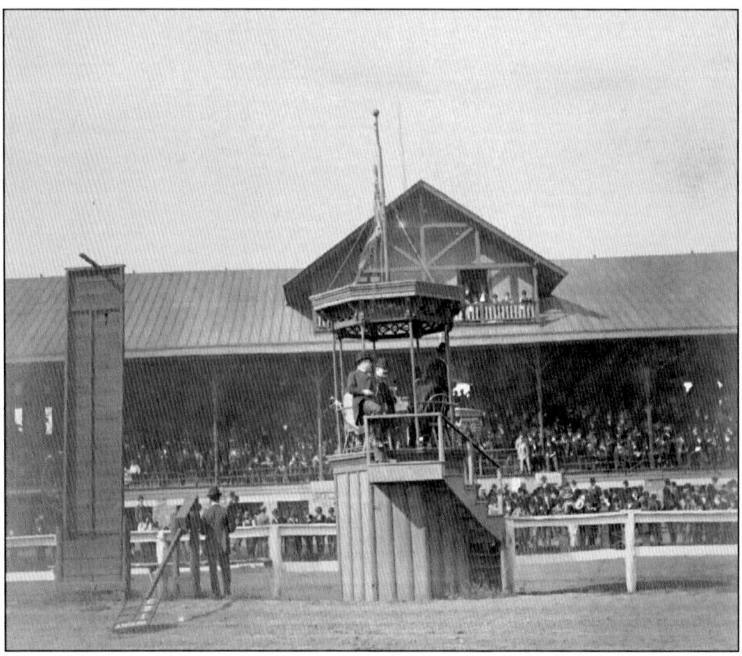

First-Class Racing. Seen in this early photograph is the octagonal race judges' stand, located at the finish line, and the wooden grandstand, both completed in 1872. The Kentucky Association track's most memorable race was in 1876 when Price McGrath's Aristides, the previous year's winner of the first Kentucky Derby, defeated Richard Harper's magnificent Ten Broeck in a two-horse race.

"Jack" Keene. John Oliver Keene was an international Thoroughbred trainer who spent years in Czarist Russia and Japan before returning to his family farm near Lexington. Keene dreamed of having a private track where he could entertain and race his horses against friends' stables. He built a track and a combination clubhouse/barn/home out of local limestone, but the Great Depression stopped his project. He offered his facility and 148 acres to a group of horsemen and businessmen looking for a location for a new racetrack.

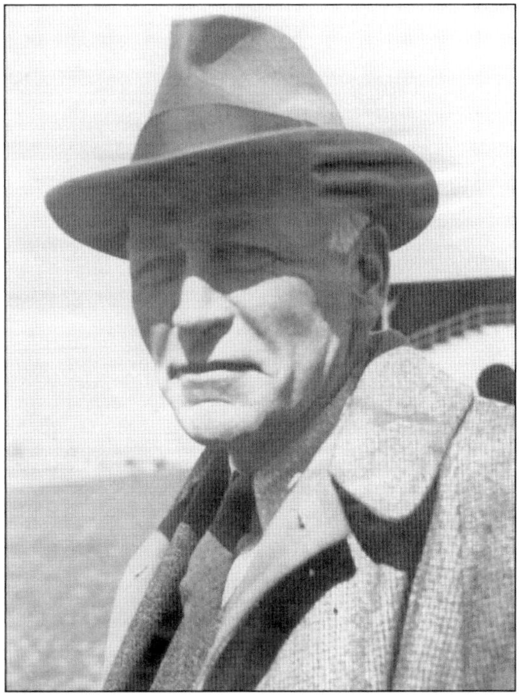

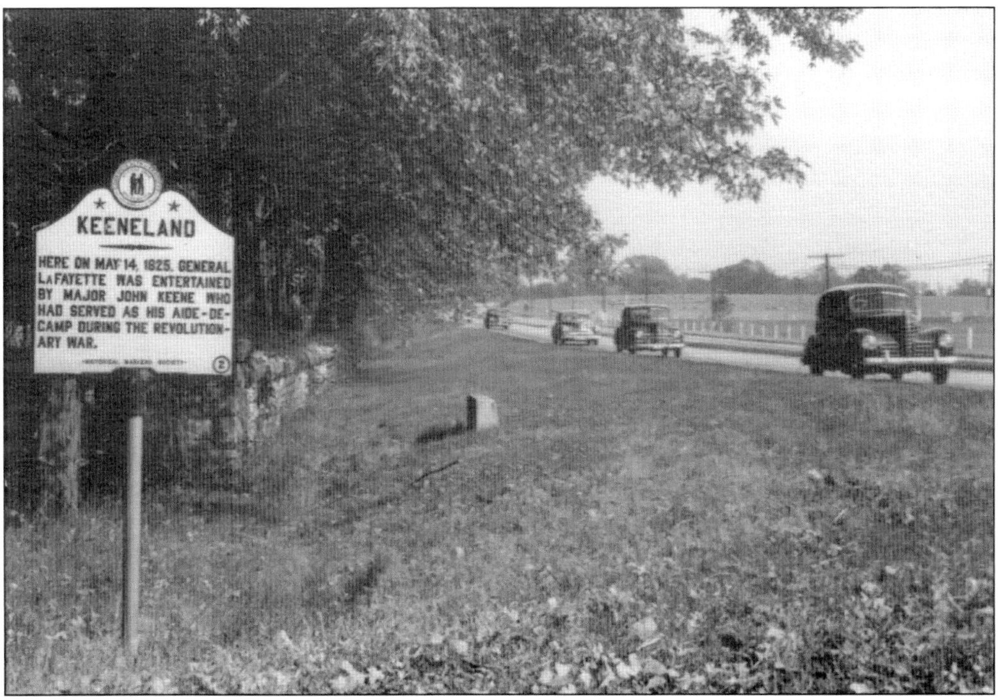

Lafayette Slept Here. The Keene family was prominent in the Lexington area since the late 1700s when Francis Keen arrived from Virginia with a land grant and an appetite for owning part of the Bluegrass countryside. The Marquis de Lafayette was a houseguest in 1825, visiting John Keene and family. Keene had not served as his aide, as the Versailles Road historical marker incorrectly states in this 1948 photograph, but his father-in-law had.

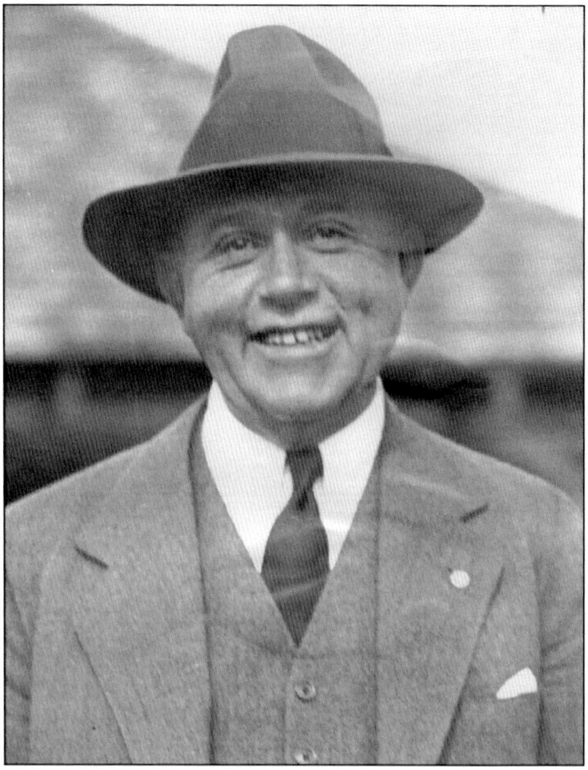

Hal Price Headley. The 107-year-old Kentucky Association's gates were not even closed before local horsemen like Hal Price Headley (pictured) and Louie A. Beard were seeking investors for a new racetrack organized to promote the sport and the community, not provide profits for the founders. As the owner of the 2,500-acre Beaumont Farm, Headley was one of the century's most successful Thoroughbred horsemen. He was elected as the Keeneland Association's first president.

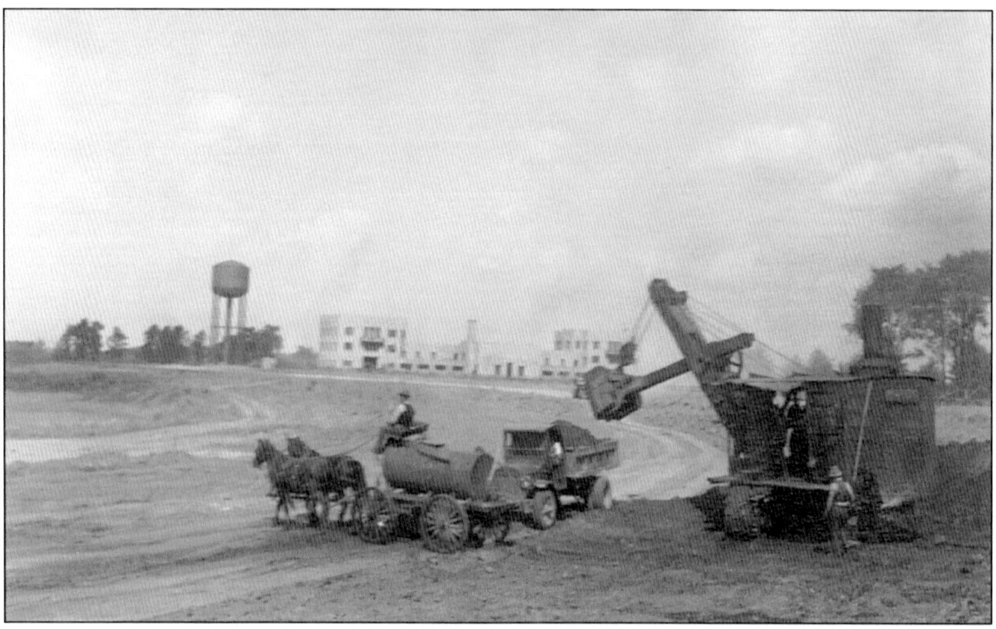

Steam Shovels and Borrowed Mules. Hal Price Headley loaned some of his Beaumont Farm's mules for the construction and track renovation that began in 1935, immediately after the purchase of the Keeneland property. Headley was the association's first president and provided tireless leadership for years. In 1962, he died at age 74 while supervising the training of his horses at Keeneland.

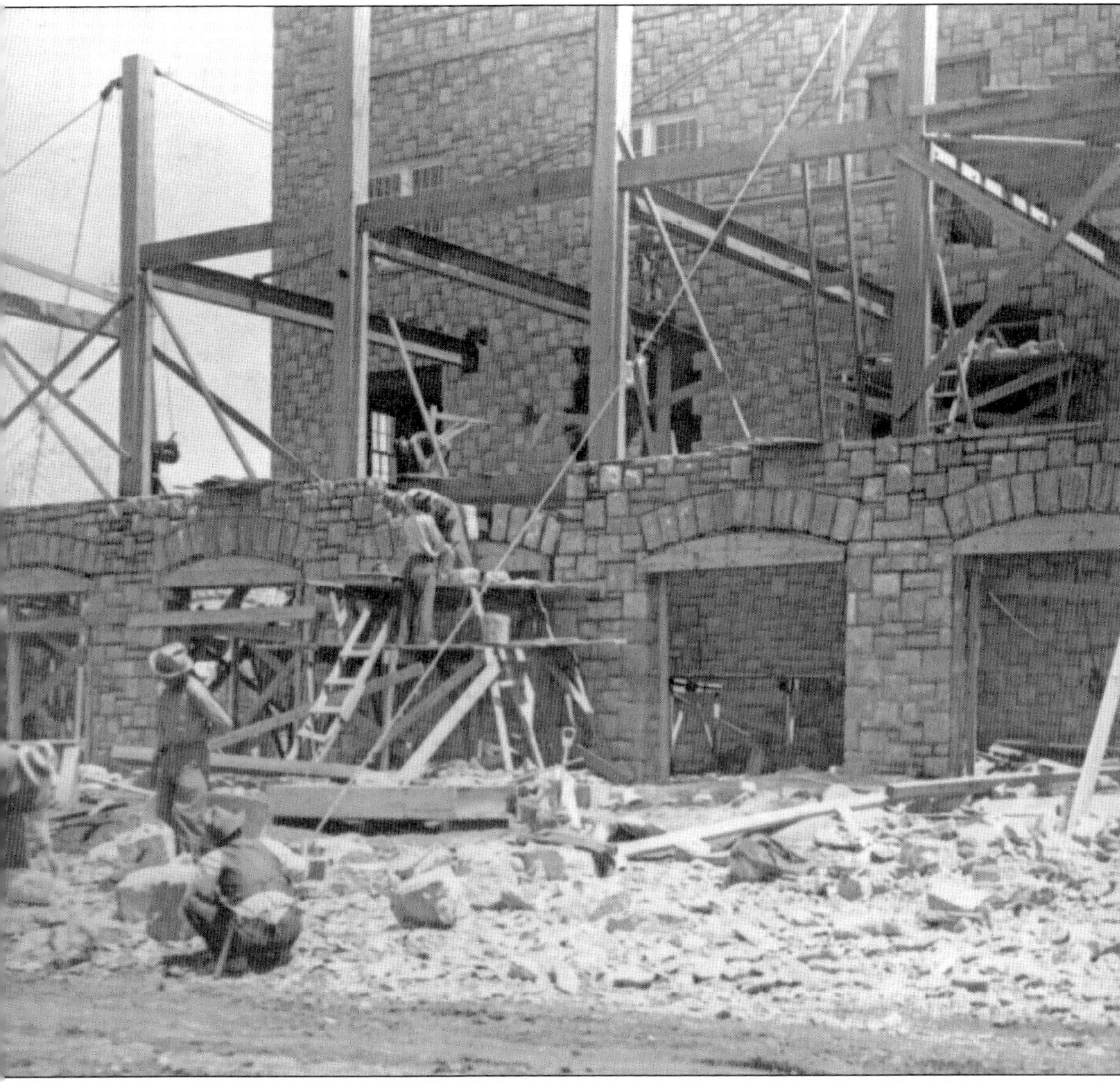

Tradition Built of Stone. From the very beginning, Keeneland's creators followed Jack Keene's practice of building with stone. Local limestone was hand cut and laid in a unique two-to-two design that Keene had begun on his original clubhouse and barns. That pattern continues to be used to this day on all new buildings and additions in the racetrack area. In this 1935 photograph, the steel framework for the clubhouse grandstand is being added. Keene must have felt some bittersweet satisfaction that the racetrack he envisioned would be constructed—but not by him. He initially had living quarters on the top floor of the clubhouse, but eventually he built elsewhere on a part of the farm he retained. Jack Keene died of a heart attack in 1943 after watching his horses work at the Fair Grounds racetrack in Detroit.

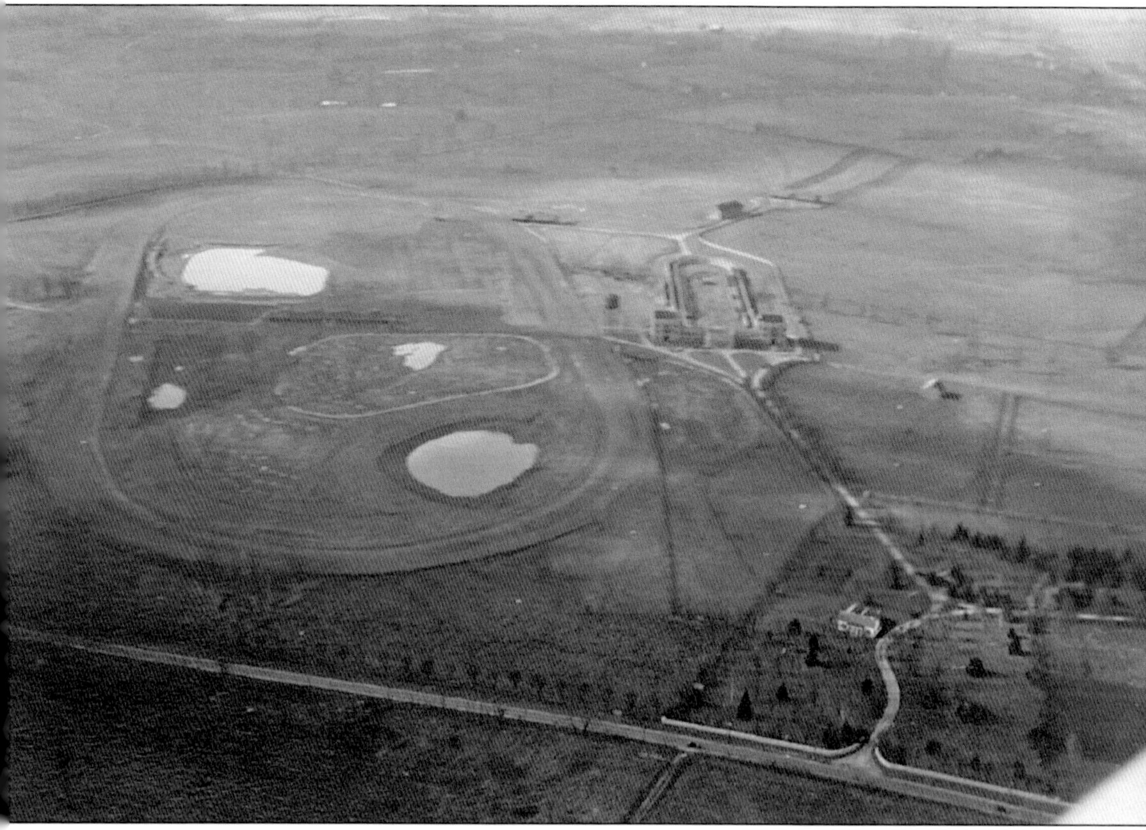

AERIAL PHOTOGRAPH, 1935. This 1935 image of Keene Stud was taken before it was transformed into Keeneland Race Course. The Keene mansion is seen in the lower right corner with its entrance off of the two-lane Versailles Road. The *N*-shaped structure at the top right is Jack Keene's stone stables with an indoor training track, anchored by two massive structures that served as his clubhouse/barn/home. The 100,000-gallon water tower sits between what would become the Keeneland Clubhouse and the rough one-and-one-eighth-mile track Keene had laid out. The ponds in the infield were filled in after the opening meet because of the sun's reflection into the crowd's eyes. It took more than 13 months to complete the changes needed to polish Keene's rough-cut diamond.

Plenty of Water. Keene built this 100,000-gallon water tower, which was supplied by a "never fail" spring between the racetrack and clubhouse/barn. It was moved to the barn area before the track's opening day. Notice the mule-drawn water wagon.

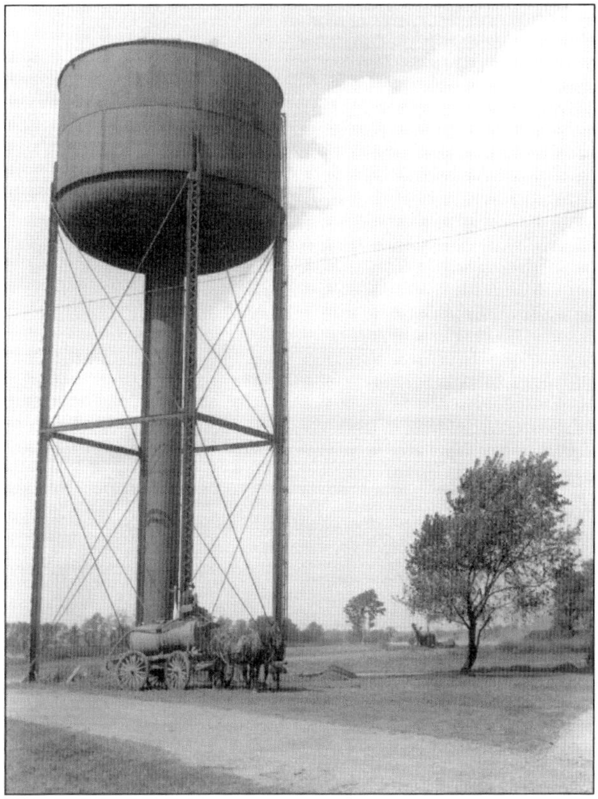

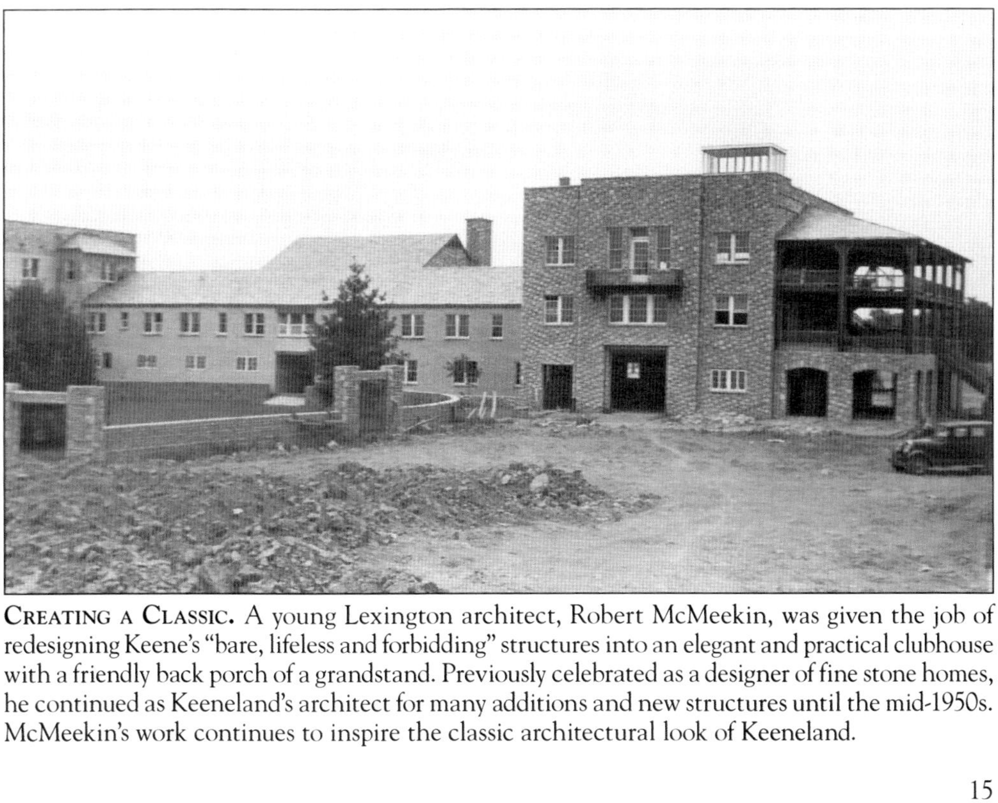

Creating a Classic. A young Lexington architect, Robert McMeekin, was given the job of redesigning Keene's "bare, lifeless and forbidding" structures into an elegant and practical clubhouse with a friendly back porch of a grandstand. Previously celebrated as a designer of fine stone homes, he continued as Keeneland's architect for many additions and new structures until the mid-1950s. McMeekin's work continues to inspire the classic architectural look of Keeneland.

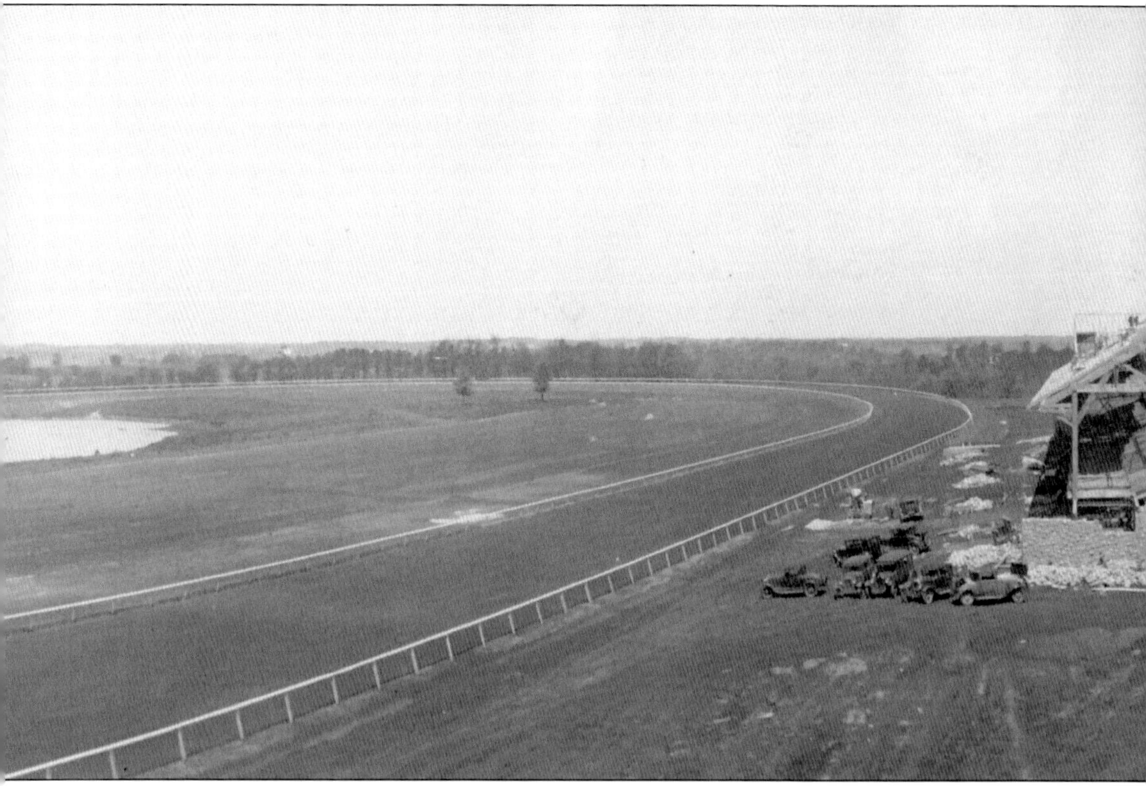

DESTRUCTION AND CONSTRUCTION. While some workmen busily worked to construct the new grandstand (center), others are tearing down the interior walls of the quarter-mile indoor training track Jack Keene had begun to build before running out of money a few years earlier. Keene had seen the combination stable/exercise tracks in Russia when he trained there in the early 1900s. The outside stone walls were cut down to chest height, and the interior walls of the unfinished

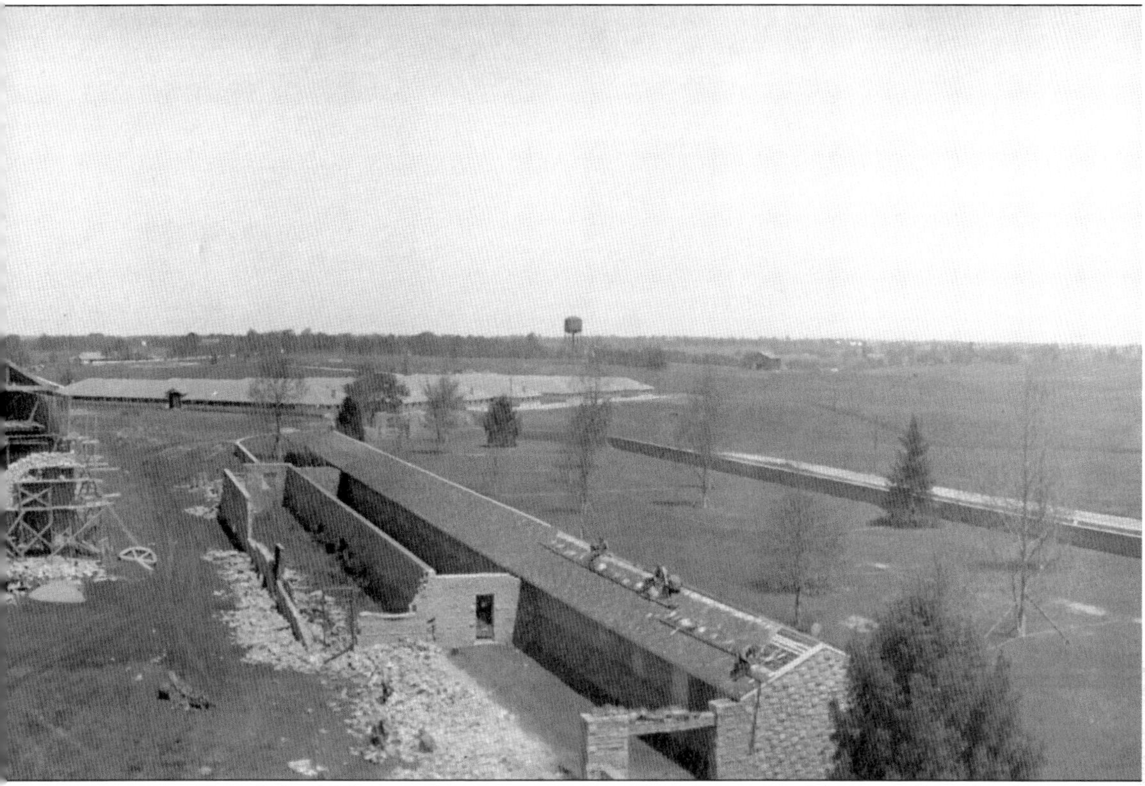

structure were demolished. The inside space was planted with trees and became Keeneland's beautiful paddock area. The original schedule had the new track opening in April 1936, but despite working 12 hours every day except Thanksgiving and Christmas, it became clear they would have to delay until October.

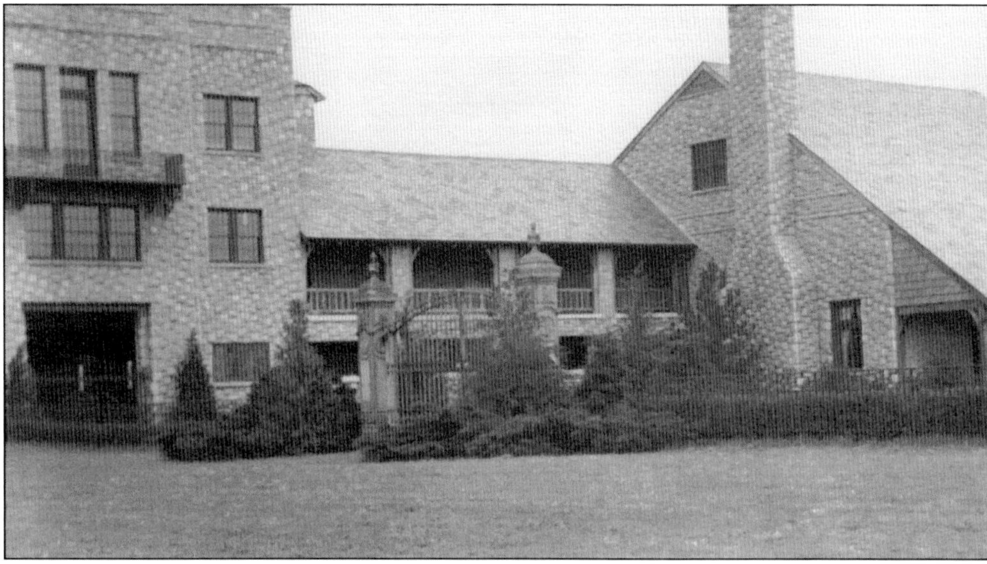

Redesigned Clubhouse. This photograph, taken in 1937, shows the clubhouse from the south-side parking lot. The rapidly growing plantings and stone architecture had already imbued a sense of age and stability to the building.

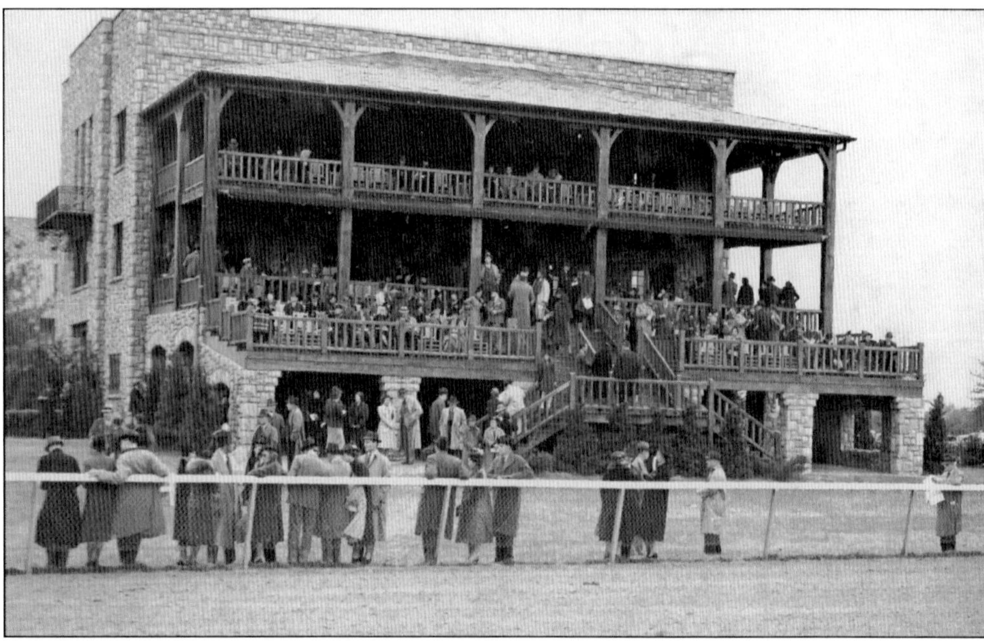

Clubhouse Porch. Blustery fall weather brought out the winter coats later during the inaugural meet in 1936. The Keeneland Clubhouse is different from other racetracks in that it is situated at the top of the stretch rather than the finish line. The location was Keene's original idea. He wanted to have a place for himself and his friends to watch their horses work each morning.

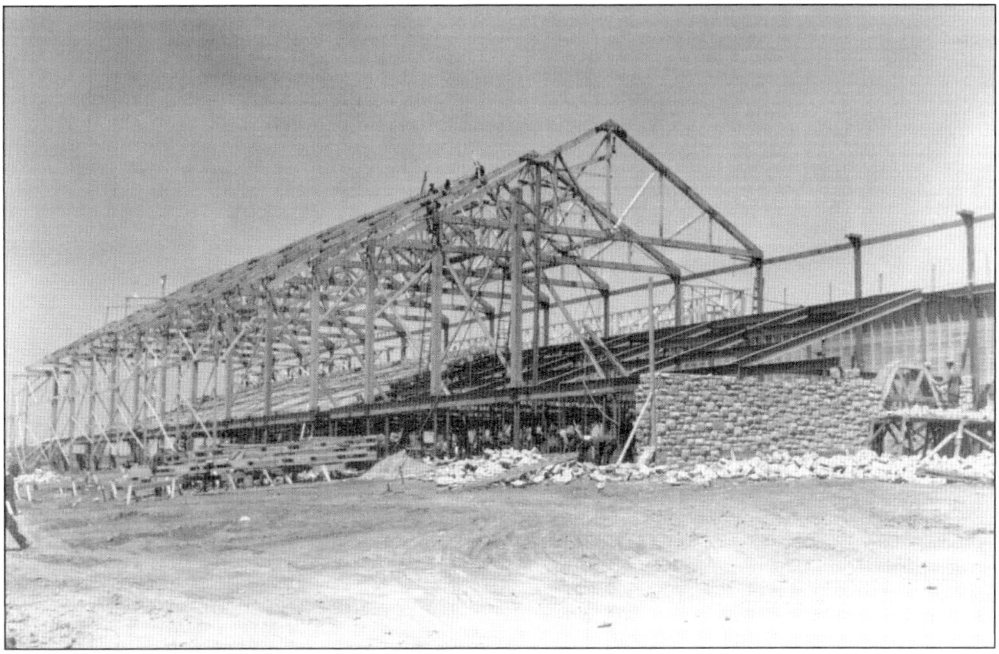

Keeneland Grandstand. Some 250 feet north of the clubhouse, a large grandstand designed by Robert McMeekin was built of steel and stone. The track's founders knew they needed to fill those seats to make Keeneland a success. The original grandstand was expanded several times.

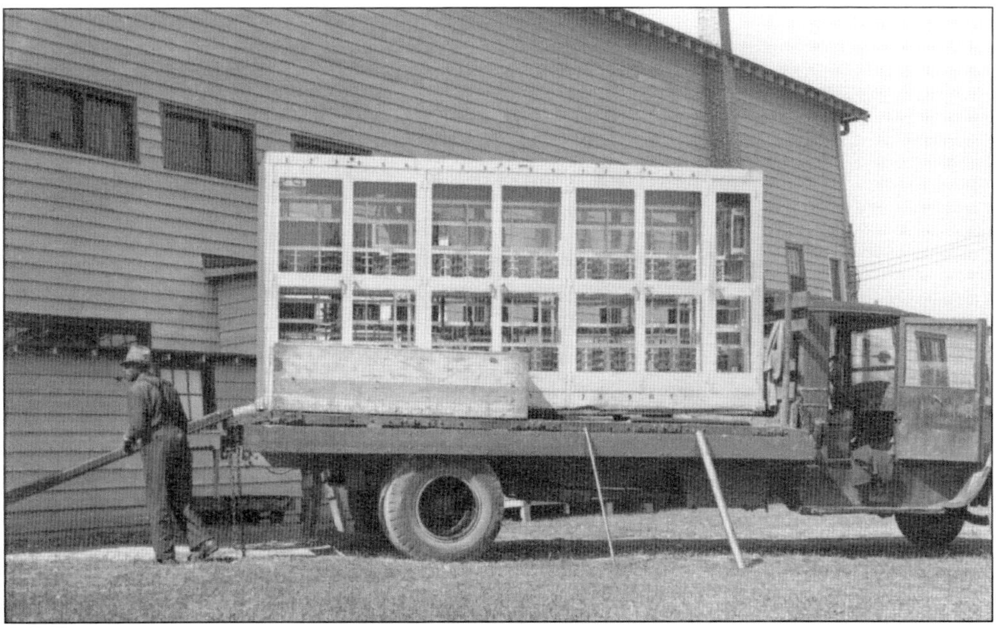

First in Kentucky. Four days before Keeneland opened for the first race, more than 15,000 curious fans showed up to see the new track and familiarize themselves with the huge totalizator board in the infield. The tote board, the very first in Kentucky, showed the post positions, odds, results, and payoffs. This information was compiled nearly instantly by an electronic, pre-computer network, which connected all the betting windows.

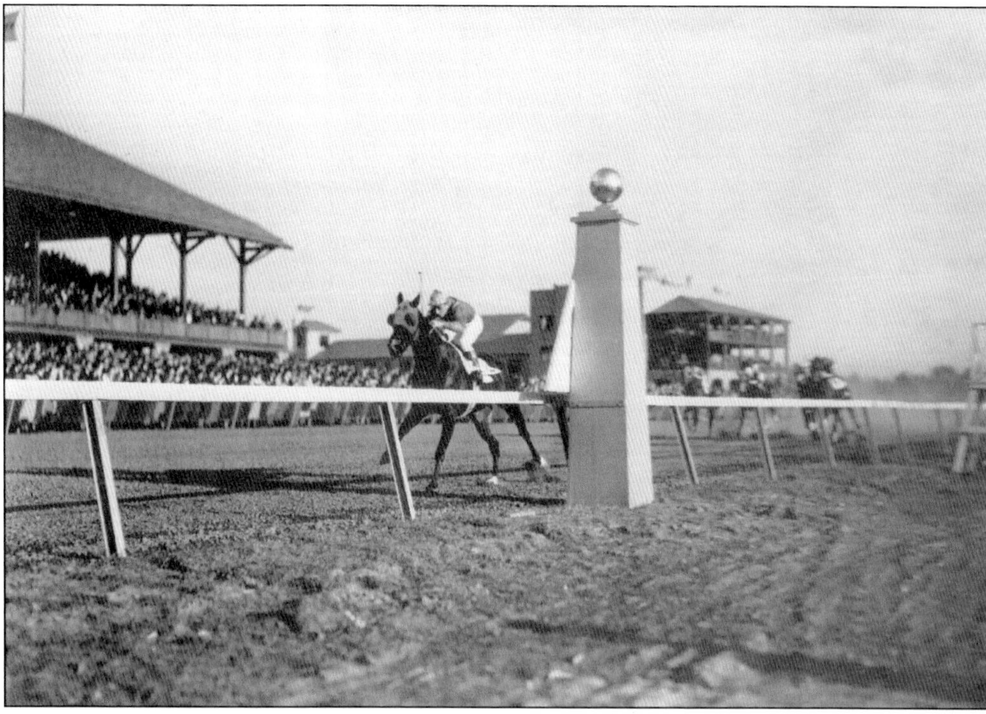

First Finish. The first winner at Keeneland on October 15, 1936, was Royal Raiment, a two-year-old gray filly by Royal Minstrel out of Brocado. She was ridden by John Gilbert, trained by J.W. Healy, and owned by John Hay Whitney. Since this race, horses have run approximately 20,000 races at Keeneland through 1961.

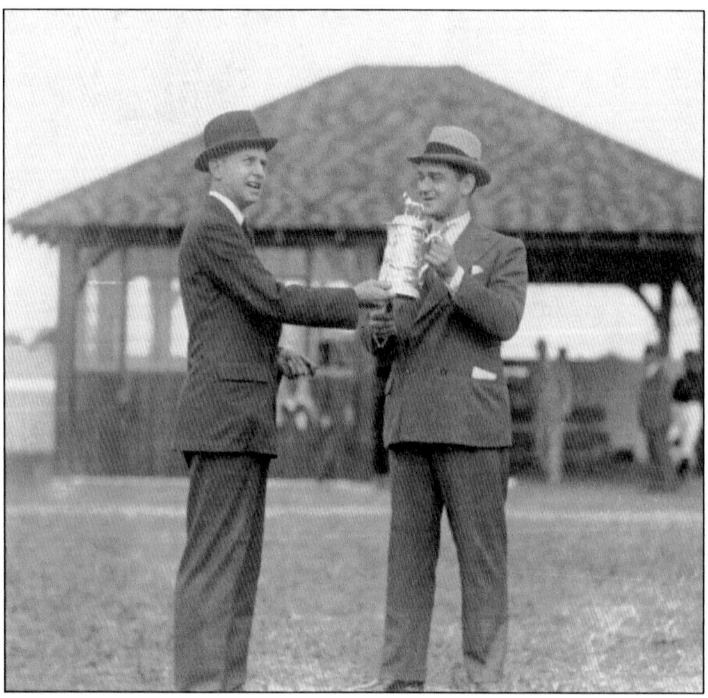

Trophy for Being First. John Hay "Jock" Whitney (right) would accomplish much more in life, but he looks very pleased to accept the fine silver trophy for owning the first winner at Keeneland from Kentucky lieutenant governor Keen Johnson. As an intelligence officer in the Office of Strategic Services during World War II, Whitney was taken prisoner by the Germans in southern France but escaped when the train transporting him to prison came under Allied fire.

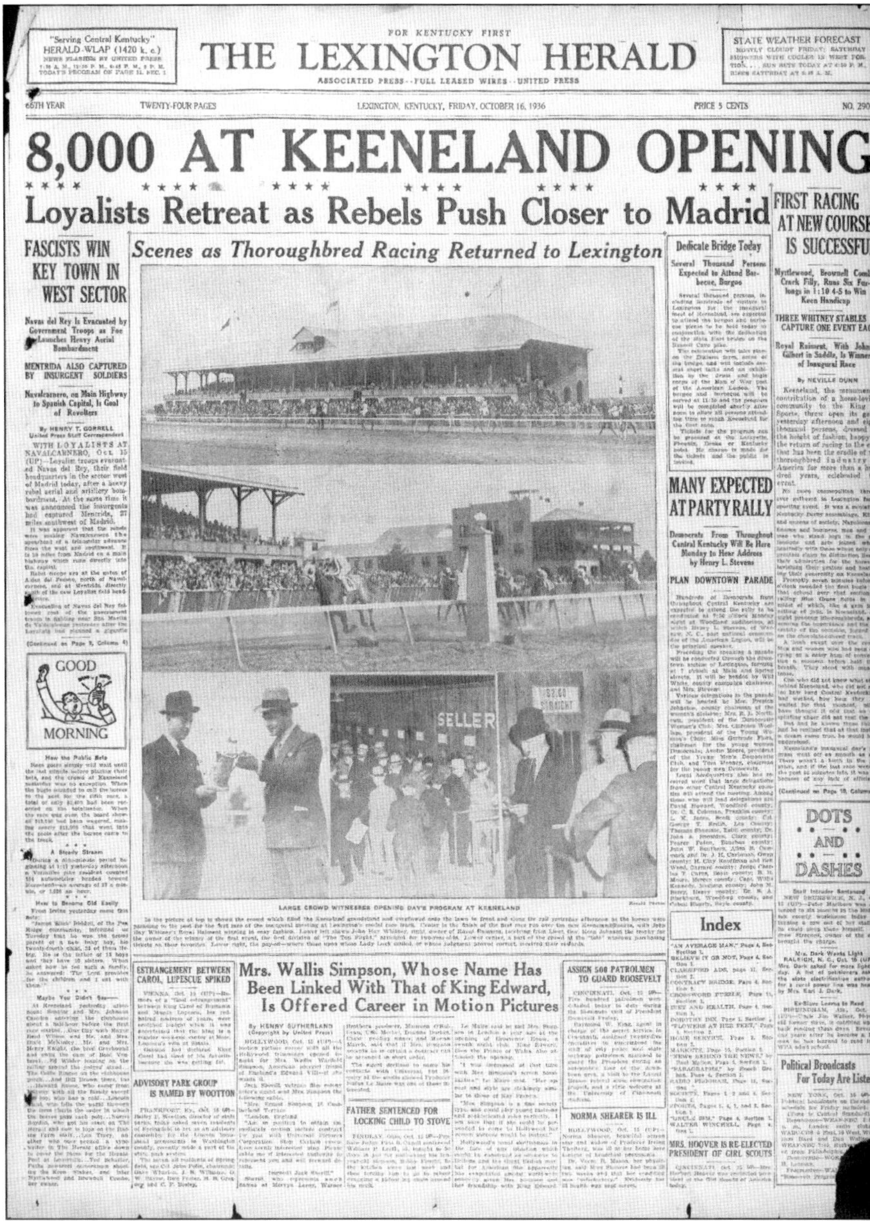

"Serving Central Kentucky"
HERALD-WLAP (1420 k. c.)

FOR KENTUCKY FIRST

THE LEXINGTON HERALD

ASSOCIATED PRESS--FULL LEASED WIRES--UNITED PRESS

STATE WEATHER FORECAST

68TH YEAR | TWENTY-FOUR PAGES | LEXINGTON, KENTUCKY, FRIDAY, OCTOBER 16, 1936 | PRICE 5 CENTS | NO. 290

8,000 AT KEENELAND OPENING

Loyalists Retreat as Rebels Push Closer to Madrid

FASCISTS WIN KEY TOWN IN WEST SECTOR

Navas del Rey Is Evacuated by Government Troops as Foe Launches Heavy Aerial Bombardment

MENTRIDA ALSO CAPTURED BY INSURGENT SOLDIERS

Navalcarnero, on Main Highway to Spanish Capital, Is Goal of Revolters

By HENRY T. GORRELL

Scenes as Thoroughbred Racing Returned to Lexington

LARGE CROWD WITNESSES OPENING DAY'S PROGRAM AT KEENELAND

Dedicate Bridge Today

Several Thousand Persons Expected to Attend Barbecue, Burgoo

MANY EXPECTED AT PARTY RALLY

Democrats From Throughout Central Kentucky Will Be Here Monday to Hear Address by Henry L. Stevens

PLAN DOWNTOWN PARADE

FIRST RACING AT NEW COURSE IS SUCCESSFUL

Myrtlewood, Brownell Combs' Crack Filly, Runs Six Furlongs in 1:10 4-5 to Win Keen Handicap

THREE WHITNEY STABLES CAPTURE ONE EVENT EACH

Royal Raiment, With Johnny Gilbert in Saddle, Is Winner of Inaugural Race

By NEVILLE DUNN

GOOD MORNING

DOTS AND DASHES

Index

Mrs. Wallis Simpson, Whose Name Has Been Linked With That of King Edward, Is Offered Career in Motion Pictures

By HENRY SUTHERLAND

ESTRANGEMENT BETWEEN CAROL, LUPESCUE SPIKED

ADVISORY PARK GROUP IS NAMED BY WOOTTON

FATHER SENTENCED FOR LOCKING CHILD TO STOVE

ASSIGN 500 PATROLMEN TO GUARD ROOSEVELT

NORMA SHEARER IS ILL

MRS. HOOVER IS RE-ELECTED PRESIDENT OF GIRL SCOUTS

Political Broadcasts For Today Are Listed

"RACING A SUCCESS." The day after opening day, Keeneland had to share the *Lexington Herald's* front page with reports on the Spanish Civil War, a planned Democratic political rally, and the flourishing romance between Wallis Simpson and England's Edward VIII, but the opening was lauded as a complete success. The paper stated, "Keeneland, the monumental contribution of a horse-loving community to the King of Sports, threw open its gates yesterday afternoon and eight thousand persons, dressed in the height of fashion, happy in the return of racing to the city that has been the cradle of the Thoroughbred industry of America for more than a hundred years, celebrated the event." On opening day, the *Lexington Herald* ran a 28-page special section full of stories about Keeneland and congratulatory ads from merchants who were hoping for a business boost from the track's opening. An ad from the Greyhound Bus Company advertised rides to the track: 25¢ one way and 40¢ round-trip.

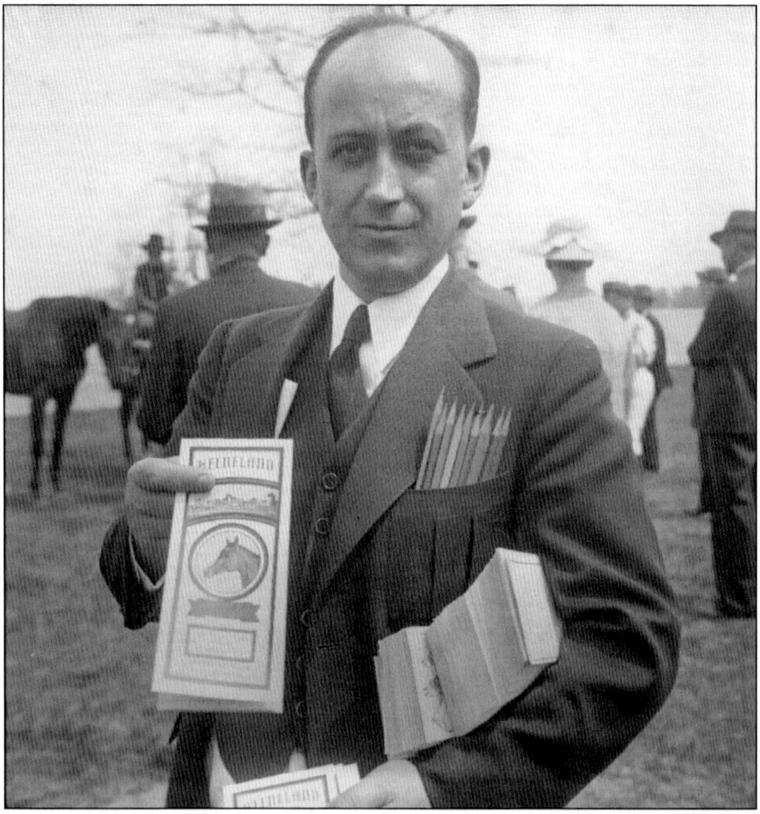

PROGRAMS AND PENCILS. This dapper program salesman, "Chick," doubtless did very well on Keeneland's opening day when more than 8,000 racing fans filled the 2,500-seat grandstand and trackside lawn. When the nine-day inaugural meet ended, the total attendance was 25,337 with $534,497 in wagers made. When the books were closed for the year, the new racetrack only showed a loss of $3.47. Keeneland never had another losing year.

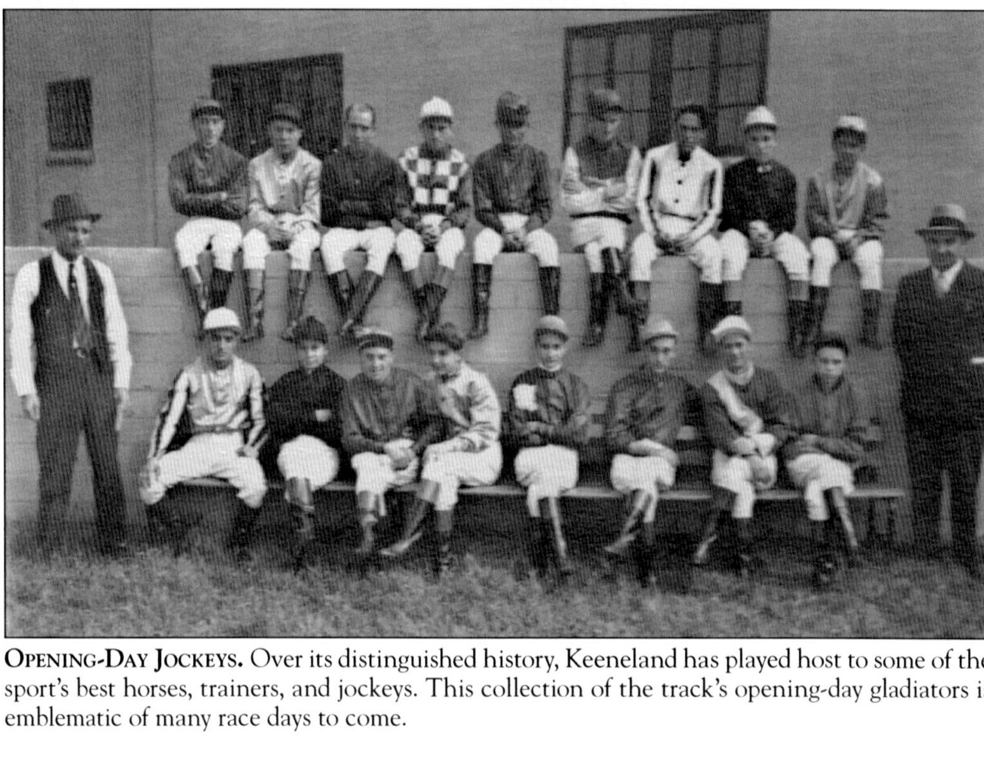

OPENING-DAY JOCKEYS. Over its distinguished history, Keeneland has played host to some of the sport's best horses, trainers, and jockeys. This collection of the track's opening-day gladiators is emblematic of many race days to come.

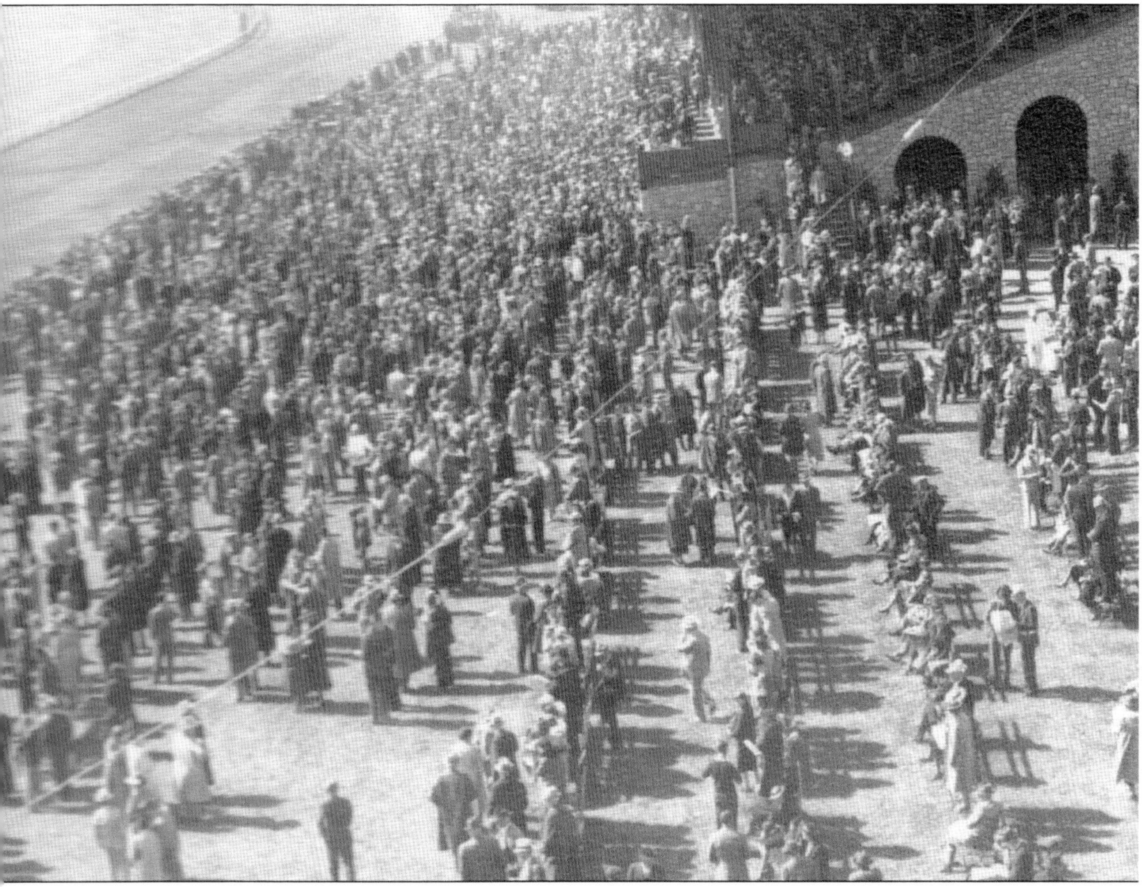

KEENELAND'S LAWN. This space between the impressive stone clubhouse and the new grandstand quickly became a popular gathering and viewing spot for the well-dressed public of the 1930s.

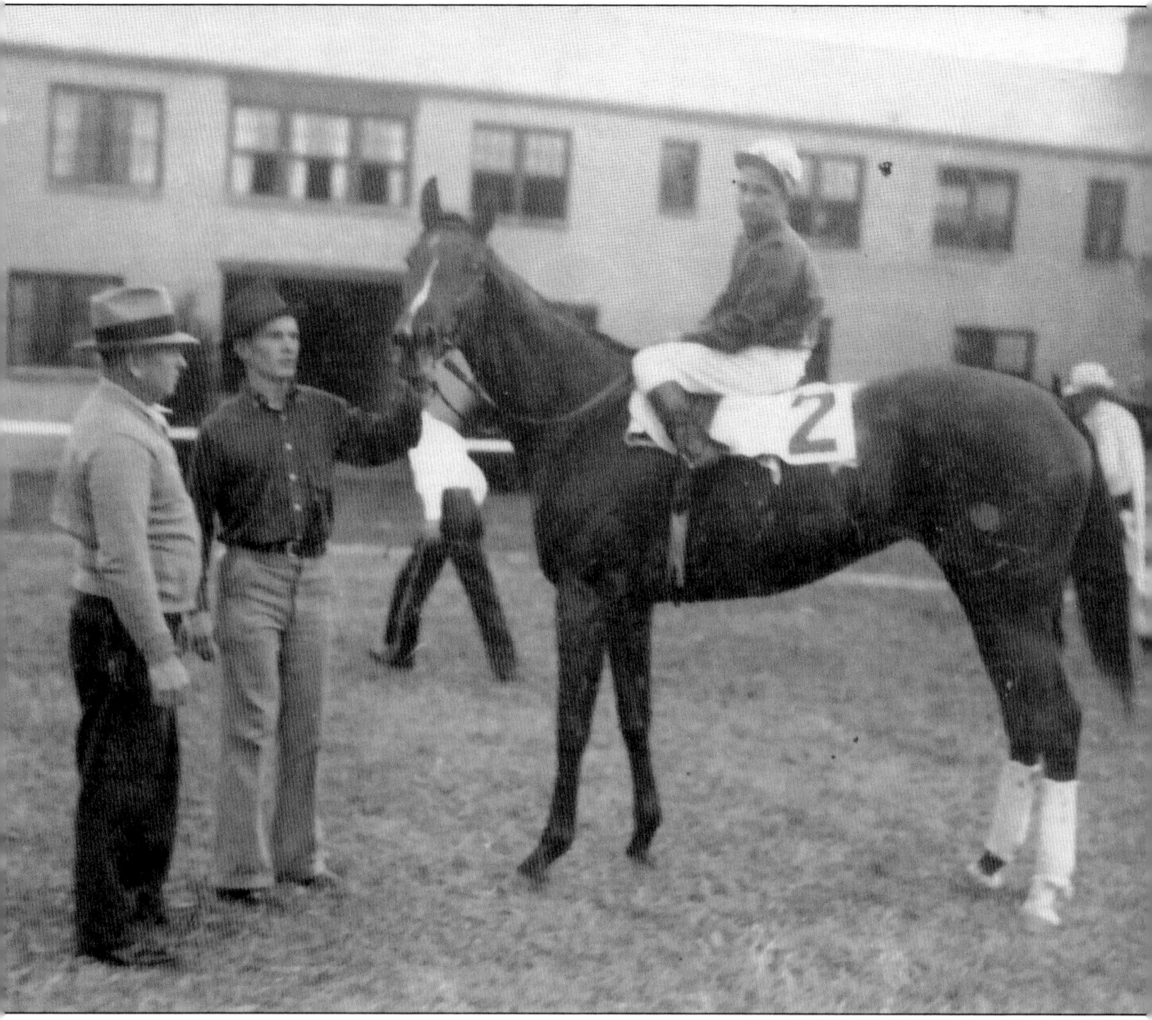

Myrtlewood. On Keeneland's first day, the featured Keen Handicap saw Brownell Combs's impressive filly Myrtlewood, ridden by George South, defeat another female and three male rivals while carrying an extra 15 to 27 pounds. Two days later, she won the first Keeneland renewal of the historic Ashland Stakes. Myrtlewood, trained by R.A. Kindred, closed out the meet and her career by winning a match race against Miss Merriment. Myrtlewood is a member of racing's Hall of Fame.

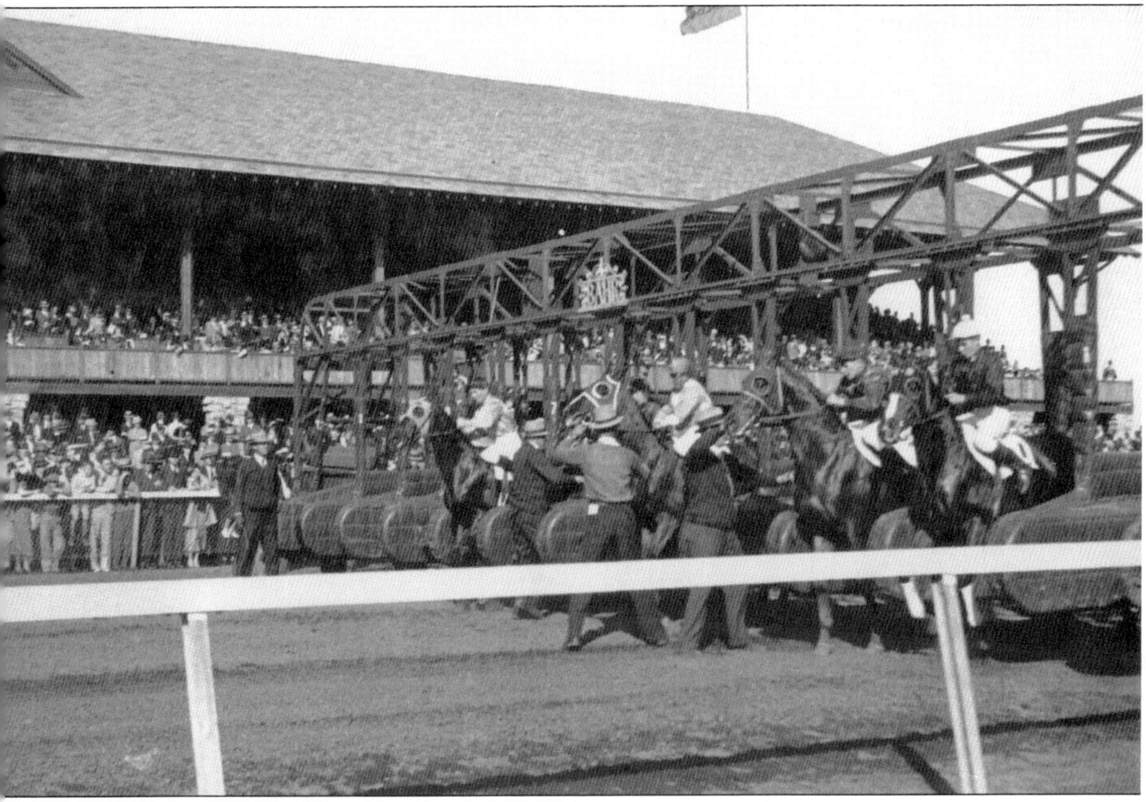

Loading the Gate. This photograph was taken during Keeneland's first meet and shows most, if not all, of the horses being backed into the starting gate. Normally, horses are led into the gate going forward. Working on the starting-gate crew is one of the most dangerous jobs on the track. On this day, it looks particularly so.

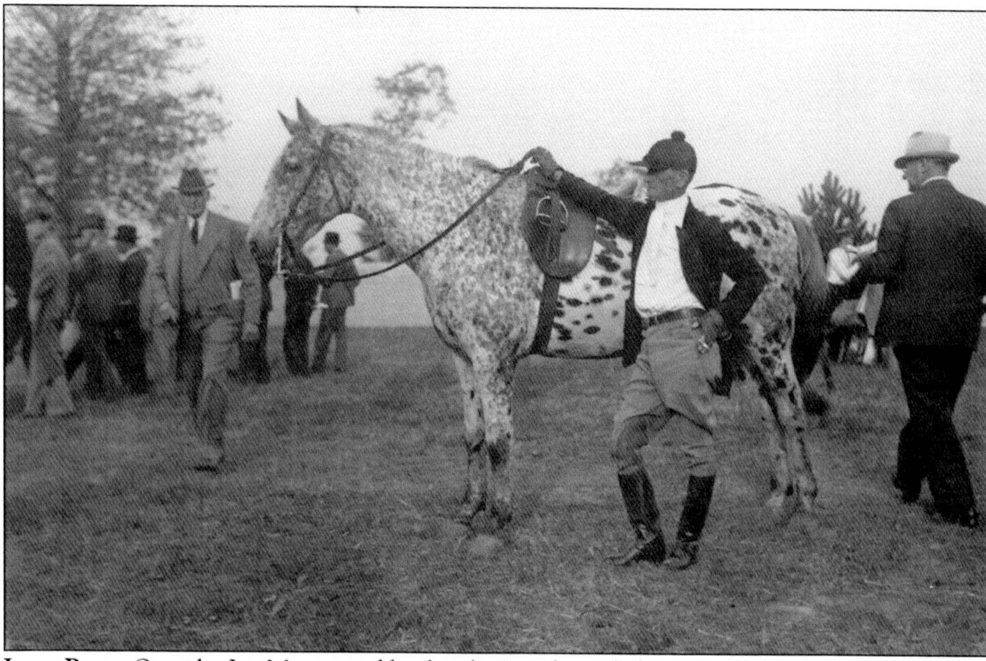

LEAD PONY. Outrider Joe Moran and his lovely Appaloosa led out the horses for the first race at Keeneland and continued to be favorites at the new track for years.

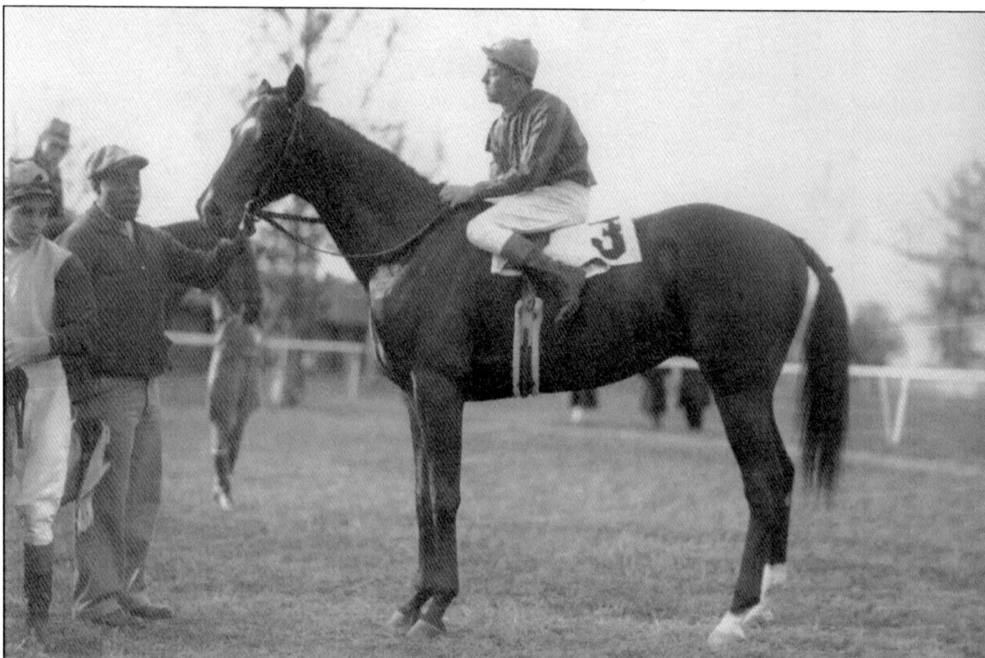

WHITE TIE. The first Lexington Stakes was a six-furlong race run for two-year-olds during Keeneland's inaugural meet. The winner was White Tie, who was owned by Manhasset Stable, ridden by Joseph Cowley, and trained by John M. Gaver. Since 1998, the Lexington Stakes has been sponsored by Coolmore, the world-famous Irish-based stallion operation. Today, the race is run as an important, springtime graded stakes race for three-year-olds.

Two

FASCINATING FACES

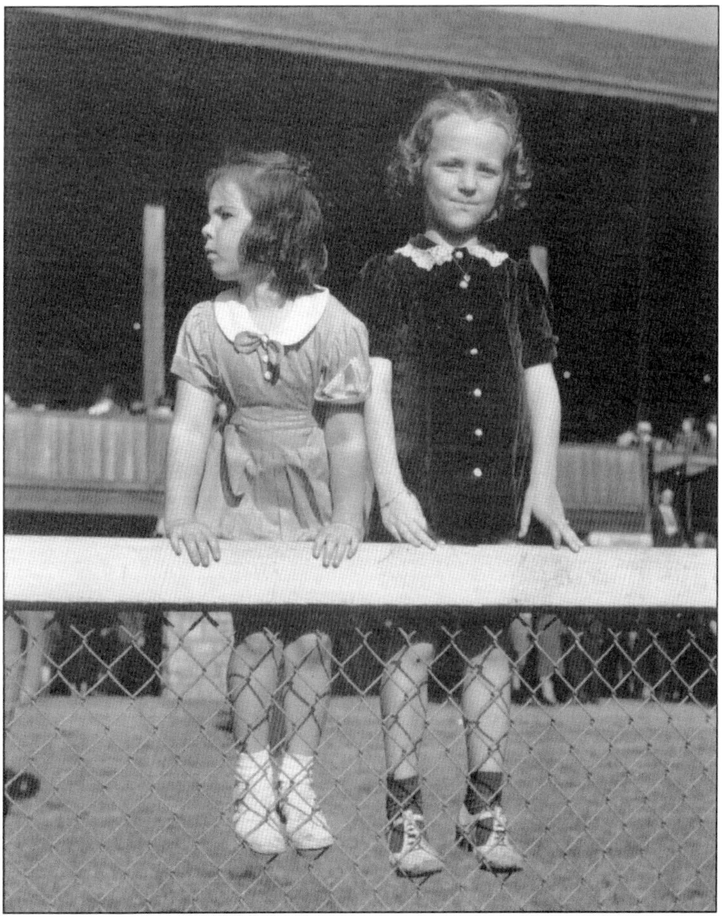

CUTE LITTLE RAILBIRDS. Children have always been a part of the Keeneland scene, unlike some racetracks around the country where only people 21 and older are allowed to enter. At Keeneland, families can spend an afternoon together enjoying fun times and building memories. These girls are two of the fascinating faces that have been seen at Keeneland since the gates first opened in 1936.

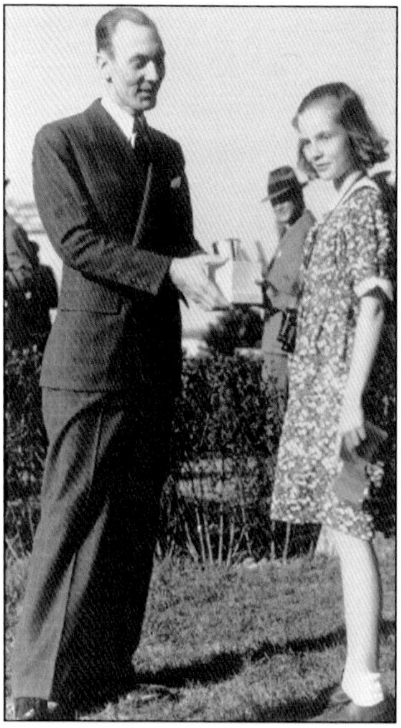

And the Trophy Goes to . . . Young Alice Headley is shown accepting the Yearling Judging Contest trophy for her father and Keeneland's first president, Hal Price Headley, from Dan Midkiff in this 1937 photograph. Twenty-five years later, Alice inherited 286 acres of farmland from her father, which she and her husband, John Chandler, developed into Mill Ridge Farms, an internationally recognized Thoroughbred operation.

Get Your Red Hots! Before the gates opened at Keeneland, Turf Catering Company of Chicago was chosen to operate the food concessions at the racetrack, which they continue to do to this day. Ben Koppel (left) and Joe Wolken, Turf Catering partners, are shown here sampling some of their company's wares. Turf Catering celebrated its 75th anniversary of providing delicious, southern-style food to Keeneland patrons in 2011.

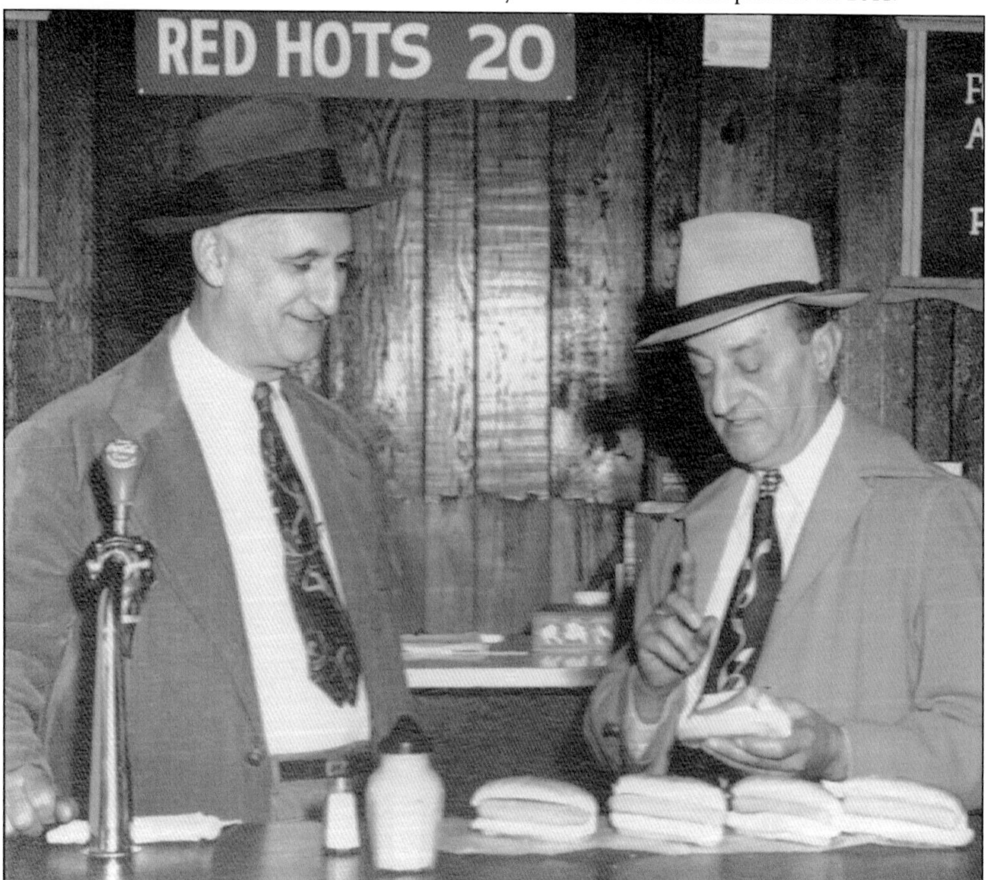

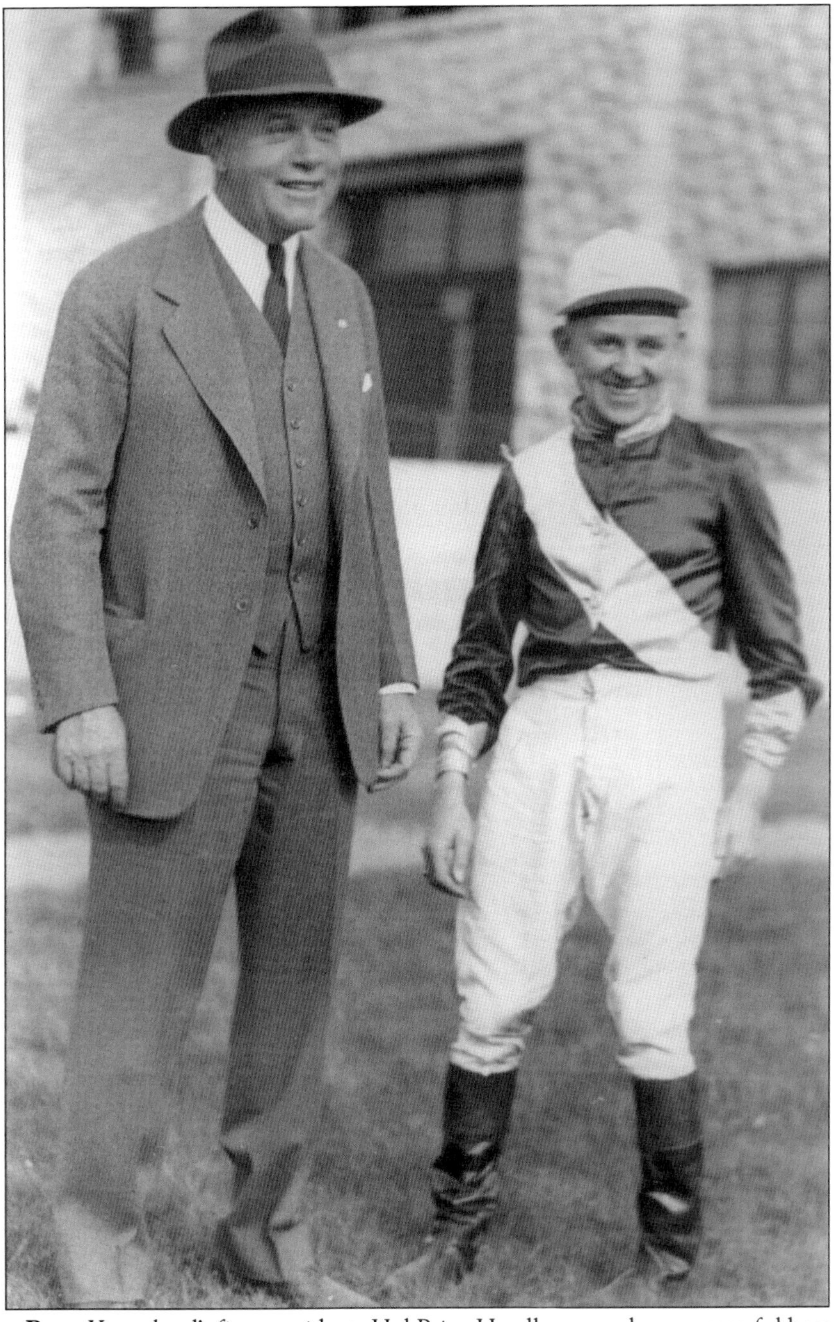

A Happy Pair. Keeneland's first president, Hal Price Headley, was also a successful horse owner and breeder and is shown here with jockey Charles Kurtsinger, who wears Headley's Beaumont Farm silks. Headley's horses earned him the leading owner title at the first four Keeneland meets. In 1959, he won his 100th race at Keeneland when his horse Rash Statement captured the Alcibiades. Headley was an integral part of the creation of Keeneland from the beginning and remained very involved up until his death in 1962, which happened at Keeneland while Headley was supervising the training of his horses. Kurtsinger was a Kentucky native best known for riding War Admiral to victory in the 1937 Triple Crown.

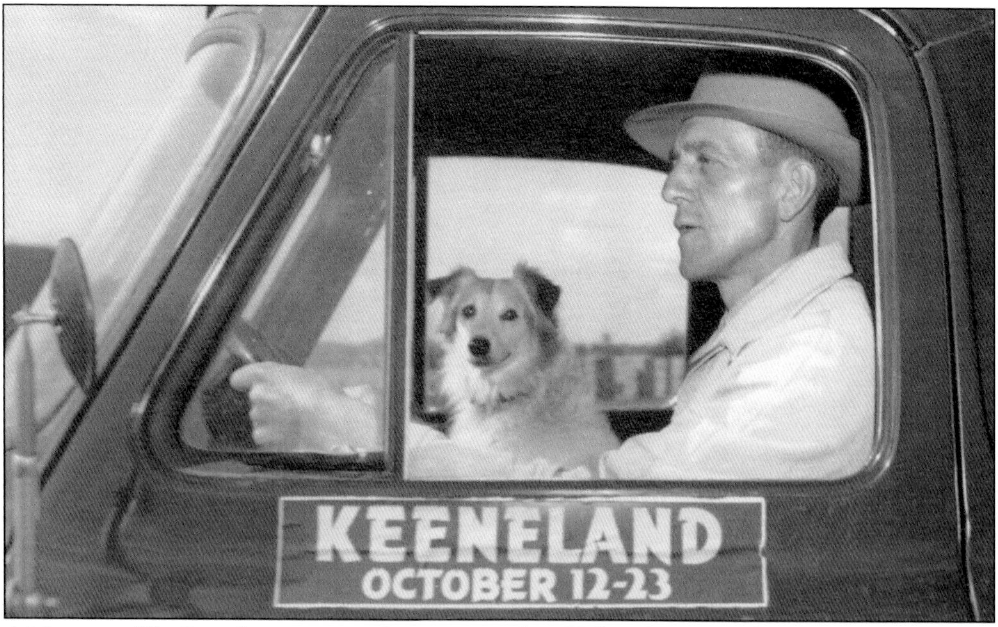

A Man and His Dog. Longtime track superintendent Hobart Burton is shown here in 1954 with his constant canine companion, Dolittle. When Dolittle died, he was buried under a tree on the Keeneland grounds. When he was named Keeneland president, Nick Nicholson remembers being shown Dolittle's gravesite, and he continues the tradition of ensuring its protection.

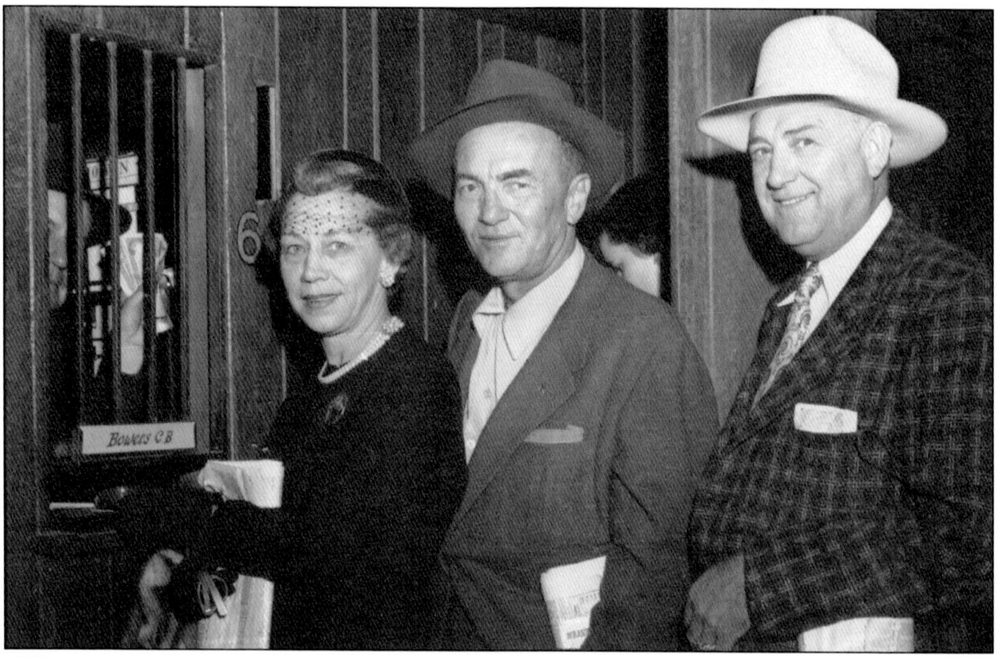

"Where Windows Clean People." That is the caption under this photograph in one of the Keeneland Library's scrapbooks. Actually, the bettors gamble against one another, and the track takes a small percentage on each bet. For example, the amount bet on a horse to win (the winning pool) is divided by the number that bet on the horse to win, and the payout is that amount less the track's percentage.

Nurse Popham. A first-aid station has been a fixture at Keeneland from the beginning to care for ill or injured patrons and jockeys. As medical care improved, a separate facility was utilized for injured jockeys, as well as providing medical care to the year-round backside residents. Nurse Helen Popham is shown here in this 1953 photograph.

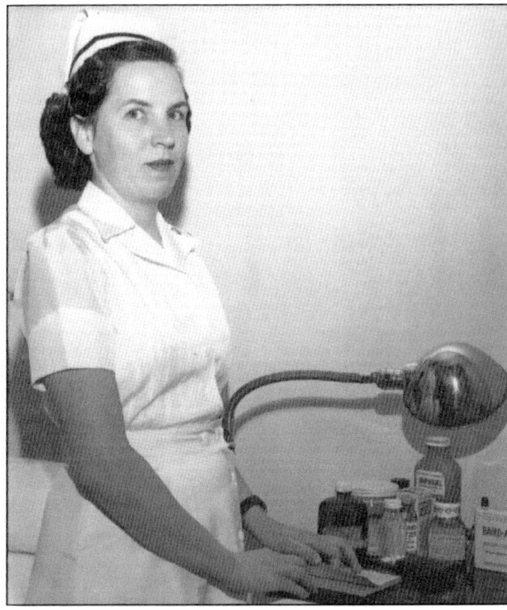

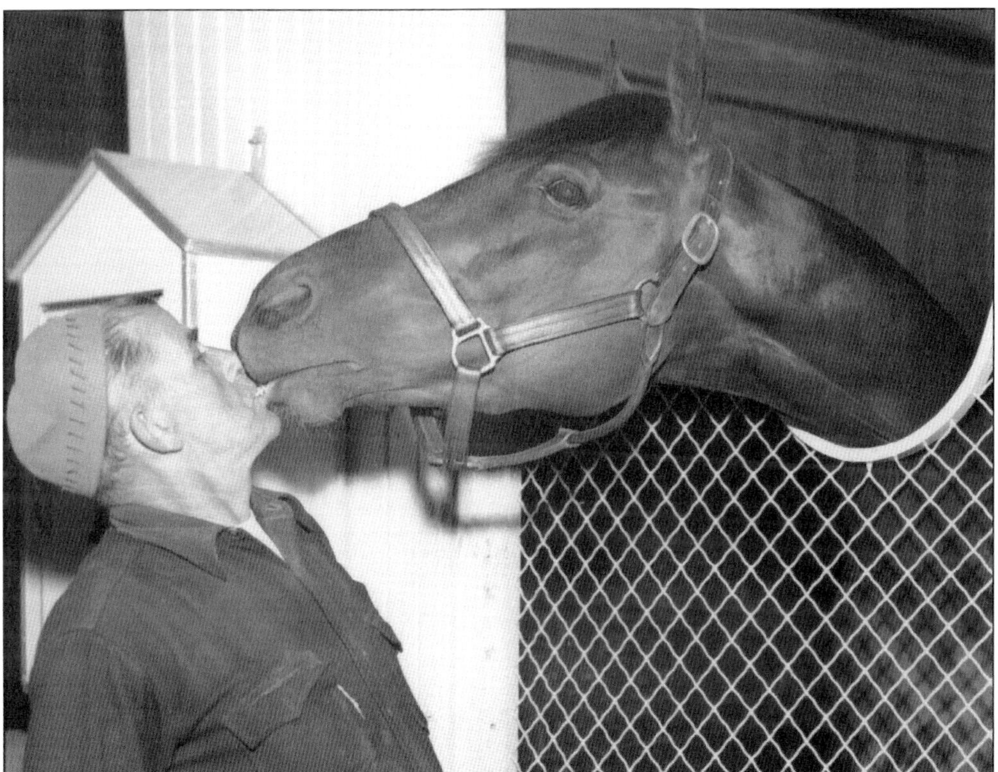

A Yummy Treat. This photograph, taken in 1959, shows groom Frank Solesky feeding a sugar cube to Tomy Lee, winner of the 1959 Blue Grass Stakes at Keeneland and the 1959 Kentucky Derby. Tomy Lee was the third horse (after Bubbling Over in 1926 and Shut Out in 1942) to win the Derby after winning the Blue Grass Stakes, but he did not race in the other 1959 Triple Crown races.

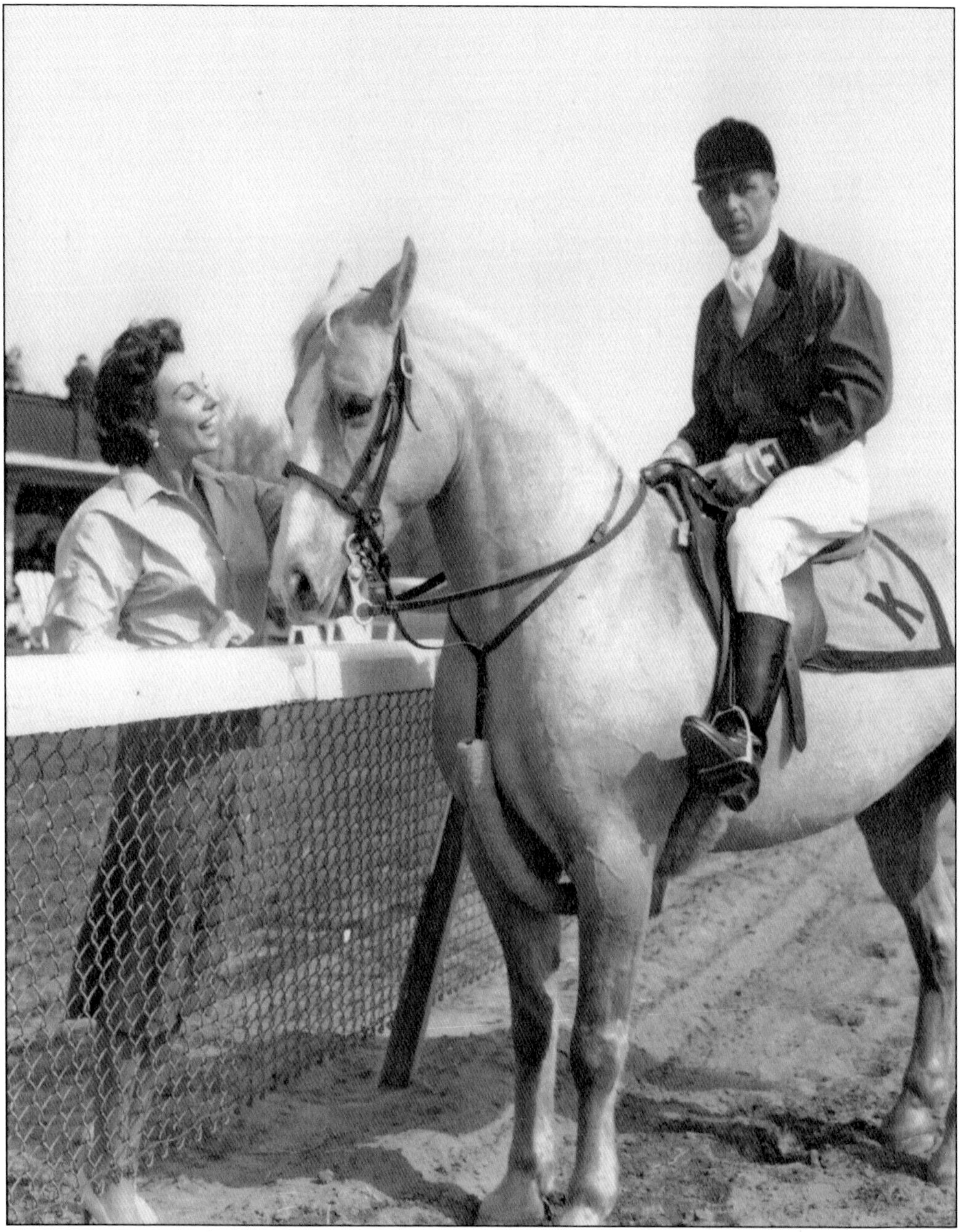

FRIENDLY HORSE. This 1956 photograph is captioned, "Miss Farraday pats Tony"; however, the identity of the man on the horse, one of Keeneland's outriders, is unknown. Outriders serve as safety officers during morning workouts to make sure that riders follow the rules and assist trainers and riders. During race meets, outriders lead the horses in the post parade to the starting gate before each race.

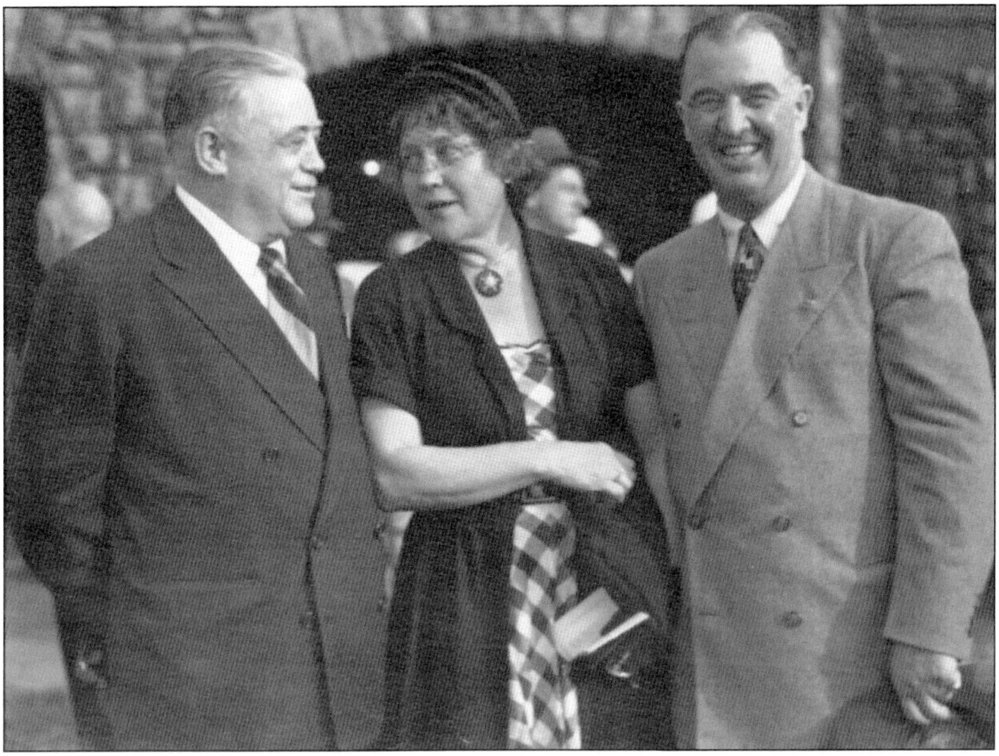

Sports Personalities. This 1953 photograph shows Bill Corum (left), Mrs. A.B. Chandler, and two-time Kentucky governor A.B. "Happy" Chandler. Corum, one of America's top sports columnists for three decades, was named president of Churchill Downs in 1949. He coined the phrase "Run for the Roses" in 1925 when describing his first Kentucky Derby. Besides serving as governor and US senator, Chandler was the commissioner of baseball from 1945 to 1952.

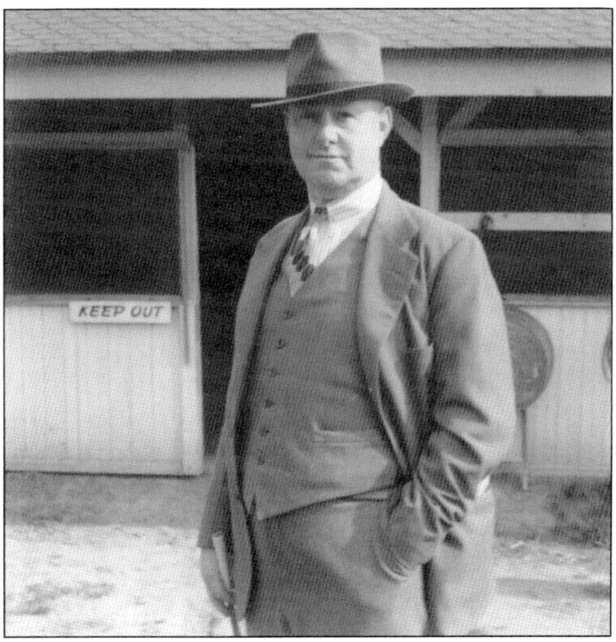

Winning Trainer. Ben A. Jones trained winners of 13 stakes races at Keeneland between 1940 and 1952. He won his first Kentucky Derby in 1938 with Lawrin and then, after taking over Calumet's stable, won five more with Whirlaway (1941), Pensive (1944), Citation (1948), Ponder (1949), and Hill Gail (1952). Both Whirlaway and Citation were Triple Crown winners. Jones is the only trainer to win six Kentucky Derbys.

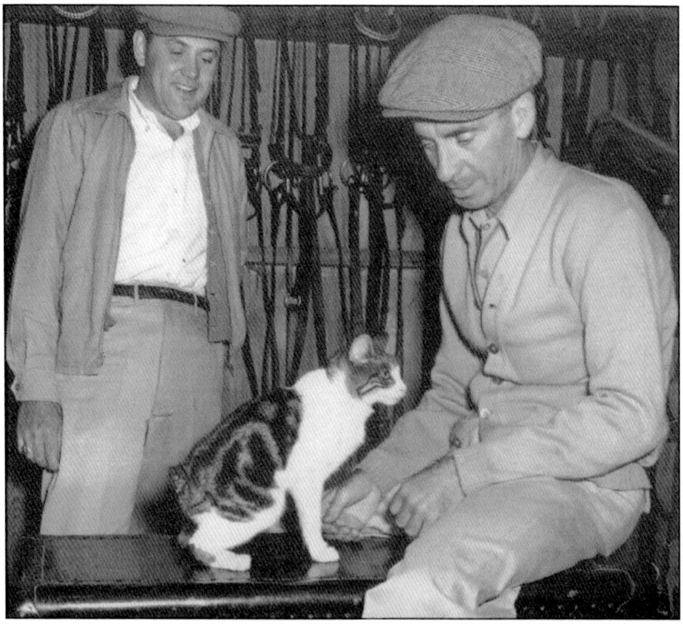

What's a Cabbitt? This is one of the more unusual stable pets that has called Keeneland home over the last 75 years. This animal was identified as the "Dixiana Stable pet 'cabbitt' " in the caption of this 1950 photograph. The photograph also shows Jack Dalzell in the foreground; the man in the background is not identified. The cat's nickname obviously came from its unusual bobtailed hindquarters.

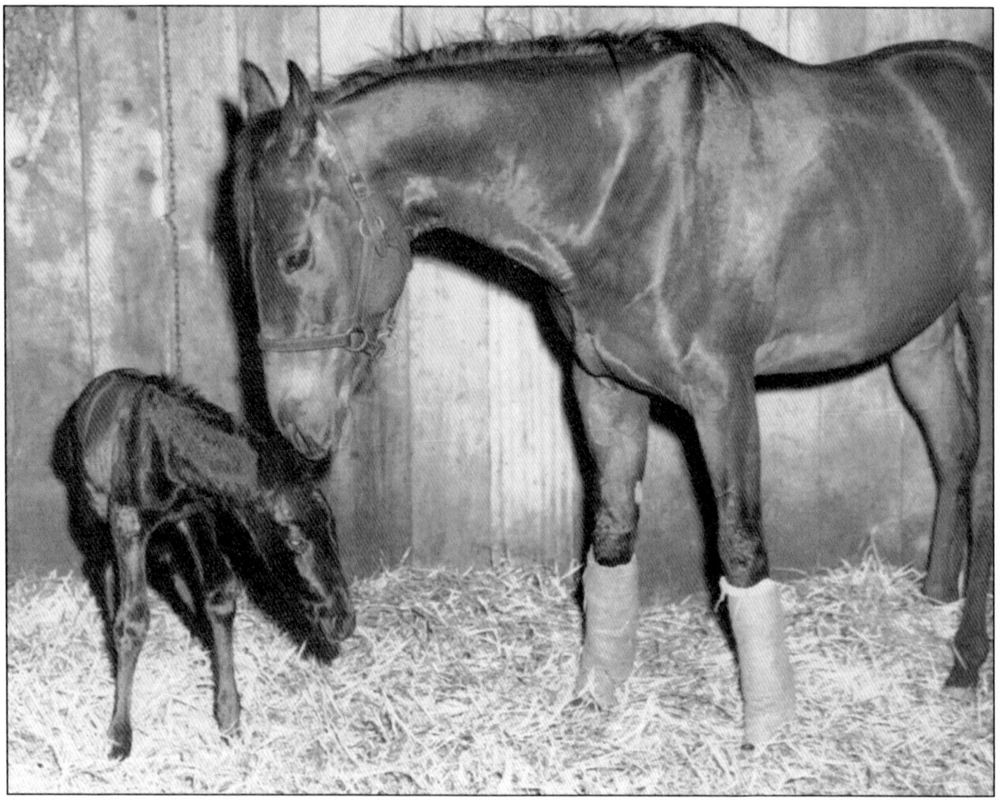

Hardworking Mom. This mare named Hashcamp worked a half-mile in 51 seconds in the morning and foaled this black filly by Zorawar, named Zocampe, that evening. That is certainly not common practice, which is why this photograph of the mare and her foal taken in 1949 ended up in the Keeneland Library's scrapbook collection.

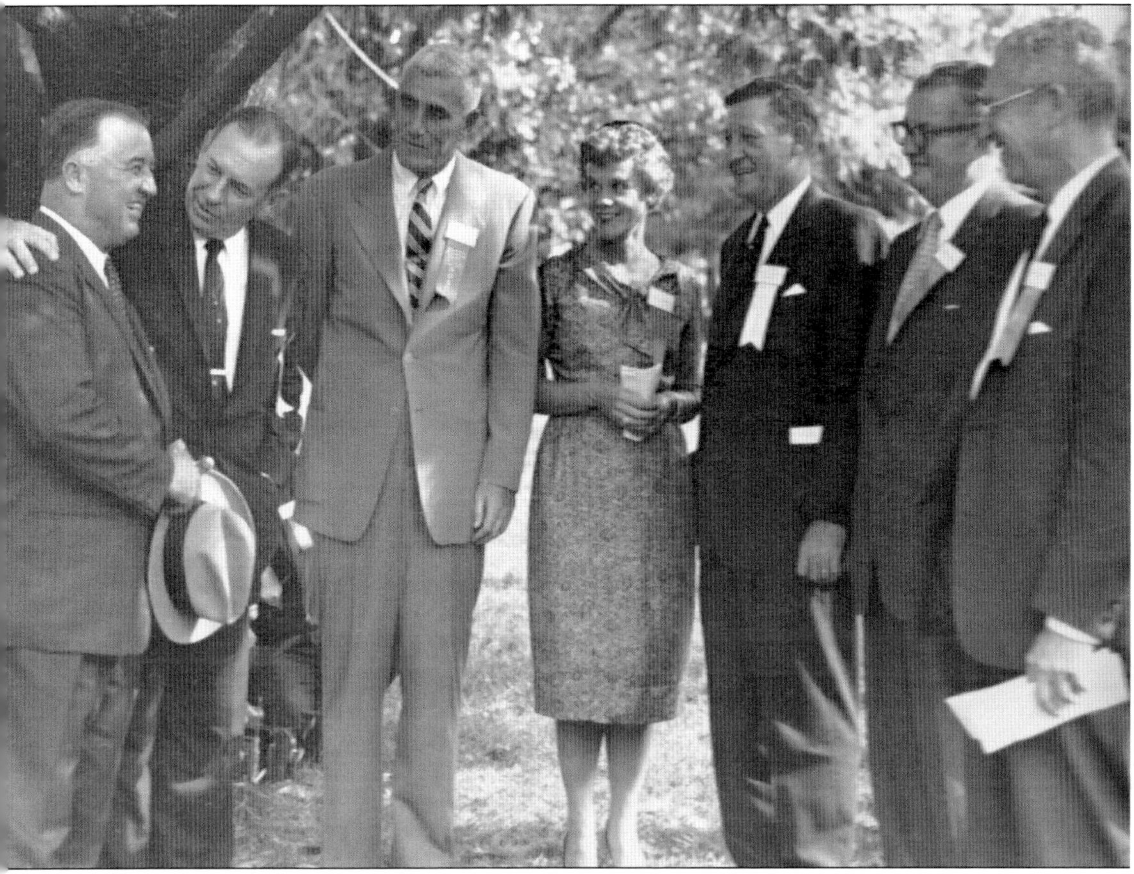

Southern Governors Visit Keeneland. In the spring of 1958, the Southern Governors Association's annual meeting was held at Keeneland, and in attendance were Keeneland Association president Louis Lee "L.L." Haggin II and his wife, Alma. Alma was a daughter of Hal Price Headley, Keeneland's first president, and she used her expertise as hostess and decorator to leave an imprint on the look and feel of Keeneland that can still be seen today. L.L. Haggin II was elected president of Keeneland Race Course in 1940 and served in that office through 1956. He served as president of the Keeneland Association from 1956 to 1970. Shown in the photograph are, from left to right, Kentucky governor A.B. "Happy" Chandler, Georgia governor Marvin Griffin, L.L. Haggin, Alma Haggin, South Carolina governor George Timmerman, Spencer Drayton of the Thoroughbred Racing Protective Bureau, and James Stewart, vice president of Hollywood Park.

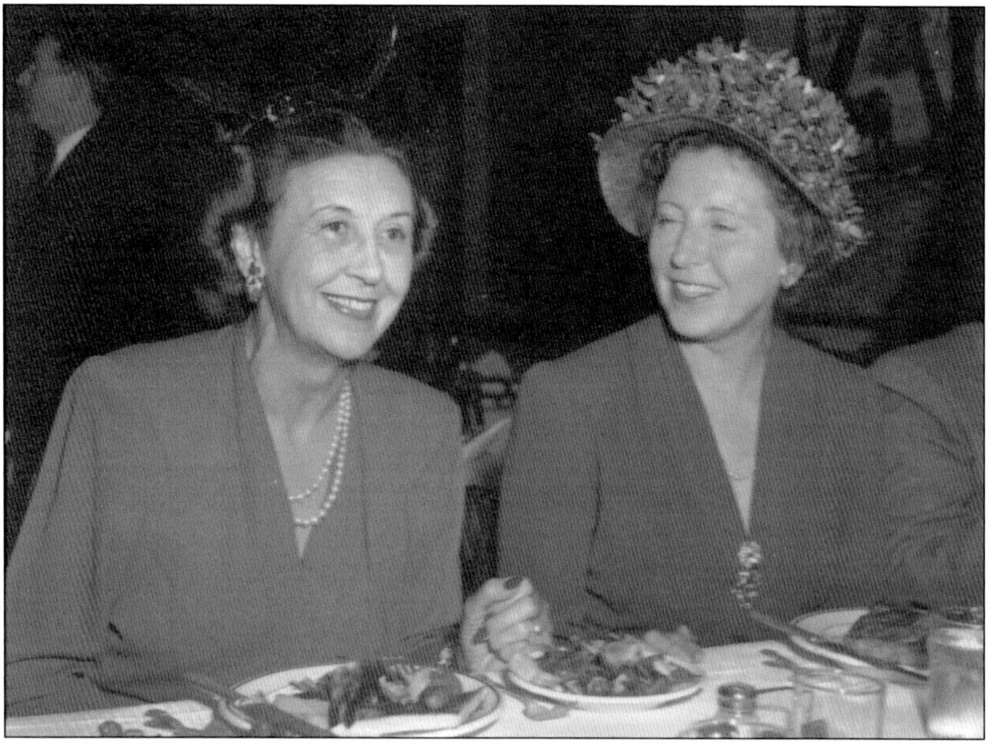

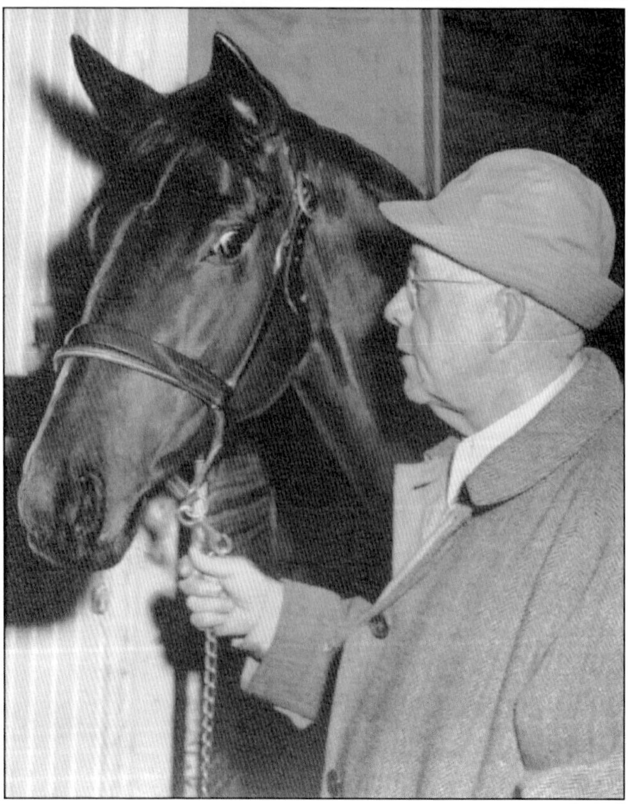

Clubhouse Luncheon. Mrs. Warren Wright (left) and Mrs. Royce Martin were obviously enjoying their luncheon at the Keeneland Clubhouse in 1946. Keeneland Club lifetime memberships are prized possessions among central Kentucky families and are passed down from generation to generation. The Keeneland Club began with 90 members, and today that number has grown to 1,000 with a long waiting list.

Eye To Eye. Pellicle takes a good look at owner Hal Price Headley in this 1946 photograph. Pellicle won multiple stakes at Keeneland, including the 1945 Breeders' Futurity and the 1946 Keeneland Special but finished a disappointing eighth place in the 1946 Kentucky Derby, which was won by Assault.

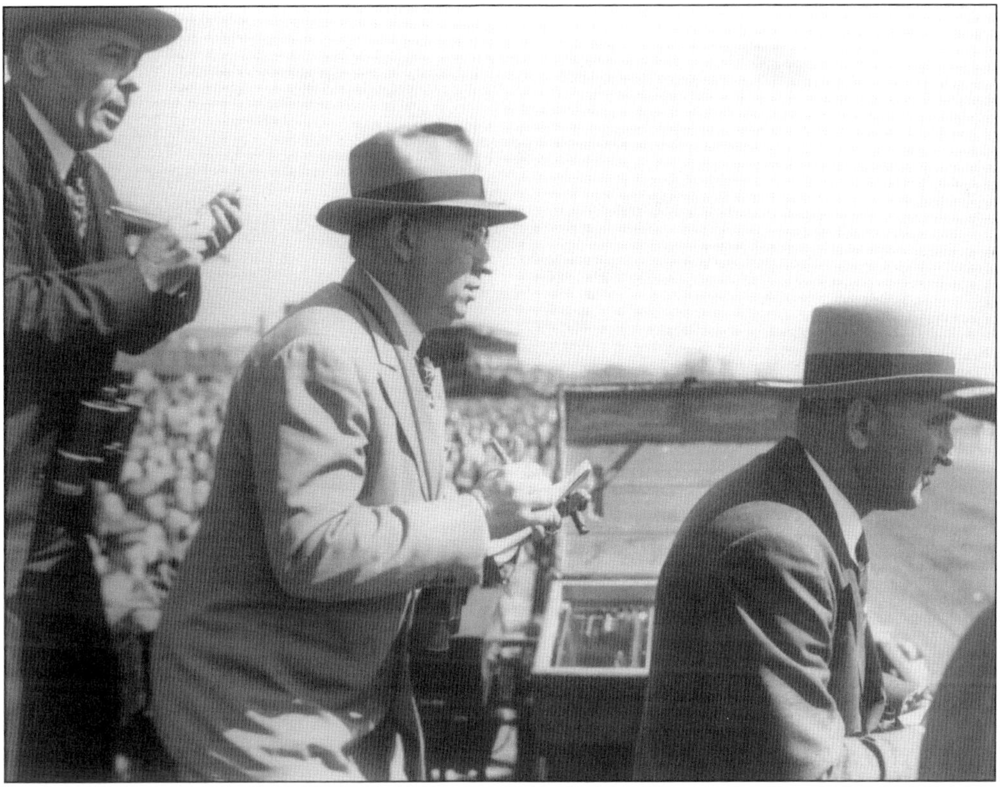

LINE OF SIGHT. Each of the three placing judges needed a clear look at the finish line in this 1949 photograph. Placing judges determine the order in which the horses finish. They communicate the numbers of the first four horses to cross the finish line to the tote board operators, who then flash the winners on the result board.

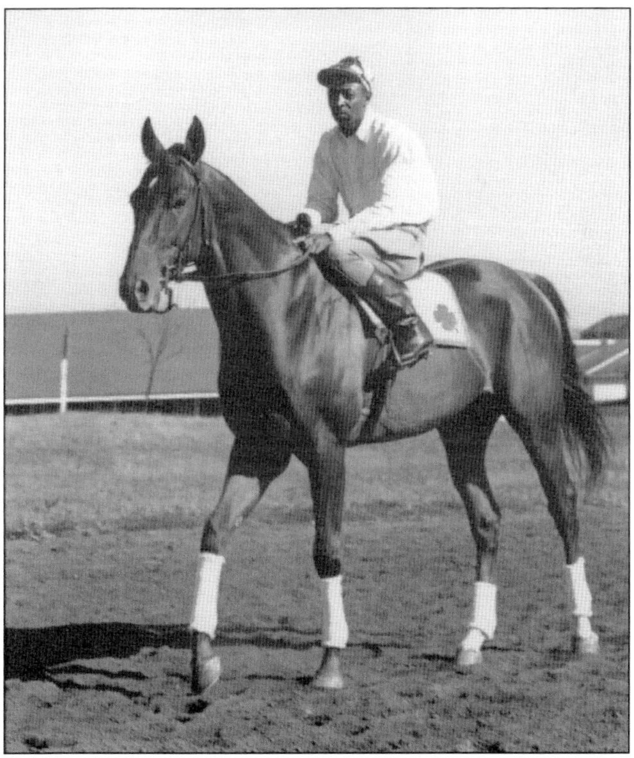

GETTING SOME EXERCISE. This 1949 photograph shows Kentucky Colonel with exercise rider Everete McCann in the saddle. Exercise riders usually work for specific trainers and gallop the trainer's horses in the morning to help them learn how to run straight, run with other horses, and switch leads. They also school the horses in the starting gate.

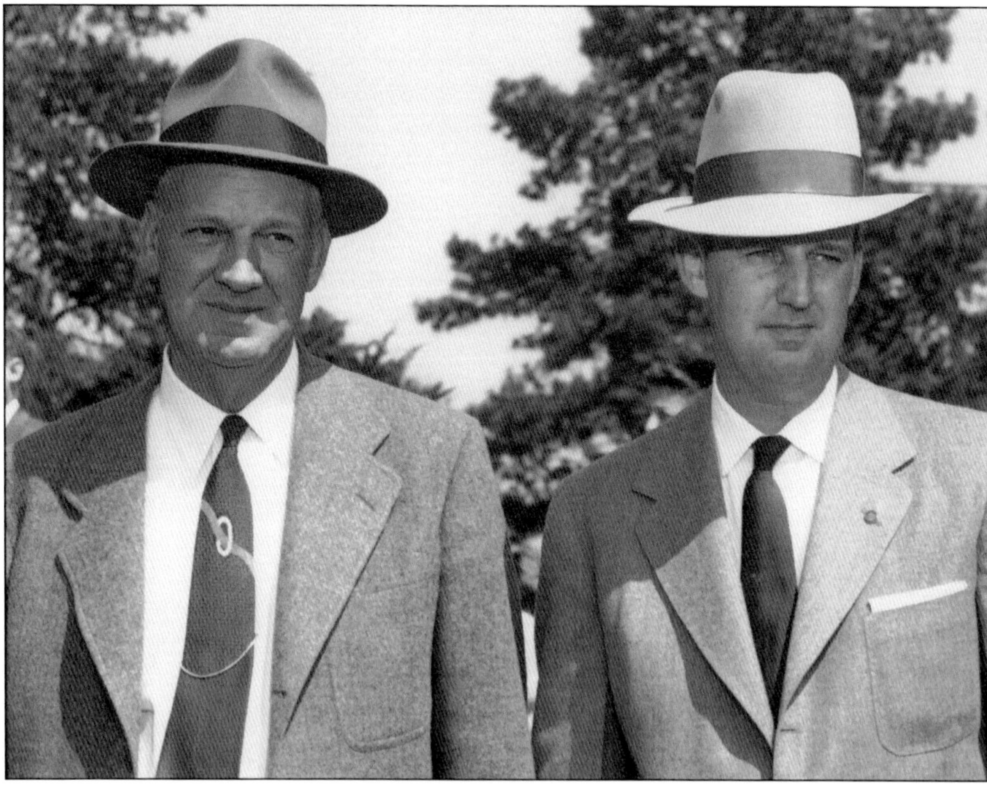

Horse Transportation Experts. This 1953 photograph shows "Scoop" Sallee (left) and Bill Sallee. Sallee Horse Vans transported horses to and from the Keeneland races and sales. The company was sold in the late 1960s to Arminda and Robert Maxwell, and since that time it has grown to be the most widely used horse transportation company in America. It remains a family-owned business, currently run by Maxwell's granddaughter.

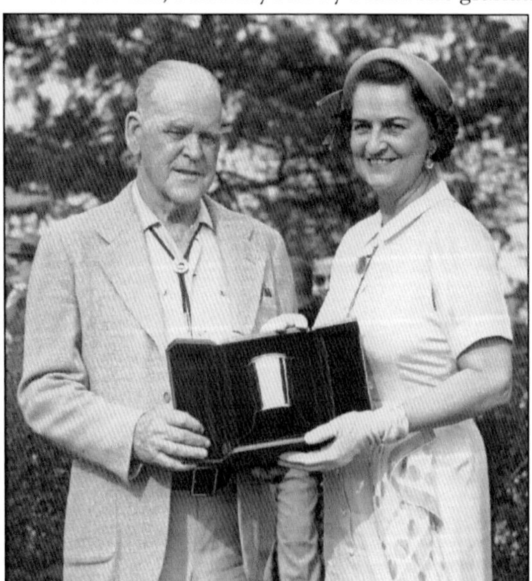

Gold Julep Cup. This photograph shows Dixiana Farm manager Ercel Ellis accepting the solid gold julep cup awarded for Safe Message's win in the 1958 Ben Ali from Mrs. George Swinebroad. Beginning with the fall meeting of 1952, Keeneland began awarding a gold julep cup to the winning owner of almost every major stakes race. Additional gold serving items are awarded after an owner has reached various levels.

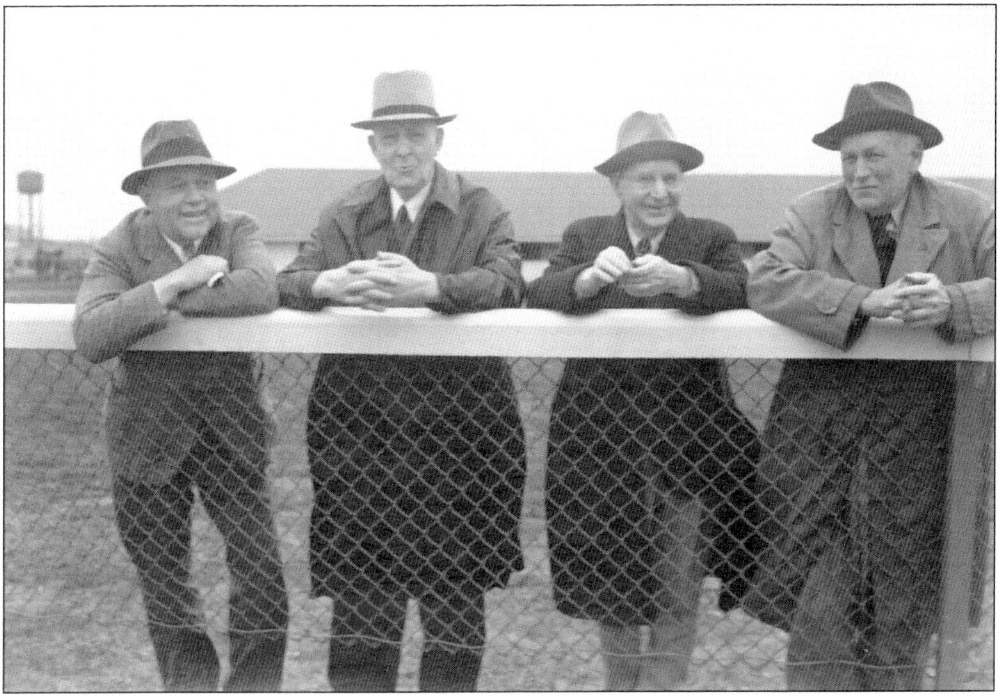

When Men Wore Hats. This nattily dressed quartet includes, from left to right, Hal Price Headley, Jack Baber, Col. Milan, and J.O. "Jack" Keene. They were photographed at Keeneland all wearing hats, which were a must for men until the 1960s. Headley and Keene were two of the men most instrumental in the creation of Keeneland.

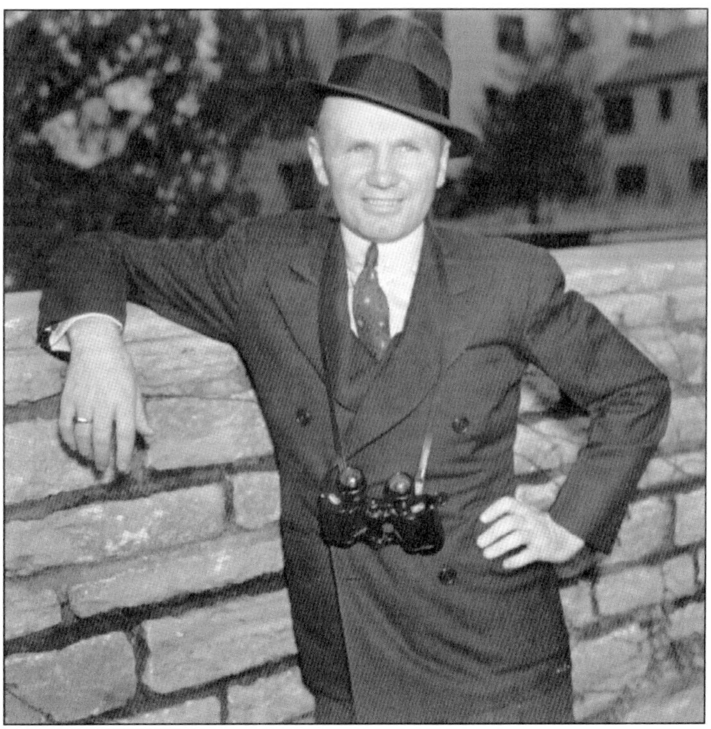

Successful Jockey and Trainer. Earl Sande began as a broncobuster and went on to be a successful jockey. He won the Kentucky Derby three times and the Belmont five times. His most famous races were the 1930 Triple Crown wins on Gallant Fox. Following his retirement, Sande became a trainer and soon owned and operated his own racing stable. He trained the 1937 and 1939 Blue Grass Stakes winners.

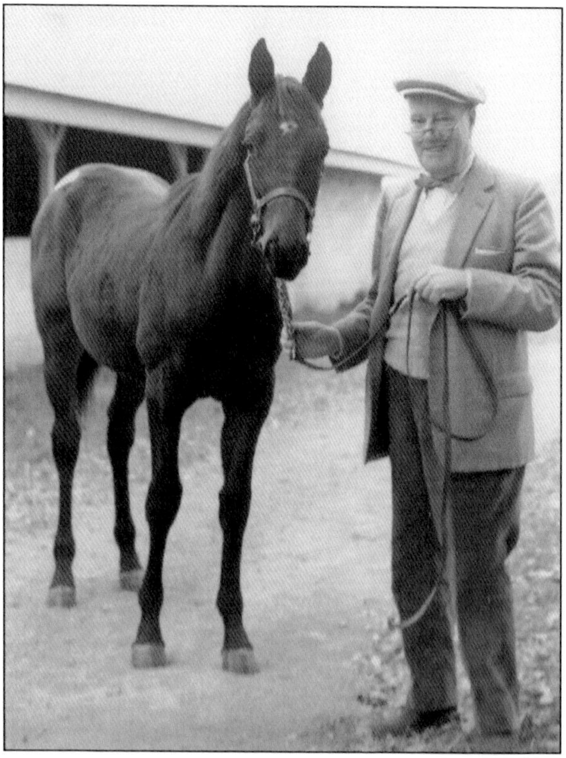

Horse Auctioneer. Humphrey Finney is shown here in 1957 with a Citation colt he purchased. A native of England, Finney enjoyed a varied career after immigrating to America in 1921. Among other things, he exhibited draft horses and procured horses for the Coast Guard during World War II. He is best known as a horse auctioneer and was chairman of Fasig-Tipton, a horse-auctioneering company, when he died in 1984.

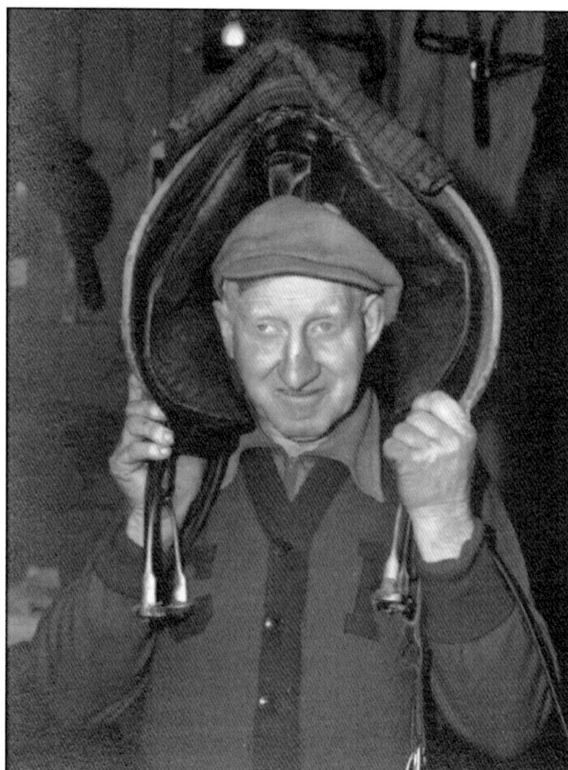

Pinky and the Saddle. Groom Pinky Brown carries a saddle in this 1949 photograph. Grooms are in charge of many aspects of the care of the horses, including cleaning tack like this saddle. They also brush, bathe, feed, and water the horses and get them ready for training or a race, clean the stalls, and sometimes walk the horses in the paddock before a race.

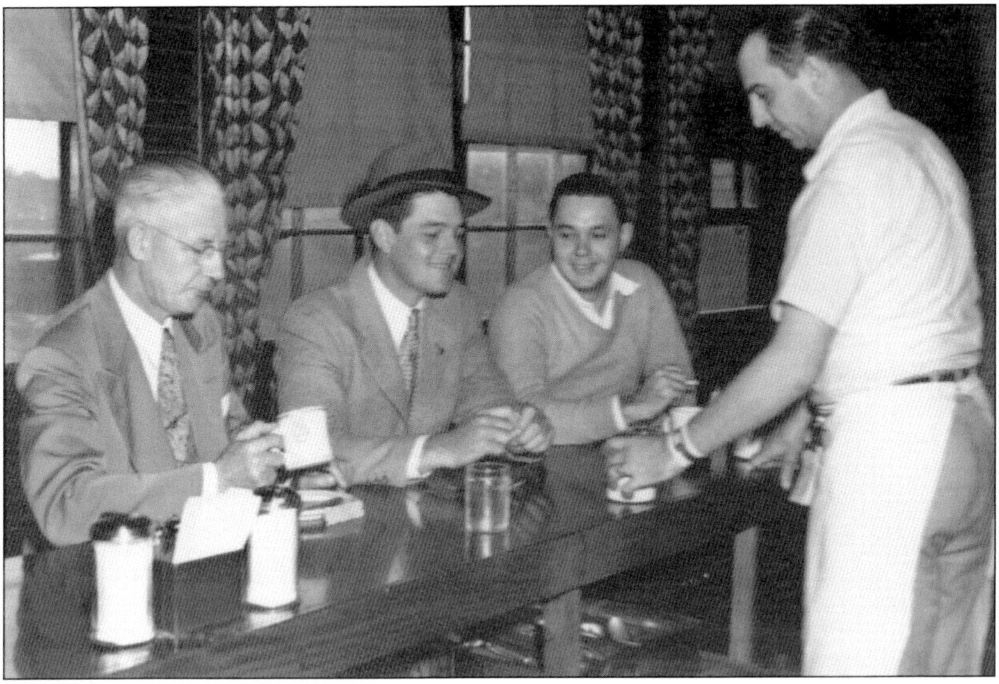

Another Cup of Joe? The Keeneland Track Kitchen was a busy place when this 1949 photograph was taken, and that has not changed today. Normally serving 80 to 100 customers each day during the off-season, the kitchen serves as many as a thousand people a day during race meets and horse sales. In this photograph are, from left to right, John Gibson, Charles Nuckols, and Alfred Nuckols enjoying a cup of coffee; the server is unidentified.

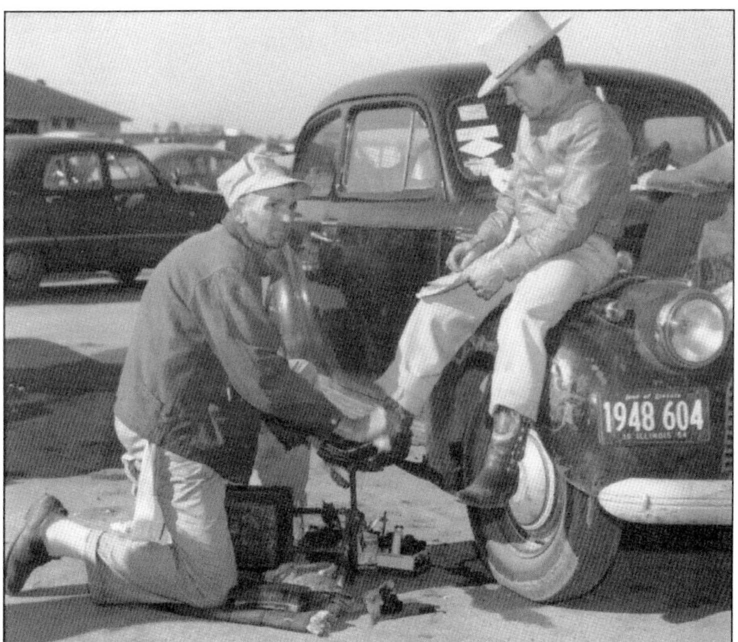

Teddy Roosevelt's Guest. Shoeshine man Zeke Montroy was a guest of Teddy Roosevelt's at the 1904 World's Fair held in St. Louis, according to this photograph's caption in the Keeneland Library's scrapbook. Unfortunately, there is no information as to why Roosevelt took him to the event. Montroy is shown here in 1954 providing a nice shine to Steve Brock's cowboy boots.

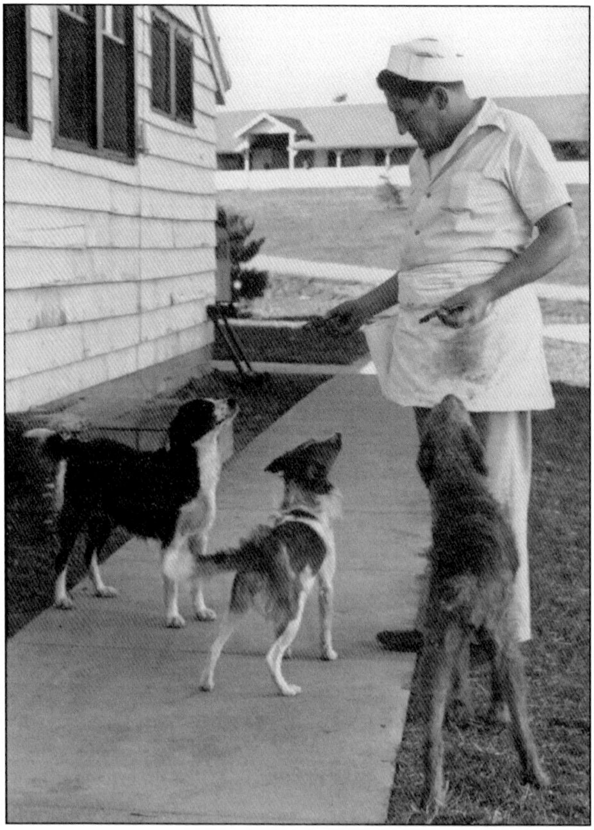

Waiting for a Handout. This 1949 photograph shows cook Pete Nekow handing out scraps to some of his canine friends behind the track kitchen. Keeneland is one of the few tracks in the country that allow the public to enjoy meals in the track kitchen alongside backsiders like grooms and exercise riders as well as track management and millionaire horse owners. Many people like to drop by the track kitchen after watching the early morning workouts.

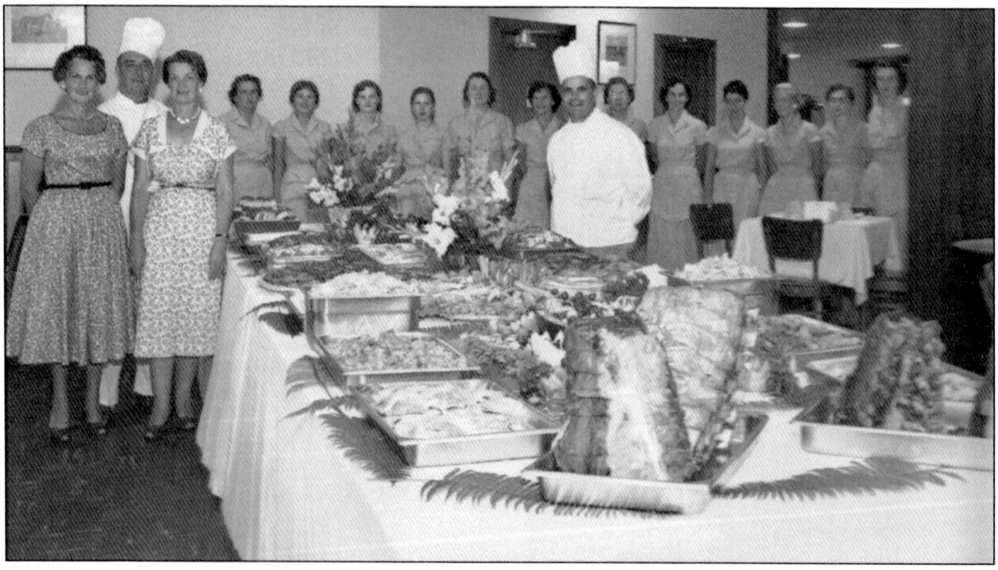

Ready and Waiting. In this photograph, taken during the 1955 fall meet, Marion and Frank (last name not provided) are shown at the corners of the table along with their staff in the grandstand restaurant. The grandstand restaurant, which seated 384 people, was added when the grandstand was enlarged in 1953, adding 1,542 more seats; that increased the grandstand's seating capacity, including boxes, to 3,849.

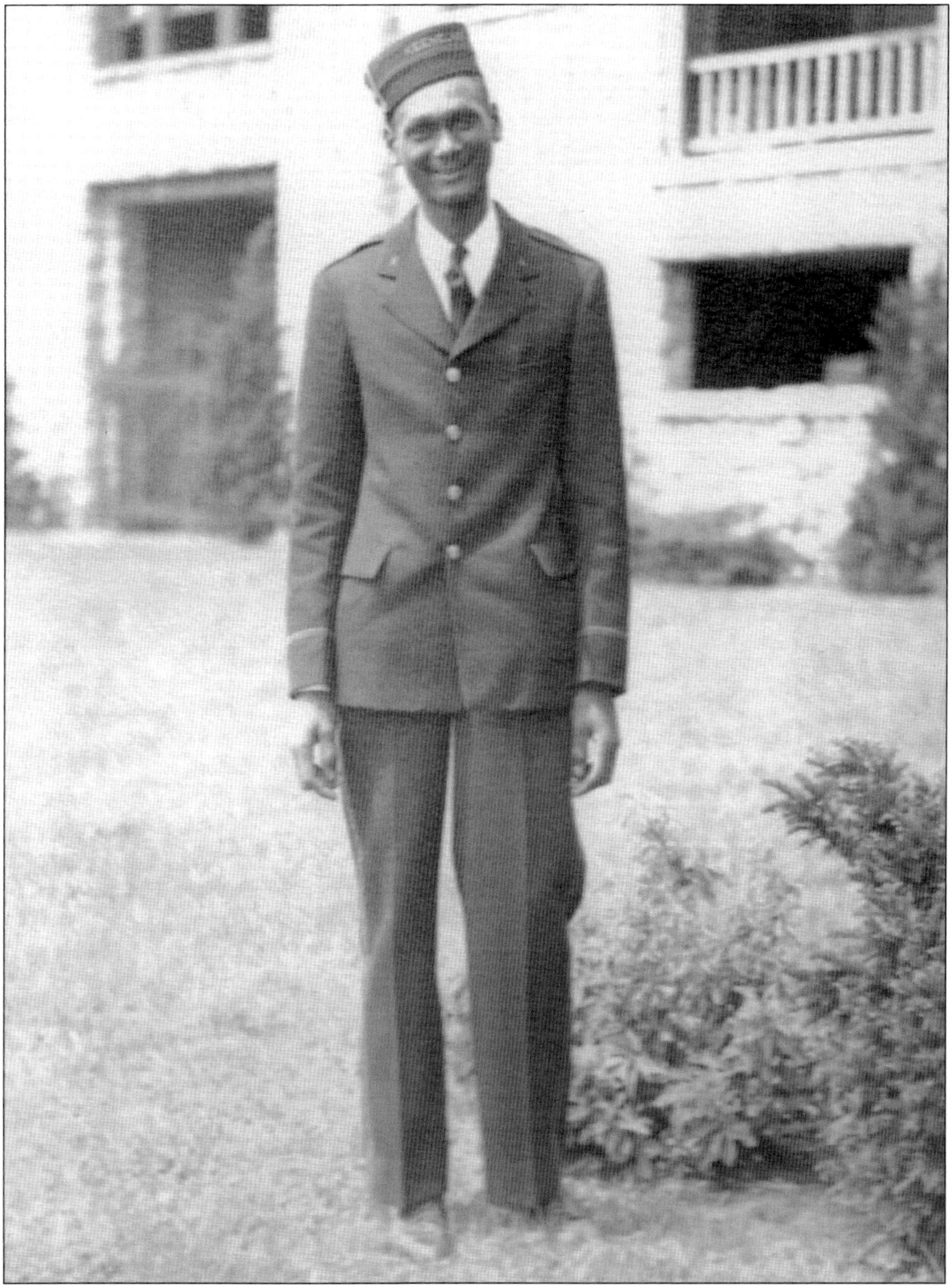

EARLY KEENELAND EMPLOYEE. This photograph, taken in 1937, only identifies the spiffily dressed usher as Oscar. Even though it is said that the original track planners envisioned a racetrack run by volunteers, in actuality Keeneland has provided both temporary and permanent employment for thousands of people through the years. Present-day Keeneland ushers guide people to their seats as they do at other tracks but also provide white parasols to protect the ladies in the private boxes from the afternoon sun. That protection can come in very handy, as the sunlight can sometimes be harsh during Keeneland's spring meet in April and the fall meet in October.

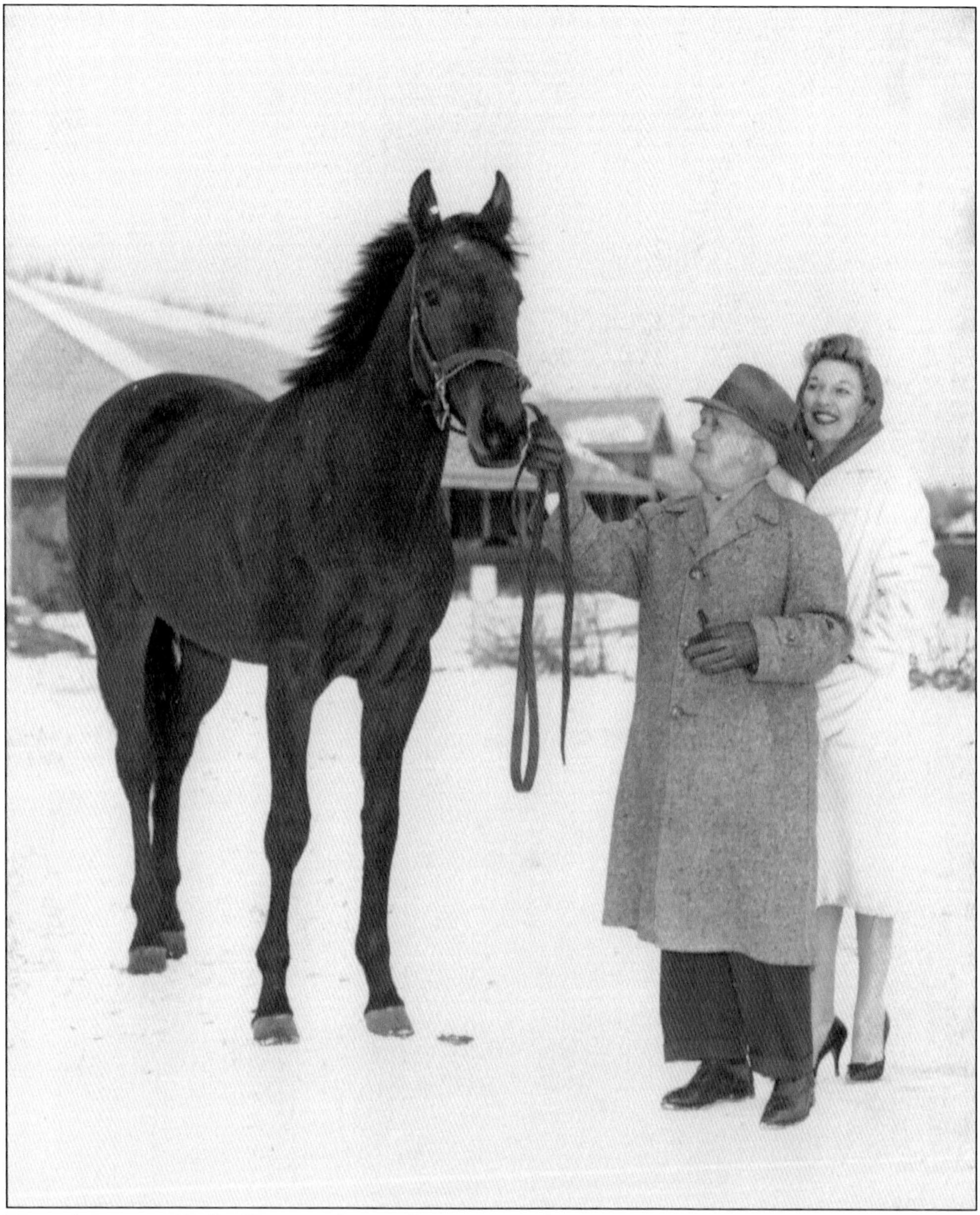

Upset's Jockey. Hall of Fame jockey Willie Knapp is shown here looking at a two-year-old named Ky. Club Tobacco on the backside at Keeneland in 1958 accompanied by Norma Copeland. Knapp was best known for his winning ride on a horse named Upset in the 1919 Sanford Stakes in New York, handing the legendary Man o'War his only defeat. Knapp's first upset came in the 1917 Brooklyn Handicap when he rode nine-year-old Borrow to victory over Regret, Old Rosebud, Roamer, and Omar Khayyam. He said his biggest thrill in racing, however, was in the 1918 Kentucky Derby, which he won aboard a 30-1 shot named Exterminator.

Three

The War Years

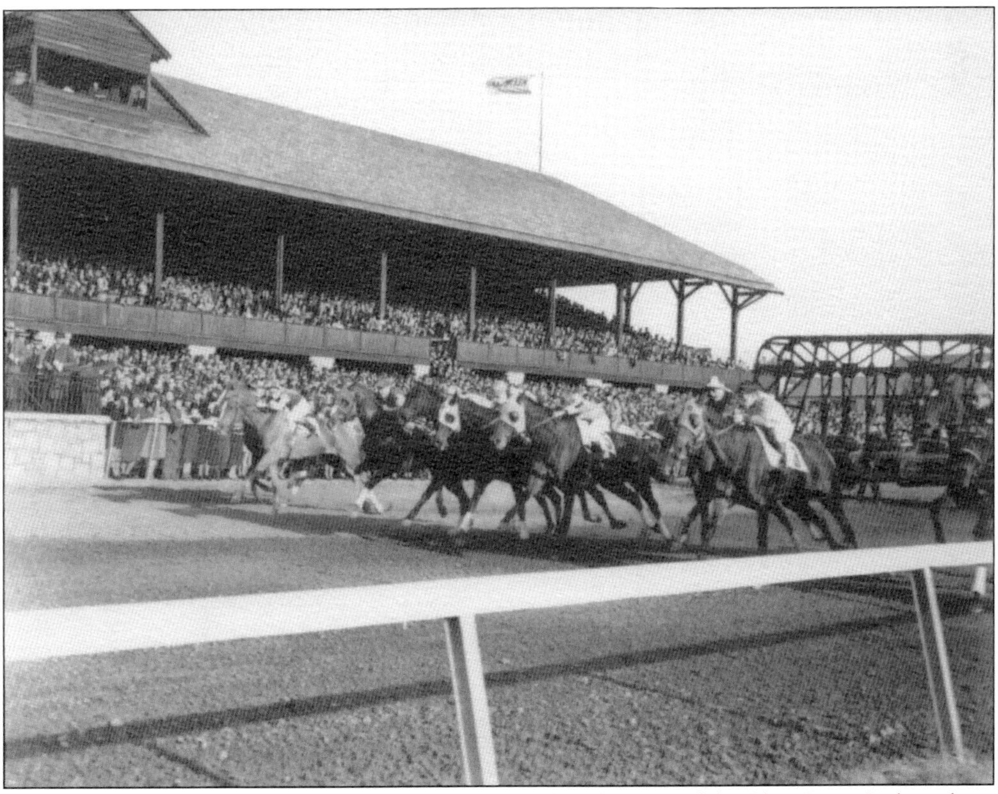

They're Off! By 1939, when this picture was snapped at the start of the Blue Grass Stakes, there was no doubt that Keeneland would be a lasting success. The Blue Grass Stakes, sponsored by Toyota since 1996, was first run at the Kentucky Association track in 1911 and is an important prep race for the Kentucky Derby. Blue Grass Day typically has the biggest handle (amount wagered) of the year.

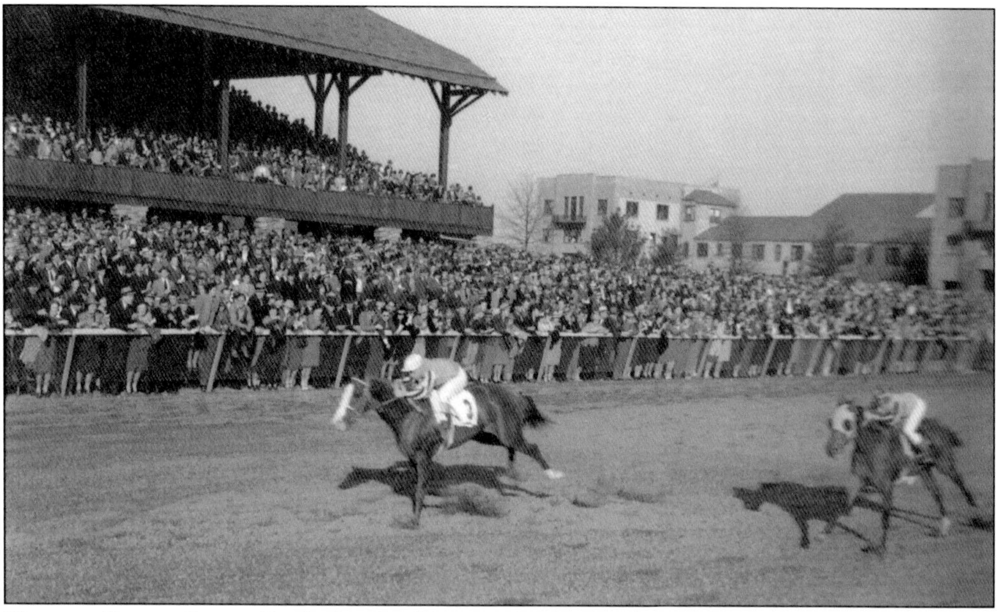

HEATHER BROOM SWEEPS IN. Jockey Basil Jones rode Heather Broom down the middle of the track to win the 1939 Blue Grass Stakes by a full length over Third Degree, ridden by Eddie Arcaro. Heather Broom finished third in the Kentucky Derby nine days later. Eleven Blue Grass winners have gone on to win the Kentucky Derby, the last being Strike the Gold in 1991.

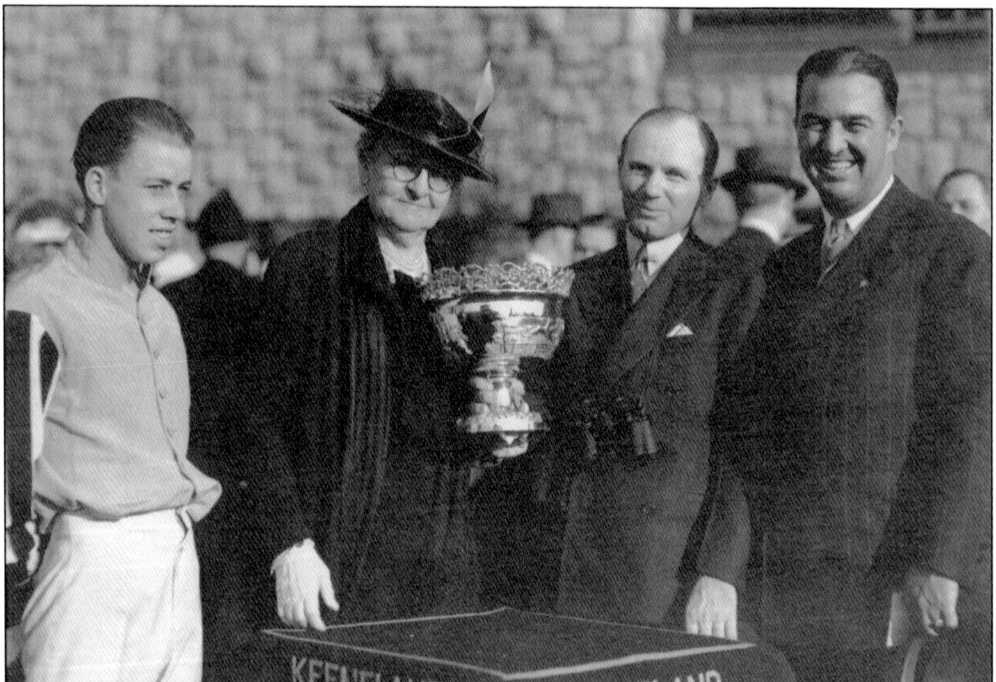

1939 BLUE GRASS STAKES. Earl Sande (holding trophy) trained Heather Broom for owner John Hay Whitney when he won the Blue Grass Stakes in 1939, with jockey Basil Jones (far left). The trophy was presented by Mrs. Brutus Clay of Runnymede Farm and Kentucky governor A.B. "Happy" Chandler (far right).

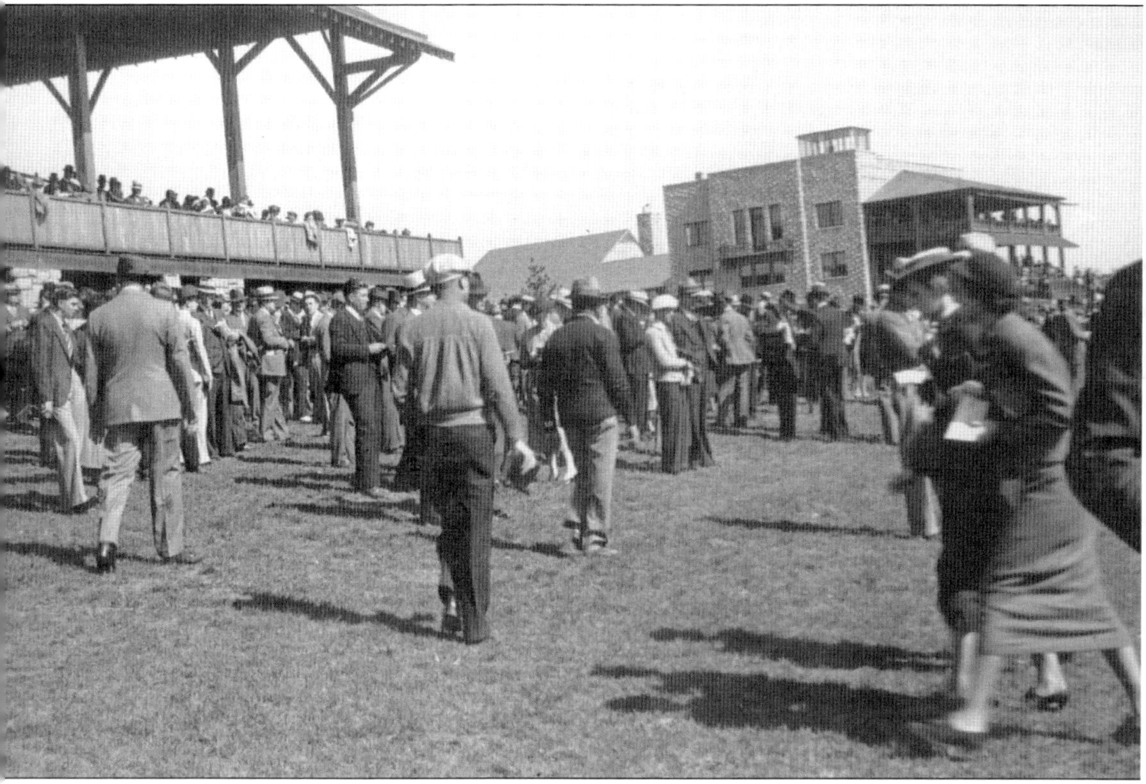

Spring Crowds. When the springtime sun shone in 1937, the crowds clustered on the lawn between the clubhouse and the grandstand. Keeneland's first spring meet featured four stakes races, three of which, the Blue Grass Stakes, Ben Ali and Phoenix Handicaps, were stakes from the old Kentucky Association meetings. The fourth, the Lafayette Stakes, was run for the first time.

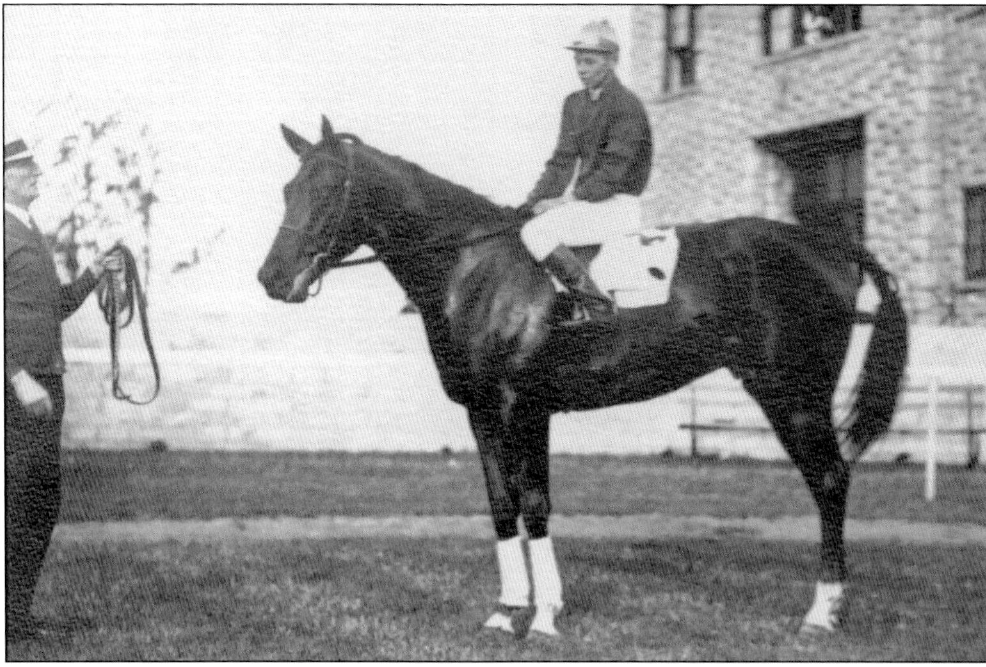

Destined for Greatness. Calumet's Bull Lea is remembered as "one of the greatest sires in Thoroughbred breeding history" by the National Museum of Racing Hall of Fame. As a three-year-old in 1938, he won the Blue Grass Stakes with Irving Anderson on board (pictured). Bull Lea entered stud in 1940 at Calumet and was the leading sire in North America for five years and the leading broodmare sire for four years.

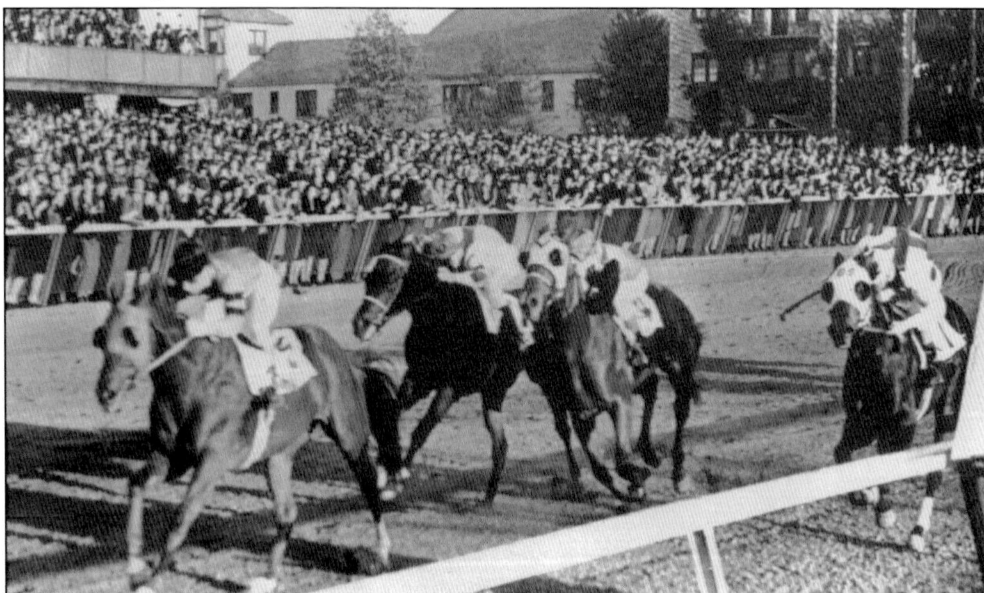

Whirlaway Winning at Keeneland. Future Triple Crown winner and two-time Horse of the Year Whirlaway impressed many at Keeneland as a two-year-old, winning the 1940 Breeders' Futurity. Hall of Fame jockey John Longden rode him at two, but Eddie Arcaro replaced Longden for Whirlaway's fabulous Triple Crown season the following year.

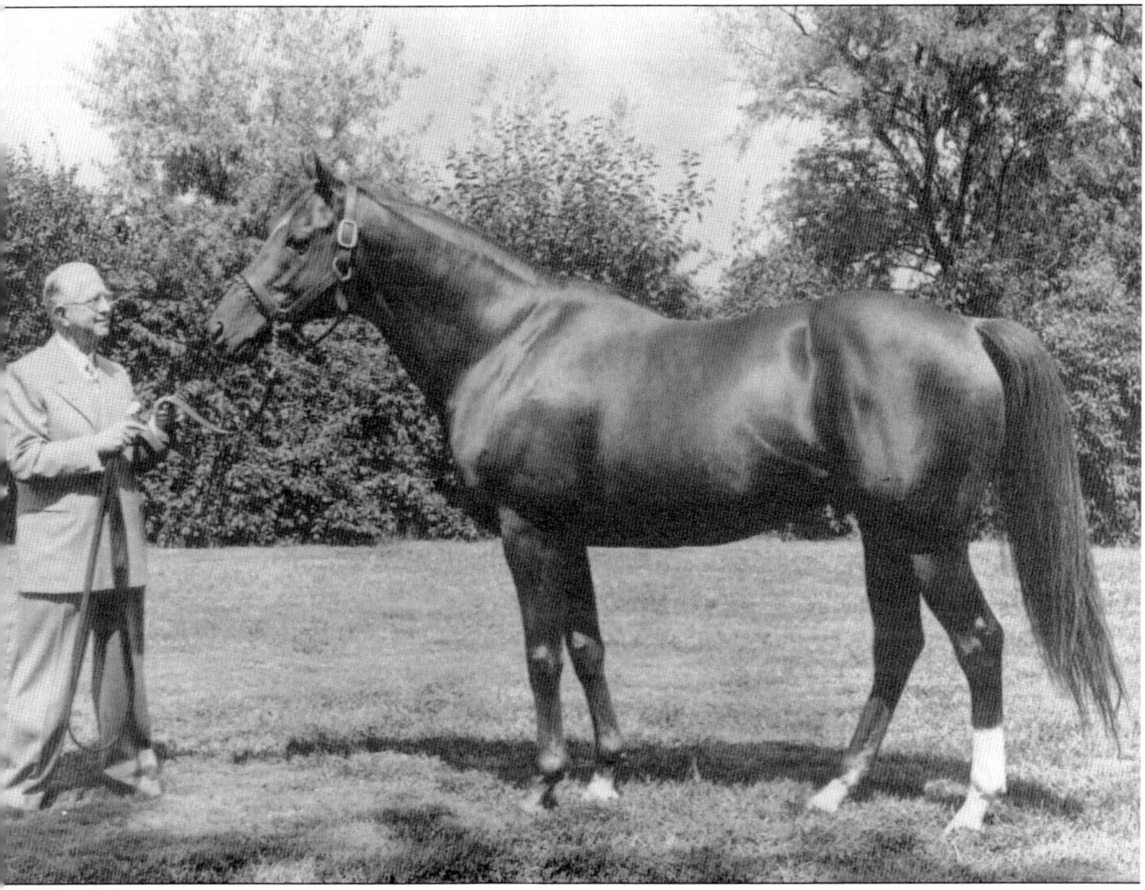

TRIPLE CROWN WINNER. Warren Wright, owner of neighboring Calumet Farm, is shown with his fabulous future Hall of Fame horse Whirlaway. This homebred won Keeneland's 1940 Breeders' Futurity and won the Triple Crown the next year. Whirlaway was trained by Hall of Fame trainer Ben A. Jones in his first year working for Wright and Calumet. He was one of several excellent horses owned by Calumet Farm and trained by Jones, but as the fifth Triple Crown winner and a two-time Horse of the Year, he stood out even among the Calumet horses. At two years of age, Whirlaway won the Saratoga Special, Hopeful, Breeders' Futurity, and Walden Stakes. In addition to the Kentucky Derby, Preakness, and Belmont, the horse won the Travers, American Derby, Dwyer, Saranac, and Lawrence Realization at three. At four, Whirlaway carried 130 pounds to victory in the Massachusetts, Trenton, Washington, and Louisiana Handicaps. He also won the Clark, Dixie, and Brooklyn Handicaps, had a uncontested victory in the Pimlico Special, and defeated Alsab in the Jockey Club Gold Cup.

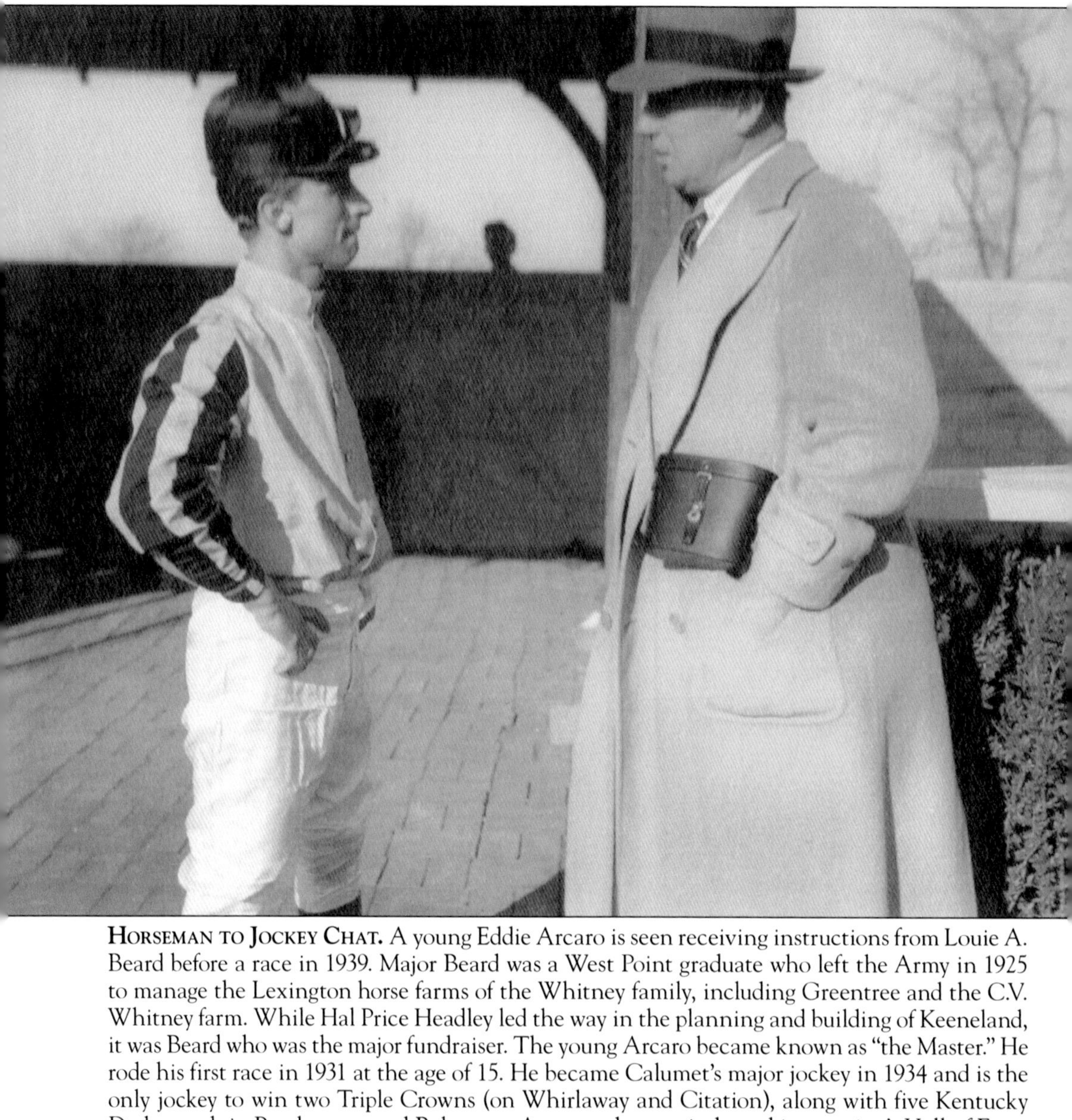

Horseman to Jockey Chat. A young Eddie Arcaro is seen receiving instructions from Louie A. Beard before a race in 1939. Major Beard was a West Point graduate who left the Army in 1925 to manage the Lexington horse farms of the Whitney family, including Greentree and the C.V. Whitney farm. While Hal Price Headley led the way in the planning and building of Keeneland, it was Beard who was the major fundraiser. The young Arcaro became known as "the Master." He rode his first race in 1931 at the age of 15. He became Calumet's major jockey in 1934 and is the only jockey to win two Triple Crowns (on Whirlaway and Citation), along with five Kentucky Derbys and six Preaknesses and Belmonts. Arcaro, who was inducted into racing's Hall of Fame in 1958, rode his last race at the age of 45 in 1961. In 24,092 races, Arcaro had 4,779 wins, 3,807 seconds, 3,302 thirds, and earnings of $30,039,543. His record of 554 stakes victories stood for 11 years until Willie Shoemaker broke it in 1972.

Jockey Tradition. Keeneland has many traditions, and none is older or more colorful than painting the jockey silks of the latest Blue Grass Stakes winner on the cast iron jockey that overlooks the paddock. This 1938 picture shows the silks of Maxwell Howard, who owned Fencing, the winner of the 1937 Blue Grass Stakes. Today, a number of other jockeys are also painted in the silks of major stakes winners.

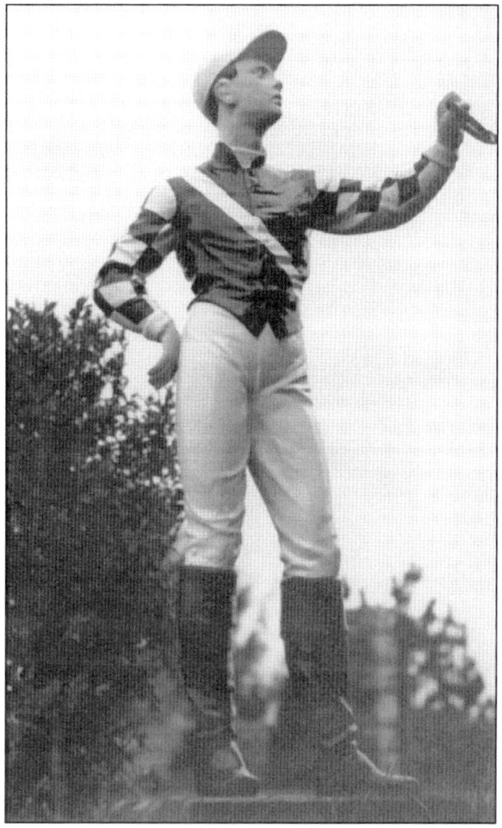

Keeneland News Stand. As the public came through the main gate at Keeneland, they were greeted with a selection of racing newspapers, including *American Racing Record*, *Daily Telegraph*, and the *Daily Racing Form*. The *Record* disappeared in the 1960s, and the *Telegraph* was absorbed by the *Daily Racing Form* in 1971. The *Daily Racing Form* archives at the Keeneland Library is comprised of approximately 5,400 hardbound volumes representing more than 113 years of racing history.

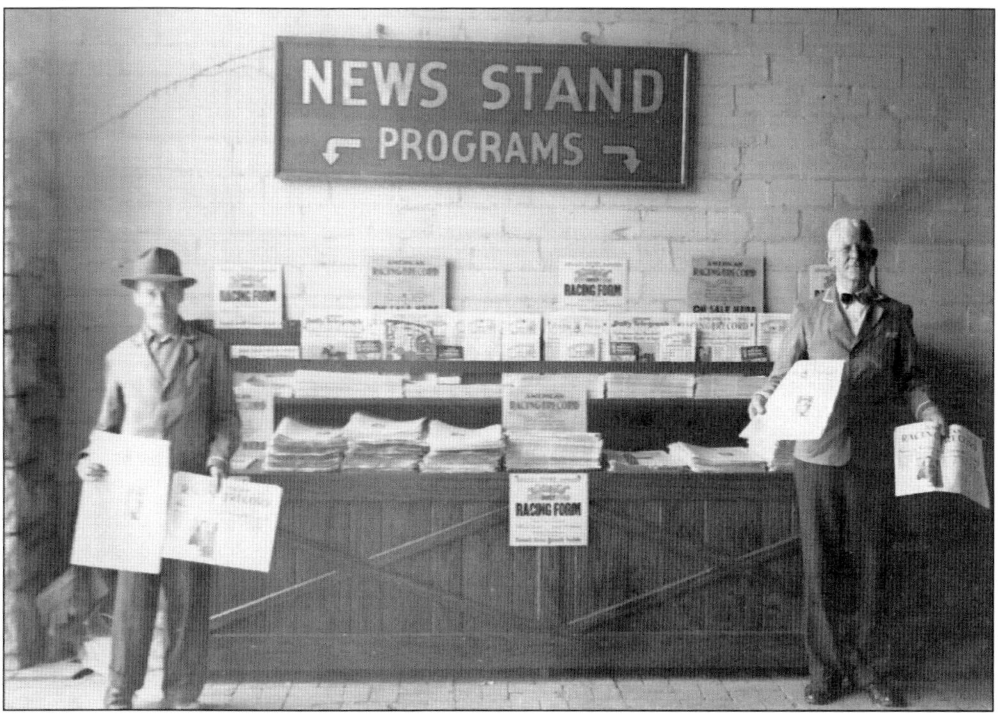

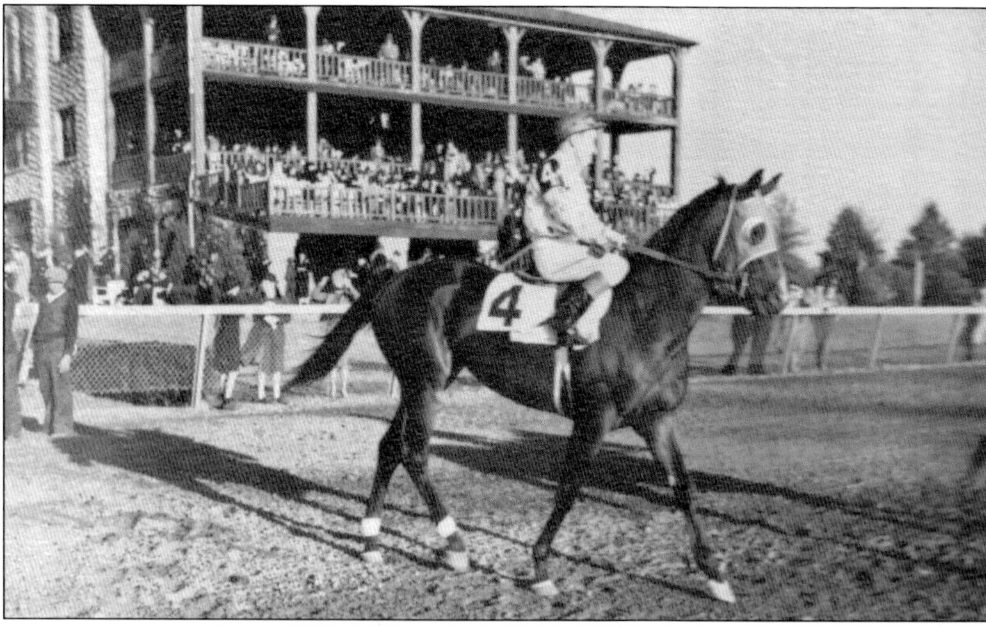

BREEDERS' FUTURITY. Johnstown was bred at Claiborne Farm by Arthur Hancock Sr. for William Woodward's Belair Stud. He is seen here entering the track with Jimmy Stout aboard before winning the 1938 Breeders' Futurity. Johnstown's most successful season came at the age of three when he won the Wood Memorial, followed a week later by the Kentucky Derby. Johnstown won 14 of his 21 lifetime starts and is in racing's Hall of Fame.

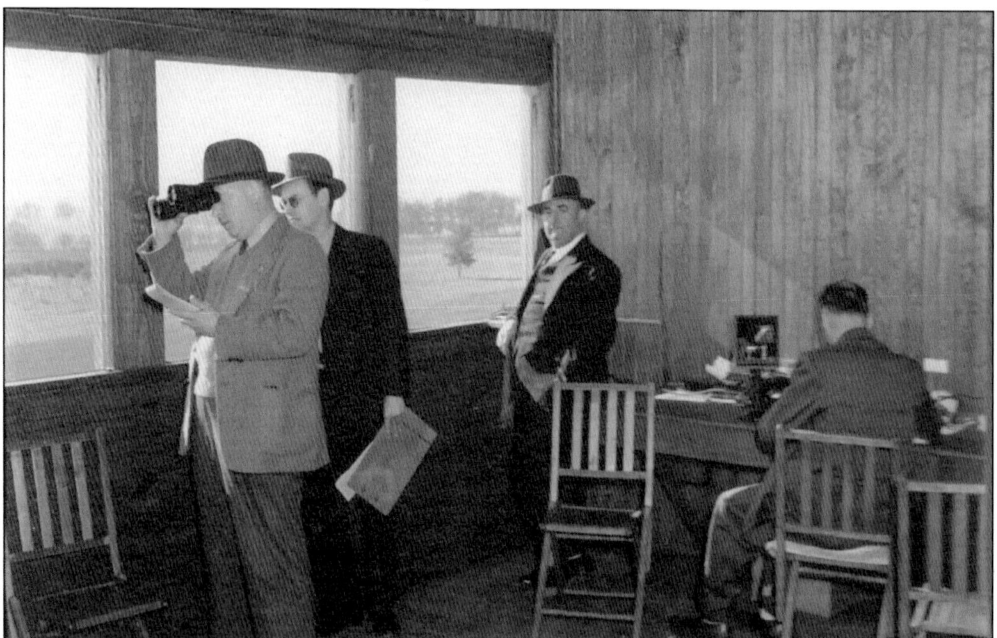

PRESS BOX. The ink-stained denizens of the press seemed to be enjoying the newly paneled Keeneland press box in this 1939 image. Racing results and current racing news were as important to Lexington newspapers then as they are today. As Keeneland's marquee races gained stature, more and more out-of-town turf writers requested press passes.

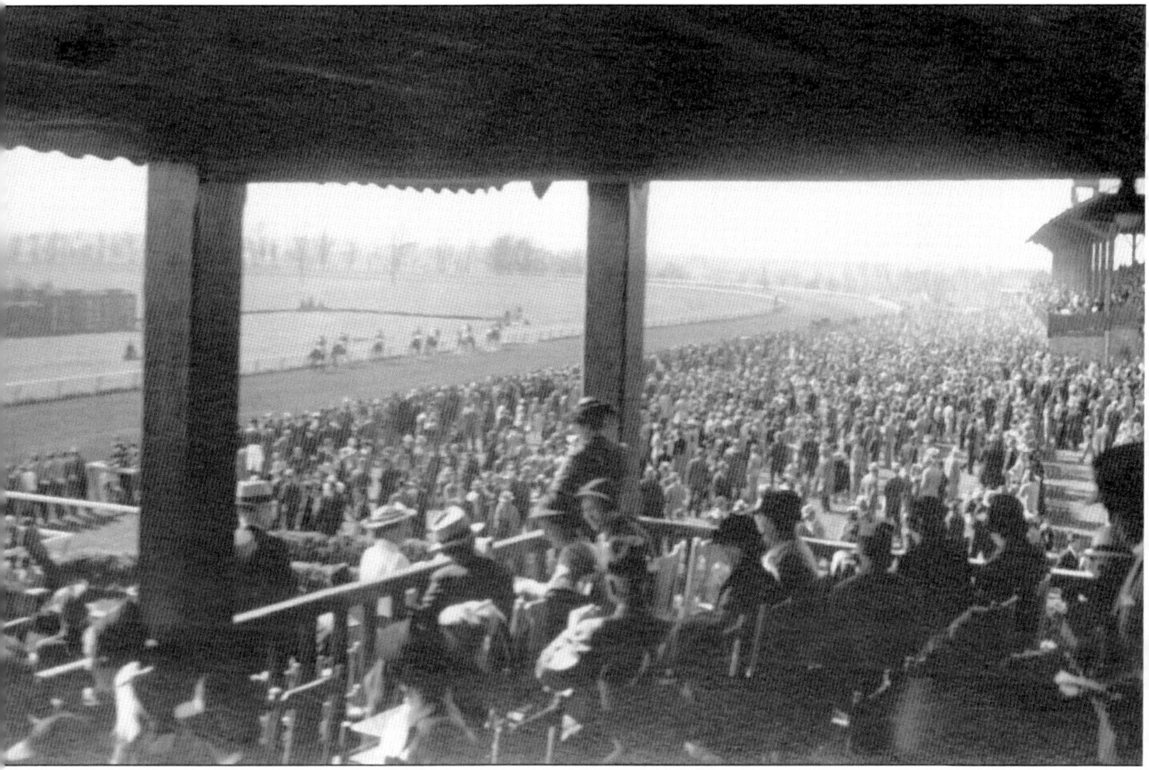

CONTINUED SUCCESS. Just three years after opening, despite a slowly recovering economy, Keeneland was drawing large crowds, as seen here in 1939. This photograph was taken from the clubhouse porch that overlooked the Keeneland lawn and the path horses used to enter the track. Within a few years, the space was filled by the grandstand addition that attached to the clubhouse, and the horses then entered the track through a tunnel beneath the seats.

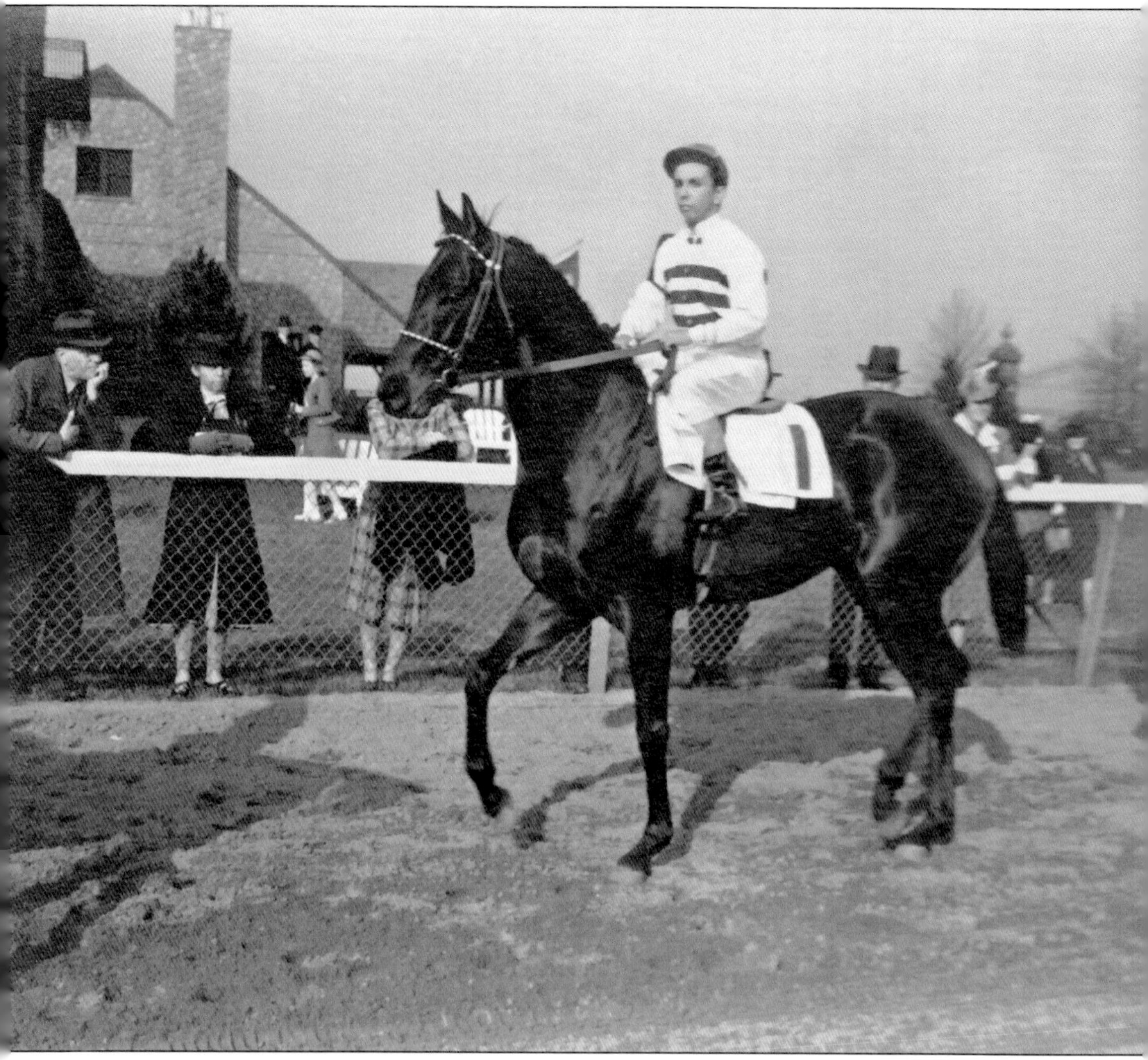

Bimelech. The 1940 Blue Grass Stakes was won by E.R. Bradley's Bimelech in a three-horse race, one of the smallest Blue Grass fields ever. He was trained by William Hurley and ridden by F.A. Smith. After he won the Blue Grass and Derby Trial Stakes, Colonel Bradley believed he might have his best Derby colt in Bimelech, but in a stunning upset he lost by one and a half lengths to Gallahadion, a horse he had beaten in the Derby Trial. Bradley found redemption after losing the Kentucky Derby when Bimelech rebounded a week later to win the Preakness before capturing the Belmont. Bradley already had four Derby trophies from winners: Behave Yourself (1921), Bubbling Over (1926), Burgoo King (1932), and Brokers Tip (1933).

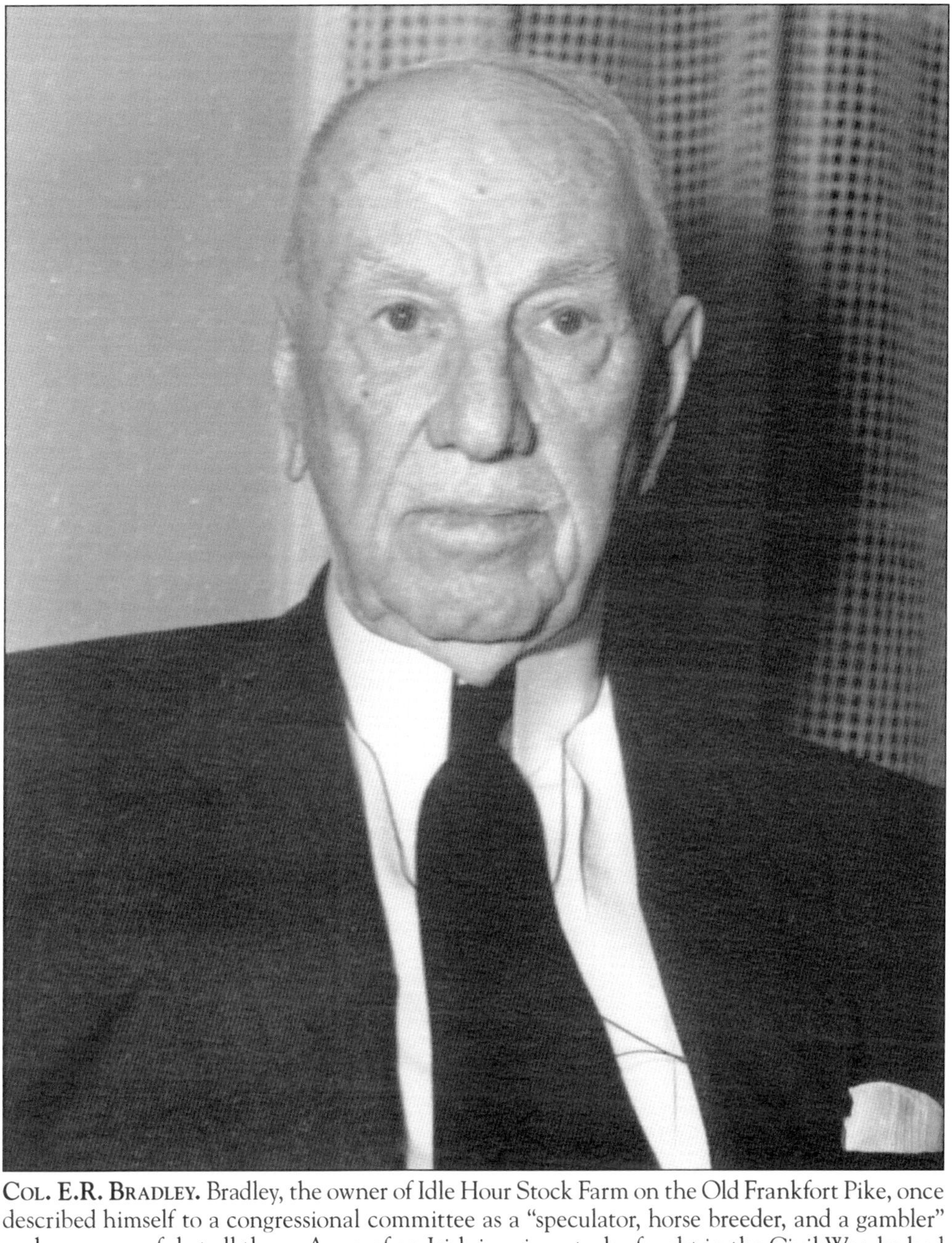

COL. E.R. BRADLEY. Bradley, the owner of Idle Hour Stock Farm on the Old Frankfort Pike, once described himself to a congressional committee as a "speculator, horse breeder, and a gambler" and was successful at all three. A son of an Irish immigrant who fought in the Civil War, he had been a steel mill worker, a cowboy, a gold miner, and friend to Wyatt Earp. The rank of colonel was of the Kentucky kind and purely honorary. He ran an exclusive restaurant and casino in Florida. He owned all or part of racetracks that included Hialeah, the Fair Grounds Race Course in New Orleans, and the old Kentucky Association track. He raced four Kentucky Derby winners and had two horses come within a race of winning the Triple Crown. He was considered by many to be the most successful racehorse owner of the first three decades of the 20th century. He and his wife were also generous philanthropists. Having no children themselves, they supported a number of orphanages.

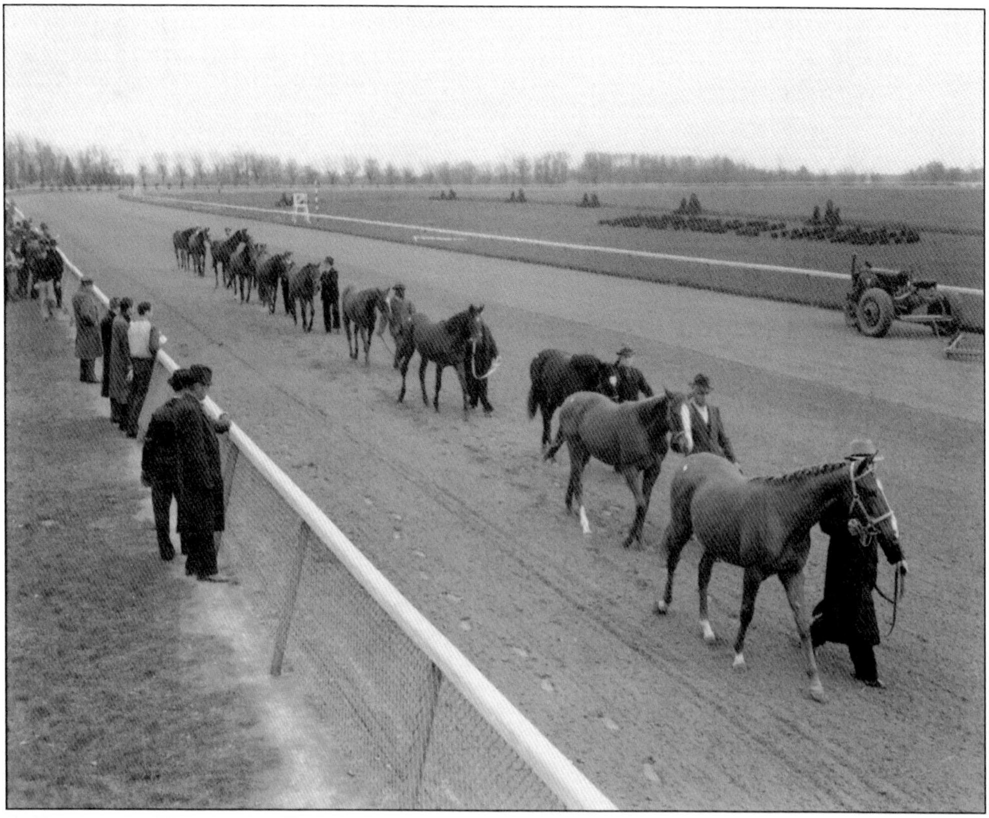

A Parade of Yearlings. Beginning in 1938, Keeneland began hosting two yearling judging contests—one for colts and one for fillies—that were sponsored by the Thoroughbred Club of America. The contests were discontinued after yearling sales began at Keeneland in 1943.

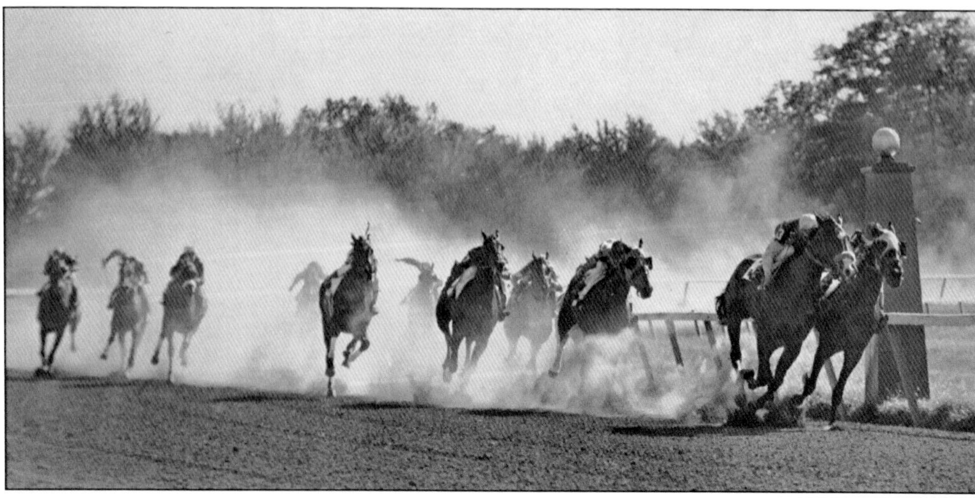

Dusty Turn. Apparently, the watering trucks seen at today's racetracks were not used as much in 1939 when this dramatic photograph was taken at Keeneland.

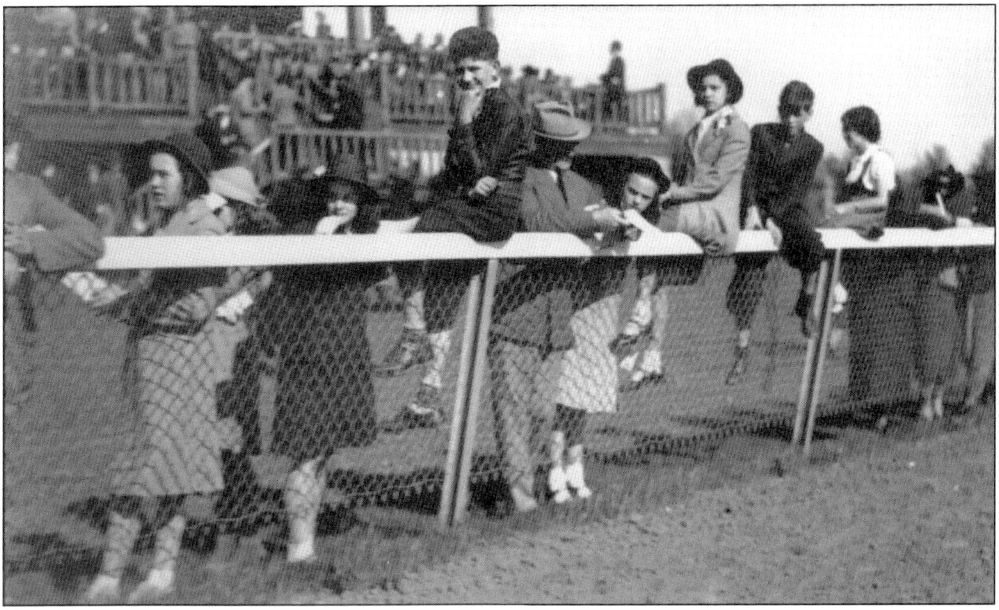

Before the "Big War." When this photograph was taken in 1938, things seemed safe and normal in America. Benny Goodman was on the radio, *Snow White and the Seven Dwarves* was big at the box office, and the Great Depression was fading, but storm clouds were gathering in Europe and in Asia. Many of the people who enjoyed Keeneland in those halcyon days soon had their lives interrupted by events far from central Kentucky.

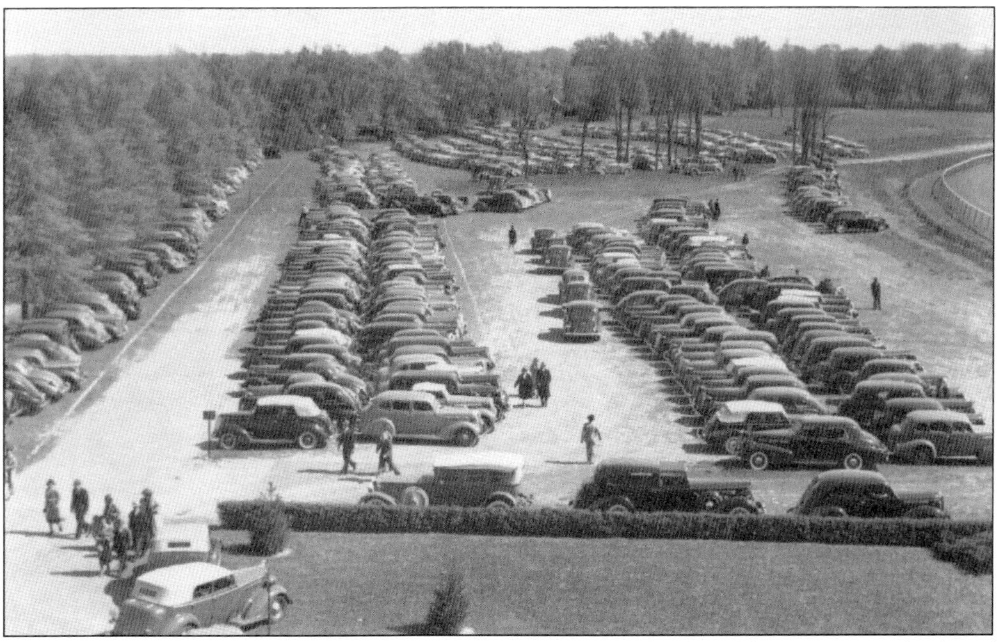

Full Parking Lot. The parking lot just south of the Keeneland Clubhouse attracted a lot of nice cars in 1939 when this image was captured. An antique car aficionado might spot a Cadillac V-12, a Packard Touring, or even a Lincoln Zephyr amidst the Crosleys, Studebakers, Pontiacs, and occasional Model T. Today, these same cars are proudly exhibited as prized antiques at the annual Keeneland Concours d'Elegance car show.

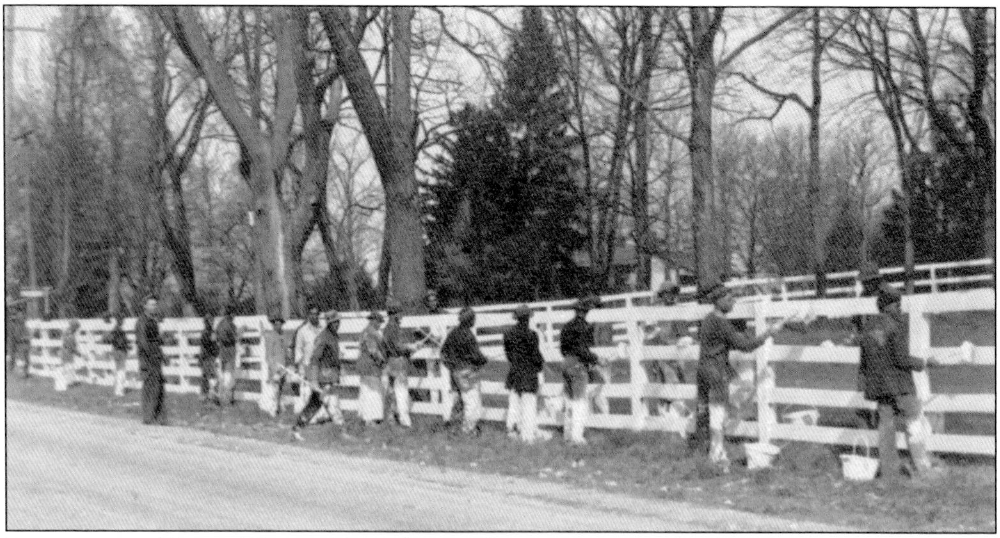

Painting the Fences White. From the very beginning, Keeneland work crews have kept the grounds park-like and well groomed as representative of a prosperous Thoroughbred industry.

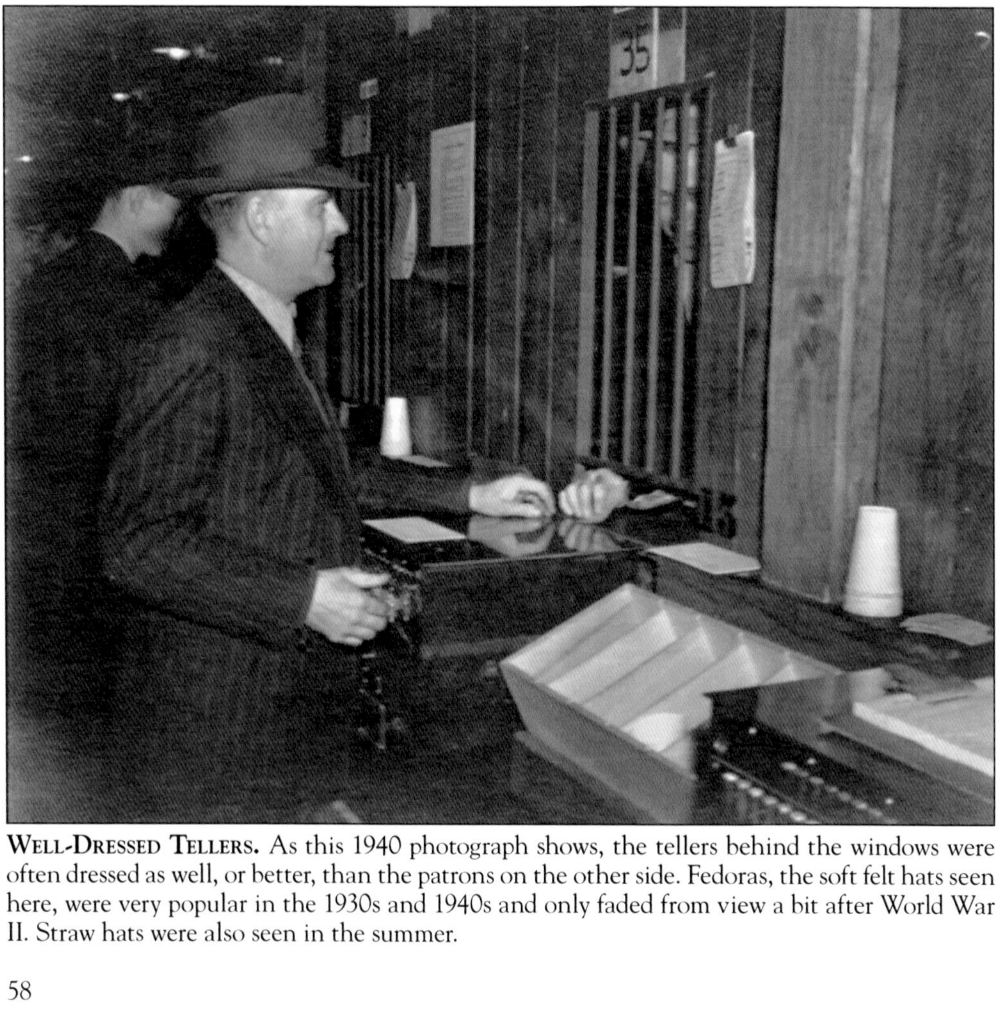

Well-Dressed Tellers. As this 1940 photograph shows, the tellers behind the windows were often dressed as well, or better, than the patrons on the other side. Fedoras, the soft felt hats seen here, were very popular in the 1930s and 1940s and only faded from view a bit after World War II. Straw hats were also seen in the summer.

Racing Secretary's Office. One of the busiest places at any racetrack is the racing secretary's office, as this 1939 photograph shows. Charles J. McLennan was Keeneland's first racing secretary. A racing secretary designs and administers the track's racing schedule, assigns handicap weights, accepts or denies all entries and entry fees, and is accountable for filing all licenses, among other responsibilities.

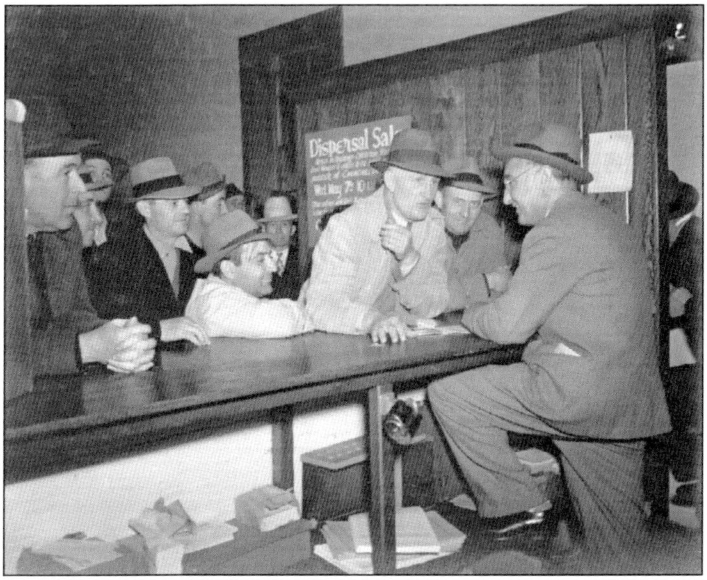

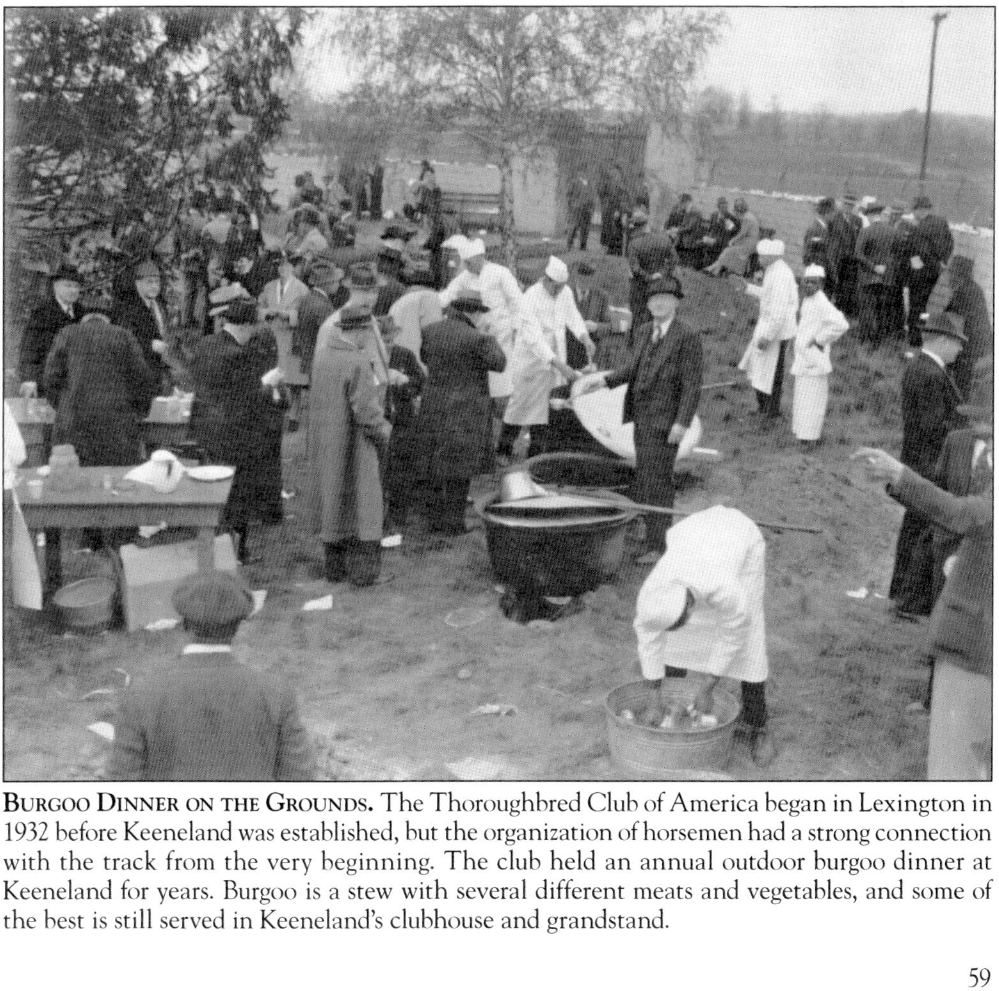

Burgoo Dinner on the Grounds. The Thoroughbred Club of America began in Lexington in 1932 before Keeneland was established, but the organization of horsemen had a strong connection with the track from the very beginning. The club held an annual outdoor burgoo dinner at Keeneland for years. Burgoo is a stew with several different meats and vegetables, and some of the best is still served in Keeneland's clubhouse and grandstand.

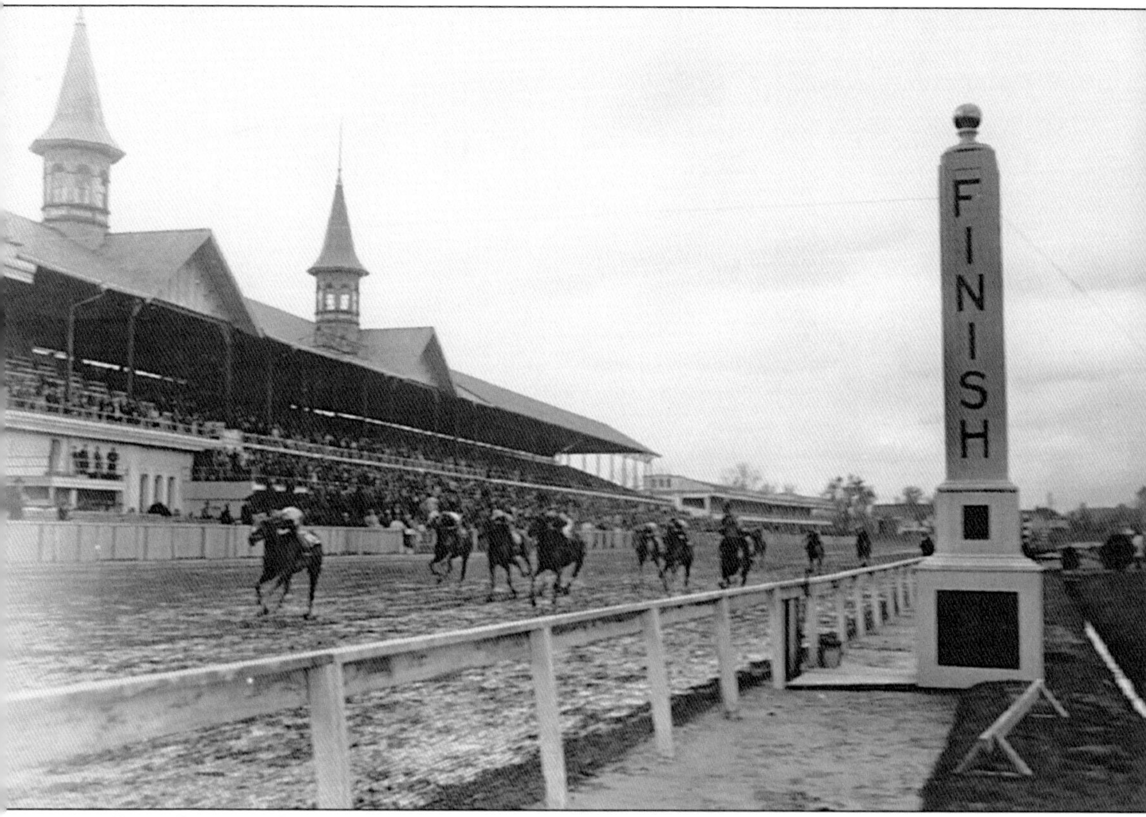

BLUE GRASS AT CHURCHILL DOWNS! During World War II, Keeneland was considered a "suburban plant," an attraction without public transportation. In 1943, the track was asked not to operate during the war because of shortages of fuel and rubber, so it leased the Churchill Downs facilities, which remained open, to hold the spring meet. Three spring meets were held at Churchill Downs from 1943 to 1945; no fall meets were held during that time. The war called away many Keeneland patrons and employees, including general manager W.T. Bishop. All the net profits from the 1942 fall meet were earmarked to help with the war, and $35,000 was given to the Lexington War Chest. Keeneland customers bought more than $27,000 in war bonds and stamps during the 1942 meeting, the last held at Keeneland until 1946.

Four

Riders Up!

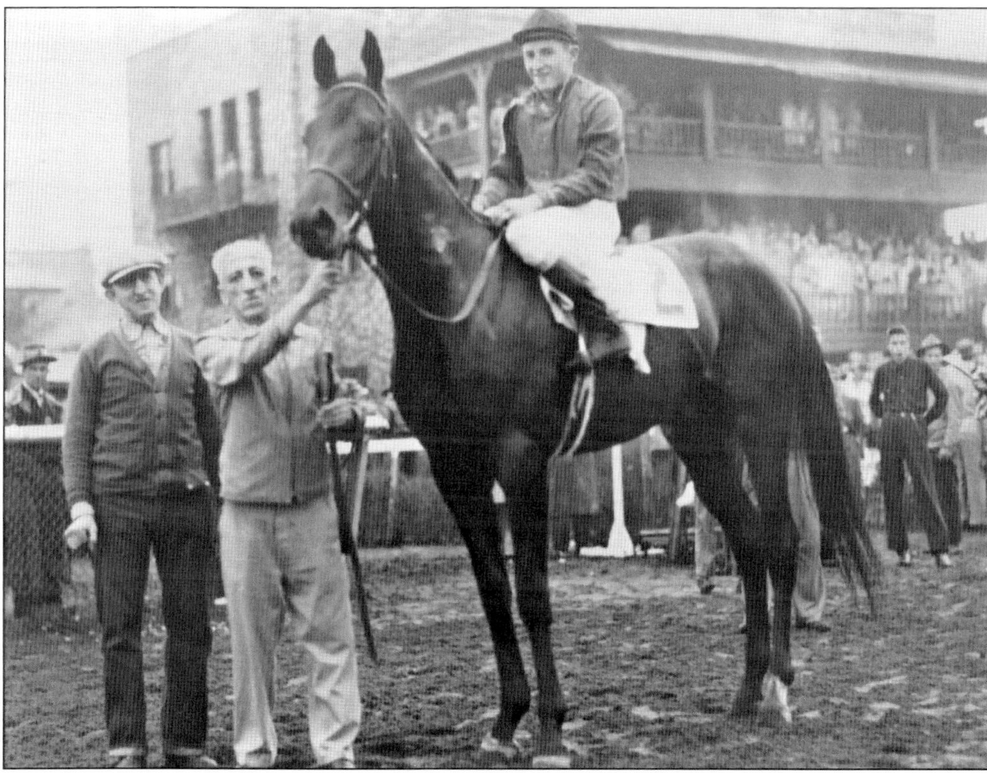

Blue Grass Beauty. Jockey Doug Dodson appears happy after winning the 1947 Blue Grass Stakes aboard Calumet Farm's Faultless. The pair placed third in the Kentucky Derby that year, but they came back to win the Preakness Stakes. Dodson scored one of his biggest successes in September 1947, when he rode the Calumet horse Armed to victory against Triple Crown winner Assault in a $100,000 match race held at Belmont Park.

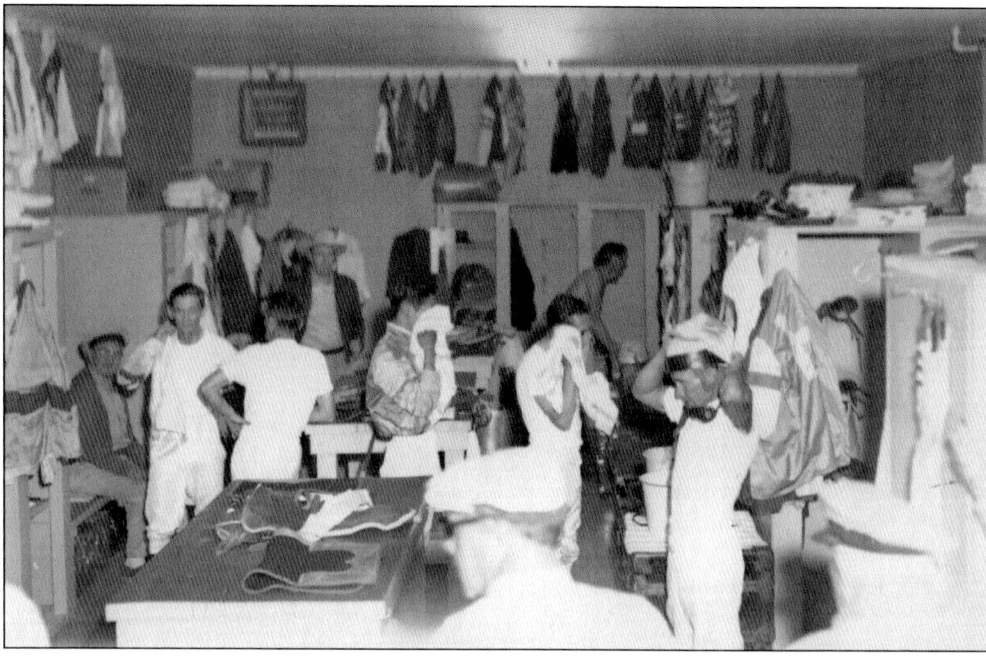

Busy Place. The jockey room at Keeneland is a busy place filled with jockeys cleaning up from their last race and getting ready for the next one in this 1949 photograph. Their valets make sure they have the right jockey silks for each race. Jockey silks are colorful tops and matching caps worn by each jockey indicating the owner of the horse they are riding. In addition, jockeys wear white breeches and riding boots.

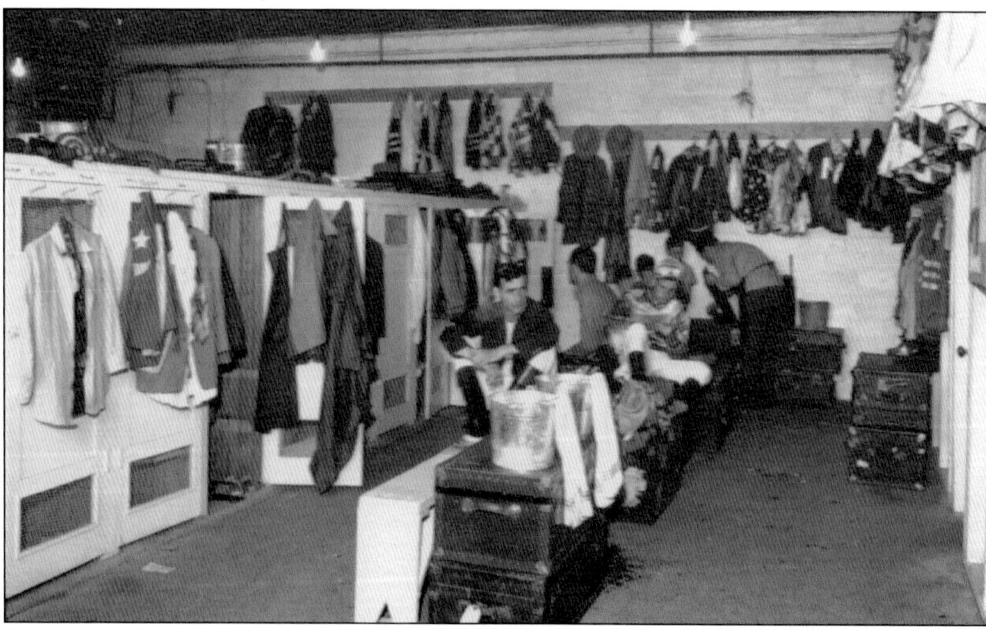

In Between Races. It is quieter in the jockey room between races, as seen in this 1949 photograph. Jockeys have to report to the jockey room an hour before their first race and remain there unless they are racing or watching a race until that day's riding assignments are finished. They also always have to report to the clerk of scales at least 15 minutes before their next race to be weighed.

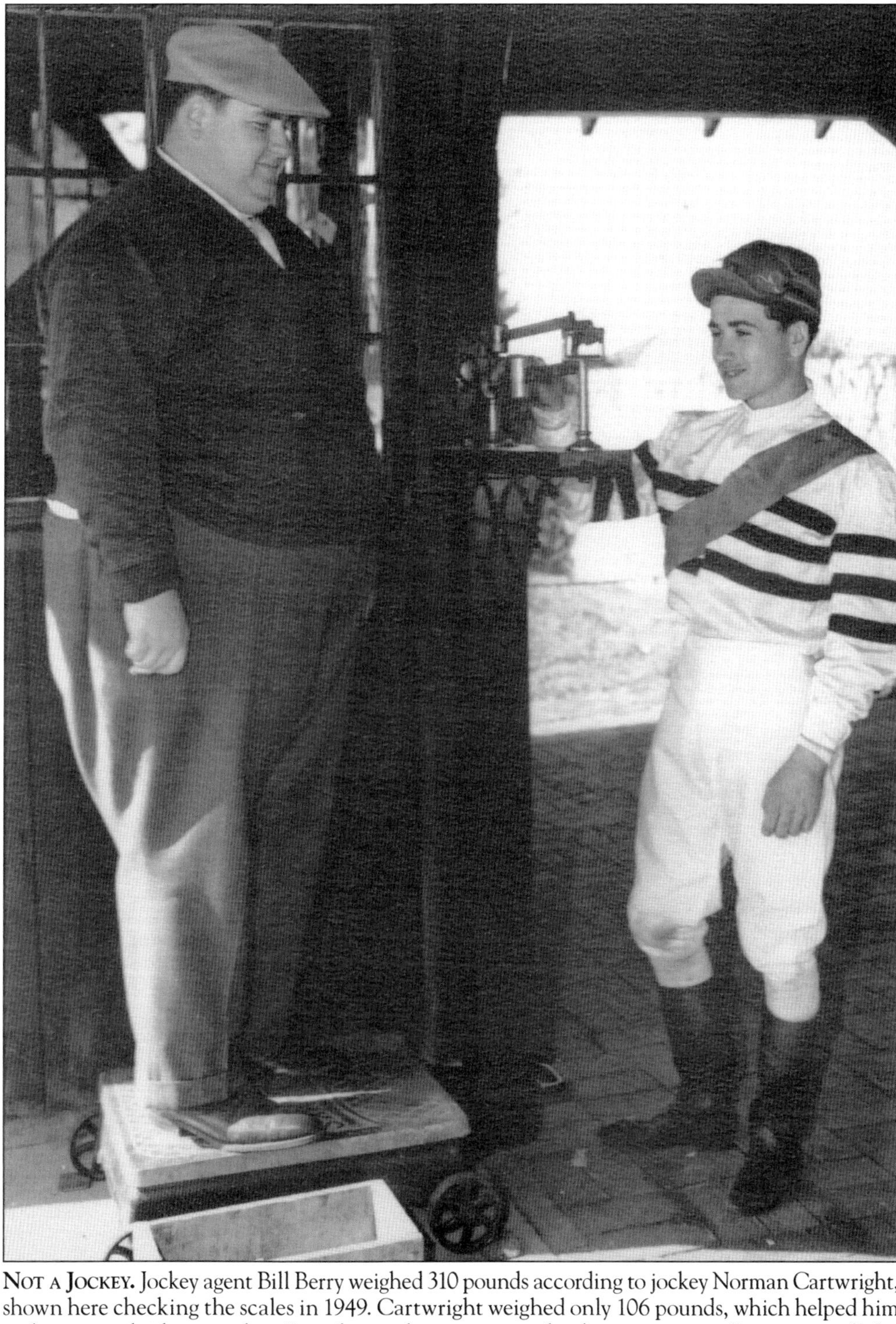

Not a Jockey. Jockey agent Bill Berry weighed 310 pounds according to jockey Norman Cartwright, shown here checking the scales in 1949. Cartwright weighed only 106 pounds, which helped him make required riding weights. Specific weights are assigned to horses in races. Sometimes, all the horses carry the same weight, and other times the horses with the better race records carry more weight in an effort to even the field.

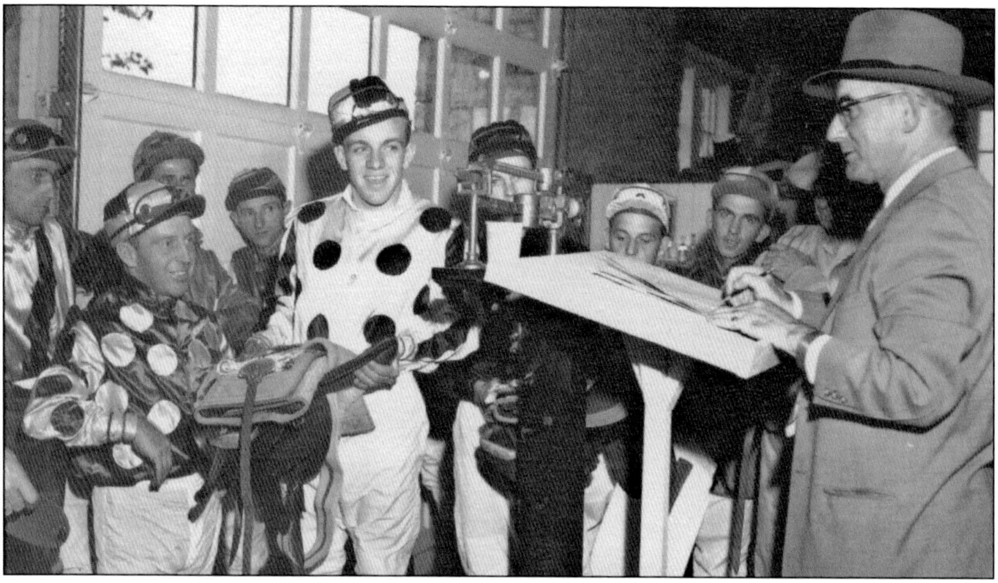

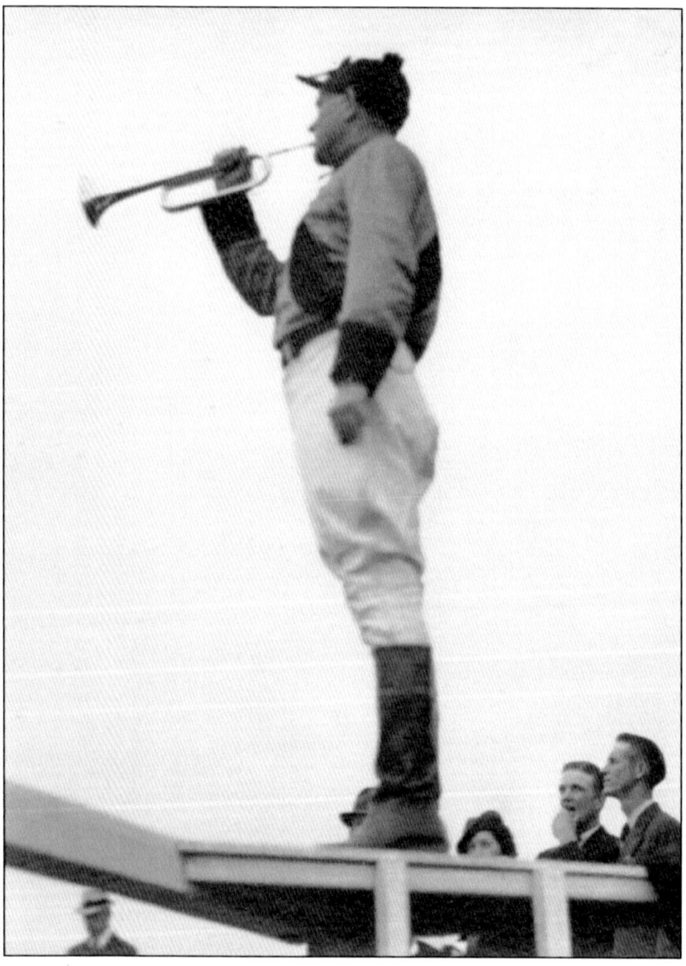

The Family Business. Johnny Adams (second from left) watches as his son J.R. Adams is weighed along with his saddle by clerk of scales Charles Gormley before a race at Keeneland in 1953. Johnny won seven stakes races at Keeneland, including three runnings of the Ben Ali Stakes (1943, 1944, and 1954) and three runnings of the Phoenix Stakes (1945, 1954, and 1955).

Call to the Post. The bugler at Keeneland plays a tune about five to ten minutes before a race, signifying that it is time for the horses to move to the starting gate for the start of the next race. This 1936 photograph is of Keeneland's first bugler, Barnes Wilhelm, playing on a raised platform. The current Keeneland bugler, Bucky Sallee, has been a fixture there since 1964.

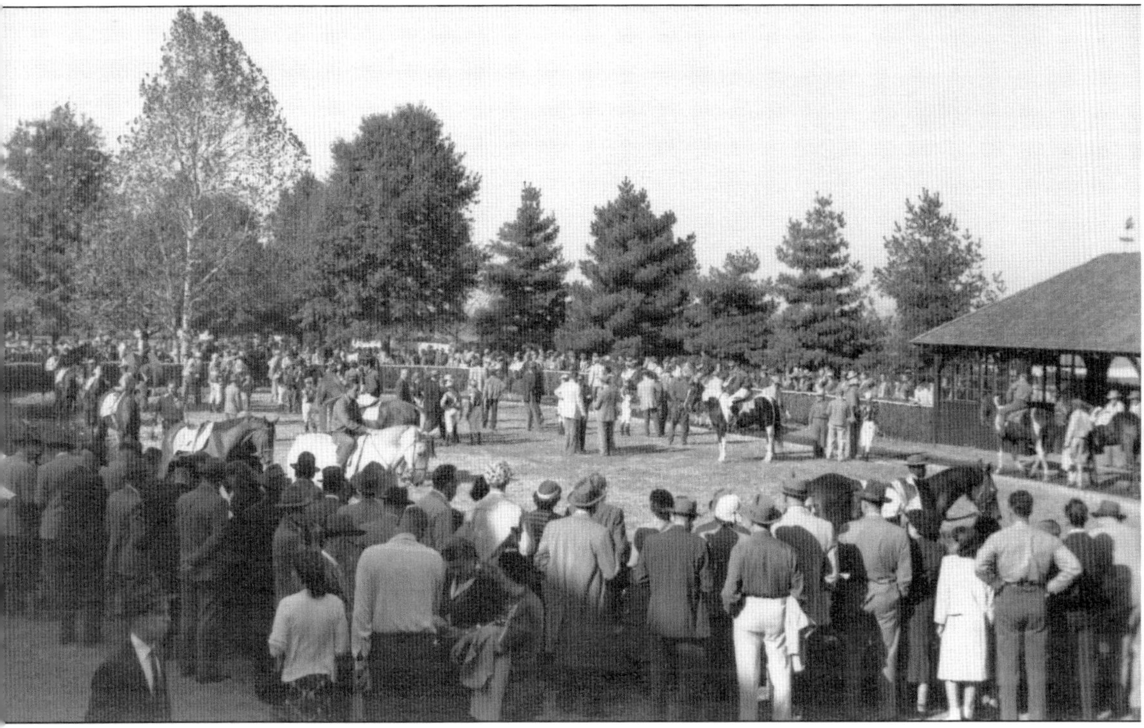

KEENELAND PADDOCK. The Keeneland paddock includes two areas: the saddling area under the trees and, next to it, a walking ring. This 1952 photograph shows the walking ring section of the paddock. Once the horses for an upcoming race are saddled, they are led to the walking ring and walked by a groom until it is time for the jockeys to mount up. In the interlude, before it is time for the jockeys to get in the saddle, owners, trainers, and jockeys mingle in the grassy area at the center of the walking ring so trainers can give jockeys any last-minute riding instructions. In the meantime, race goers outside the paddock get a chance to look over the next race's runners.

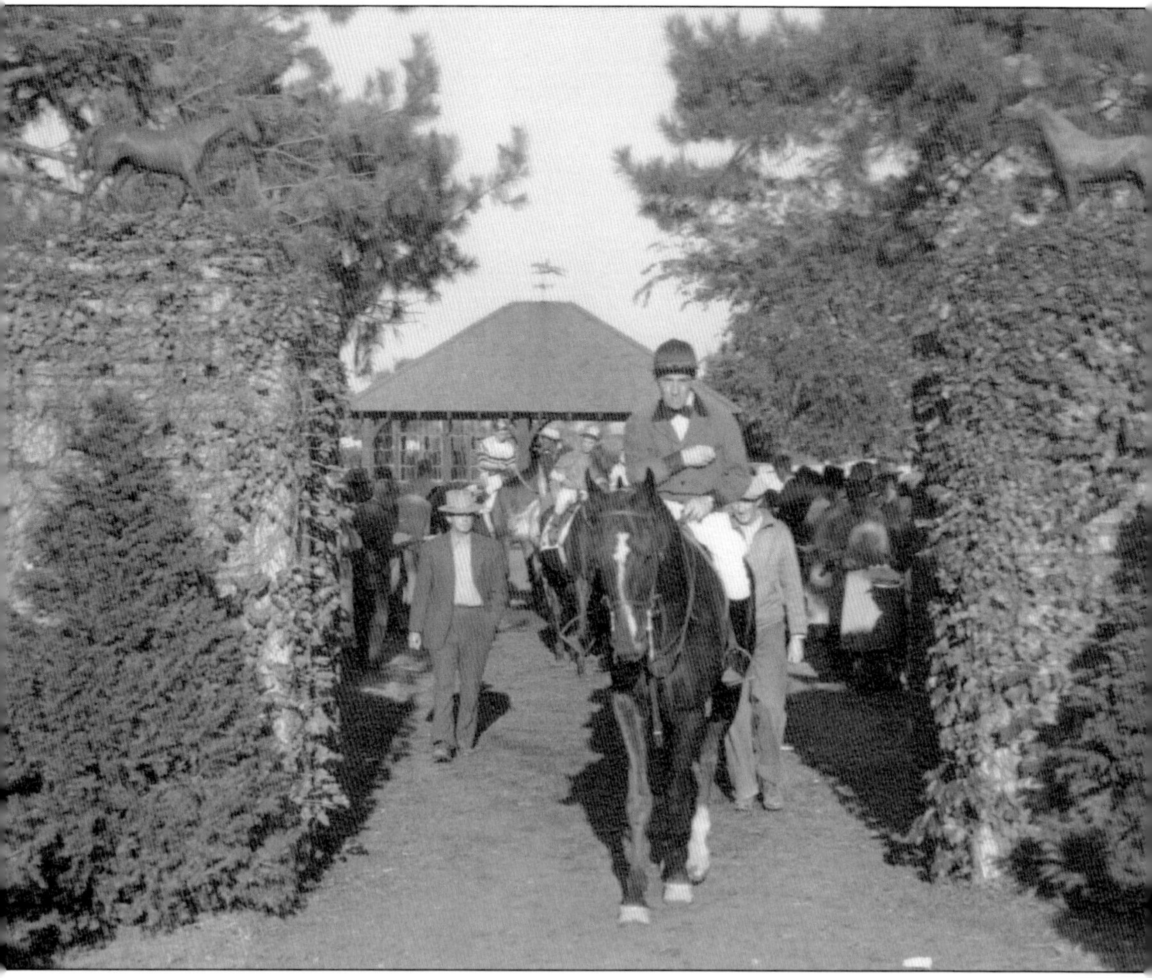

FOLLOW THE LEADER. Once the jockeys are mounted, they guide their horses in post position order (each horse's number is shown on the cloth they wear under their saddle and on the jockey's right sleeve) out to the racetrack where they are met with outriders on ponies who accompany them through the post parade to the starting gate. This 1954 outrider is identified as "Pony Boy—Smokey Hershenson," and he is shown leading the horses from the walking ring to the track through two stone pillars topped with bronze sculptures by sculptor Isidore Jules Boheur. The two sculptures are of a mare and stallion representing the ideal male and female Thoroughbred.

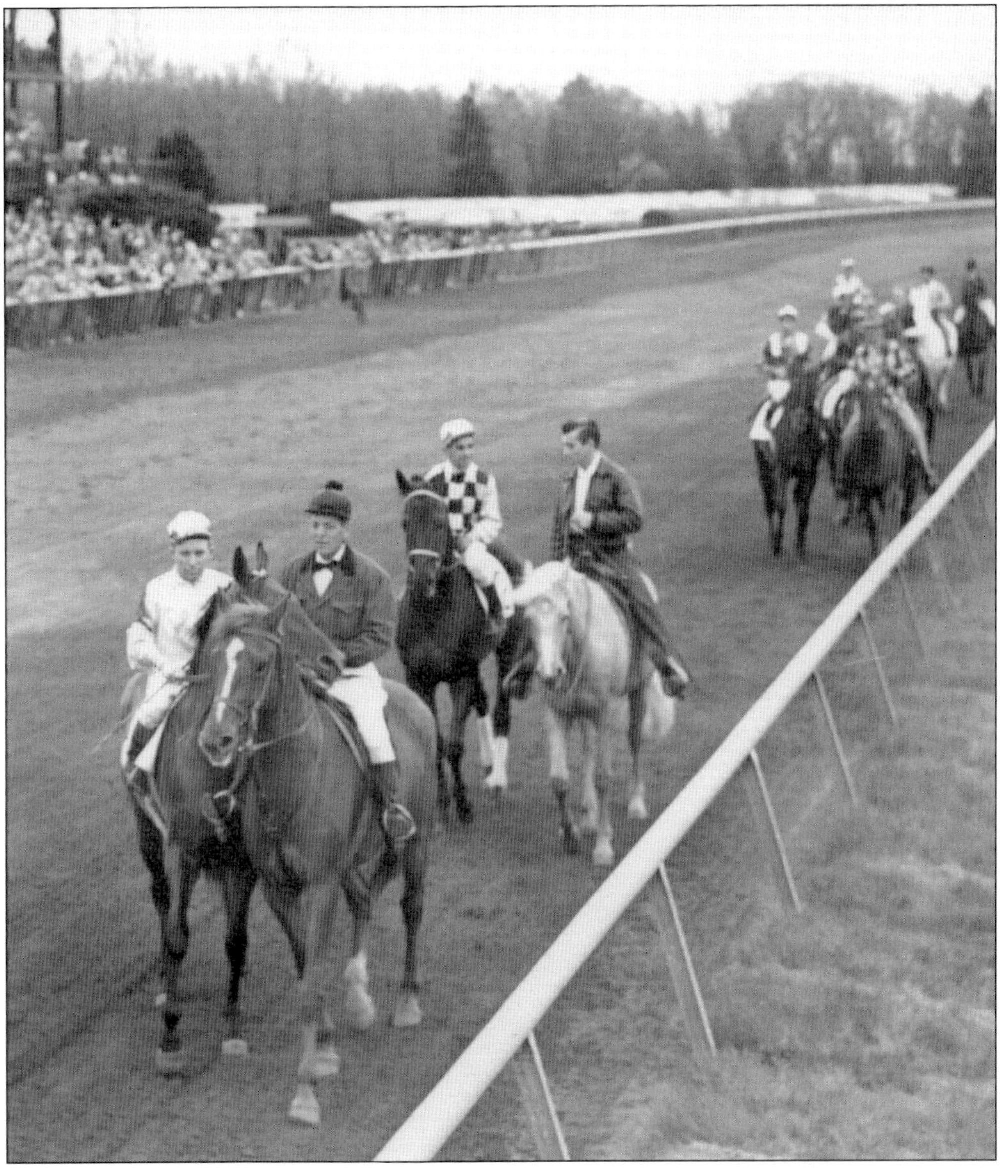

Ben Ali Parade to the Post. This photograph shows the horses who will contest the 1953 Ben Ali as they start their parade to the post near the top of the stretch. Before each race, the horses, accompanied by an outrider on a pony, are paraded down the length of the clubhouse and grandstand at Keeneland. This way, race goers can see each horse's condition and familiarize themselves with the jockey's silks. According to Thoroughbred racing lore, the first post parade took place on June 14, 1880, before the running of the Belmont Stakes. Prior to that, horses went directly from the paddock to the starting gate. The Ben Ali Stakes, named for Thoroughbred breeder James Ben Ali Haggin, was run at the Kentucky Association track from 1917 to 1922 and at Keeneland beginning in 1937 except for the years during World War II when the race was run at Churchill Downs as part of the Keeneland meets held there. In 1953, the race was won by the favorite Oil Capitol.

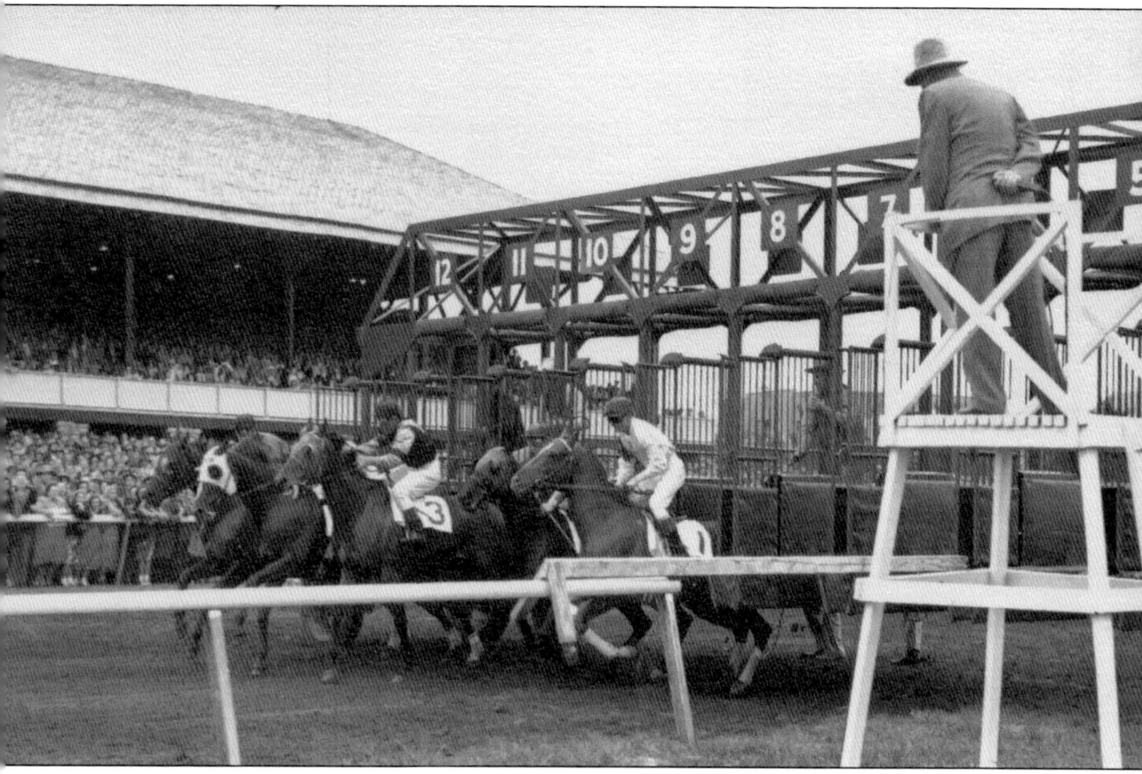

AND THEY'RE OFF! The horses in the 1951 Ben Ali are seen charging out of the starting gate, which was opened by the official starter who can be seen on the elevated stand in the foreground. The race was won by Calumet Farm's Wistful, ridden by Doug Dodson and trained by Ben Jones. She is the only mare to win the Ben Ali since it was revived at Keeneland in 1937.

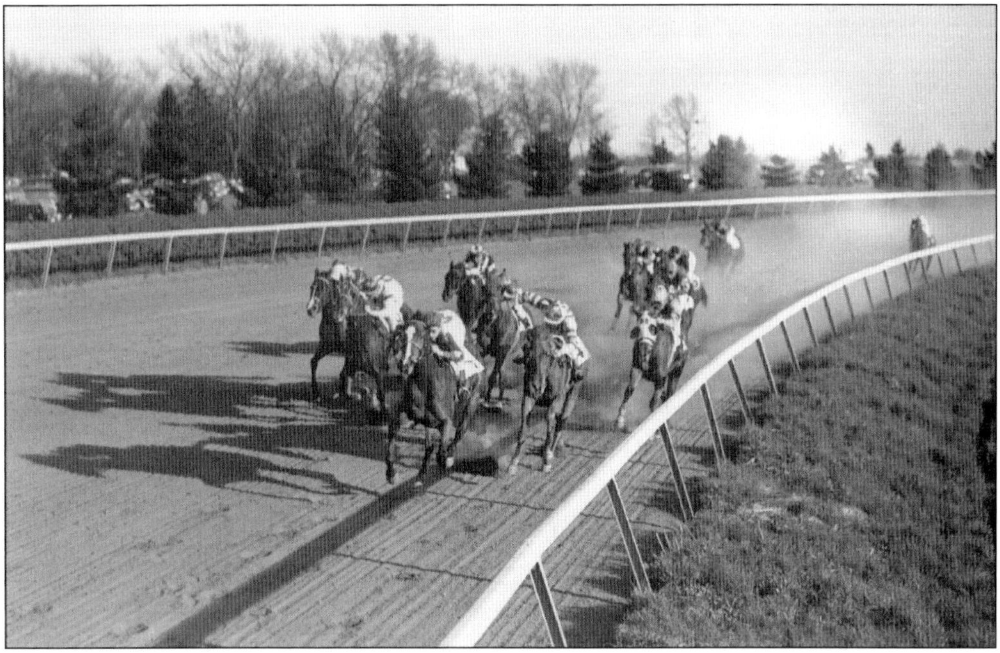

Now's the Time. The horses in this unidentified 1948 race are at the top of the stretch. The jockeys' training and experience are now put to the test as horses hurtle towards the finish line. A rider's skill at finding the right path is often the difference between victory and defeat. Most of the jockeys in the photograph are hand riding, and the jockey on the horse near the rail is using his whip.

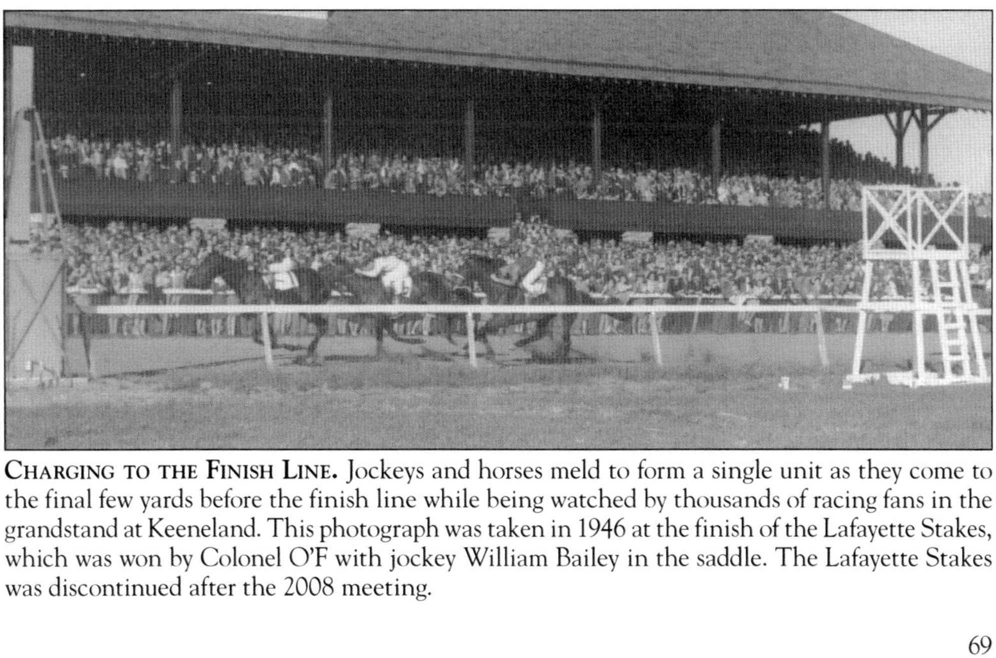

Charging to the Finish Line. Jockeys and horses meld to form a single unit as they come to the final few yards before the finish line while being watched by thousands of racing fans in the grandstand at Keeneland. This photograph was taken in 1946 at the finish of the Lafayette Stakes, which was won by Colonel O'F with jockey William Bailey in the saddle. The Lafayette Stakes was discontinued after the 2008 meeting.

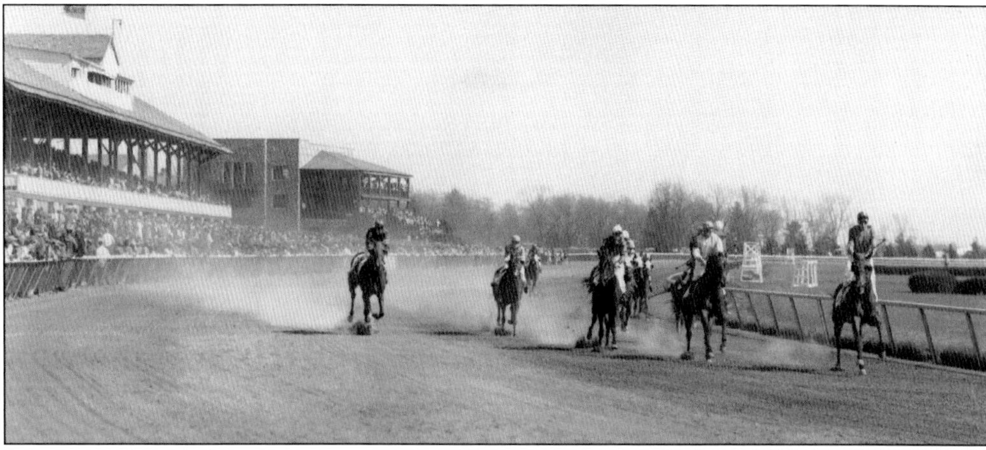

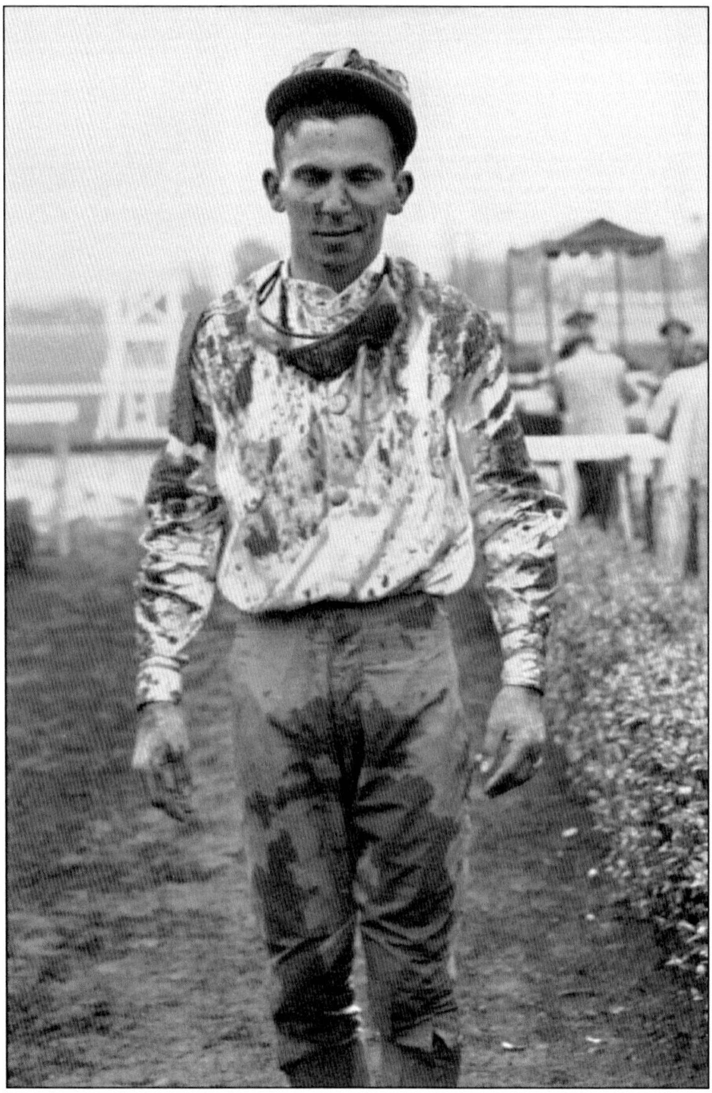

Past the Finish Line. Once past the finish line, jockeys stand up in the stirrups to let their horses know the race is over. Even the best jockeys can misjudge when to stand up—notably Willie Shoemaker, who stood up too soon in the 1957 Kentucky Derby, costing Gallant Man the win.

Muddy Work. Riding horses on a muddy track brings up a whole extra set of challenges. Many horses do not like the different footing on a wet track, and others do not like having mud flung back on them by horses in front. Horses who do well on sloppy tracks are known as "mudders." Jockeys like Al Popara, seen here in 1952, also must learn to deal with the elements.

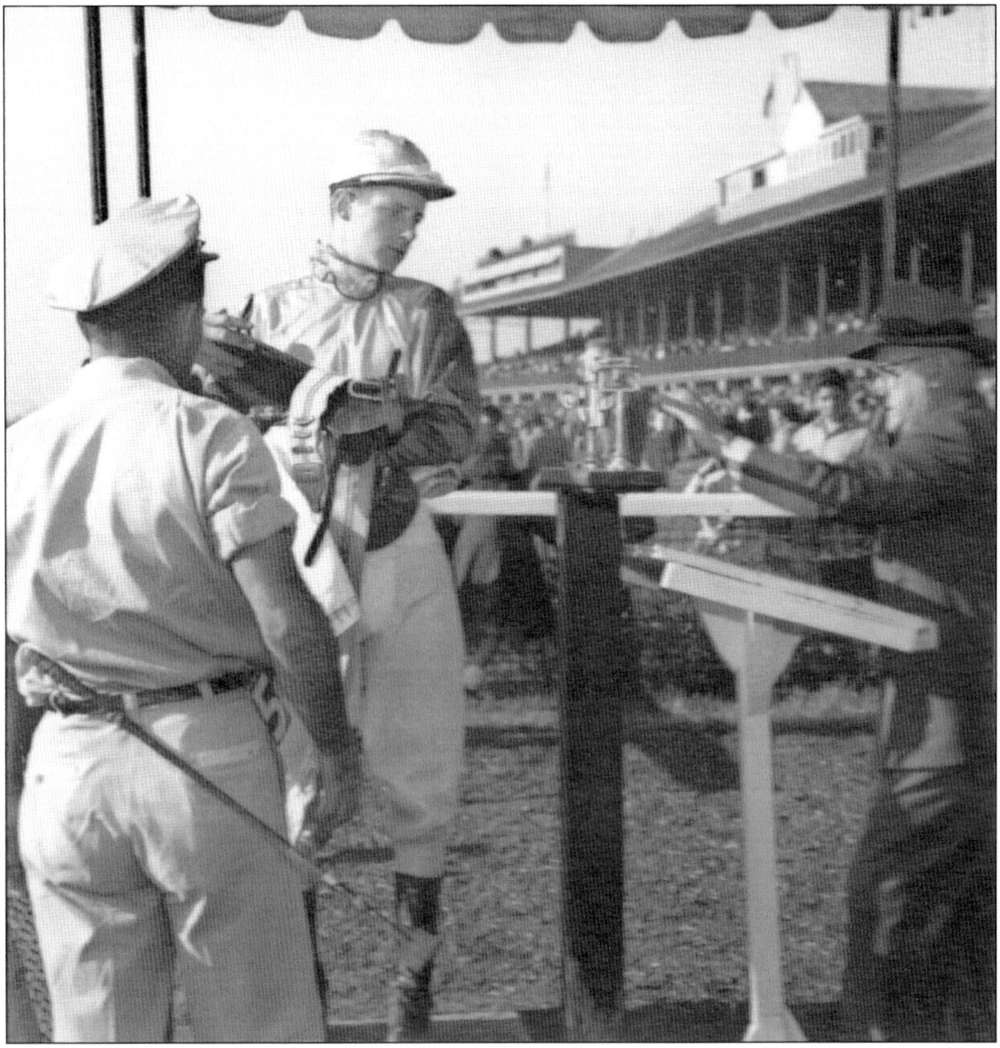

WATCH THAT SCALE. This jockey is watching closely as the clerk of scales weighs him and his saddle out after a race in 1954. The race results are not official until all the jockeys have weighed out following a race. The jockey's scale is located next to the winner's circle in full view of the racing patrons at Keeneland. The jockey's valet can be seen looking on with his client's whip tucked in his belt. Several items, including whips, helmets, and safety vests, are not included in the jockey's riding weight listed in the program.

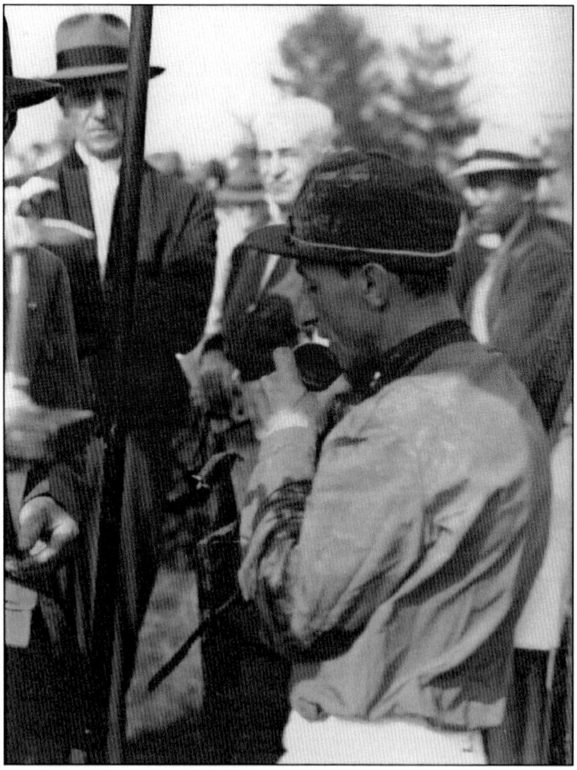

Withstanding a Claim. Jockey Eddie Arcaro is shown on the phone with the racing stewards explaining what happened after another jockey claimed a foul in a 1953 allowance race at Keeneland. The stewards sided with Arcaro, and his win on Breeze By was allowed to stand. Arcaro is the only jockey to have won the Triple Crown twice: once on Whirlaway in 1941 and again on Citation in 1948.

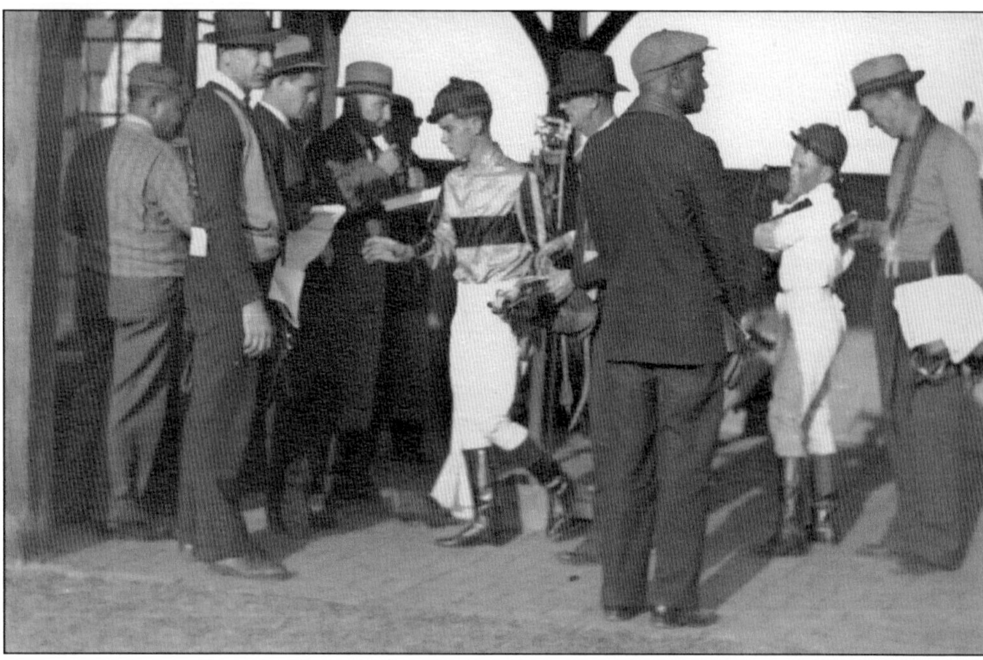

On to the Next Race. Jockeys' valets and agents wait to assist their clients after they have weighed out following a race. Now, everyone's focus turns to the next race, which provides another chance to place "in the money" and receive the jockey's share of the purse. No matter where they place, all riders are paid a set amount for each race they ride in.

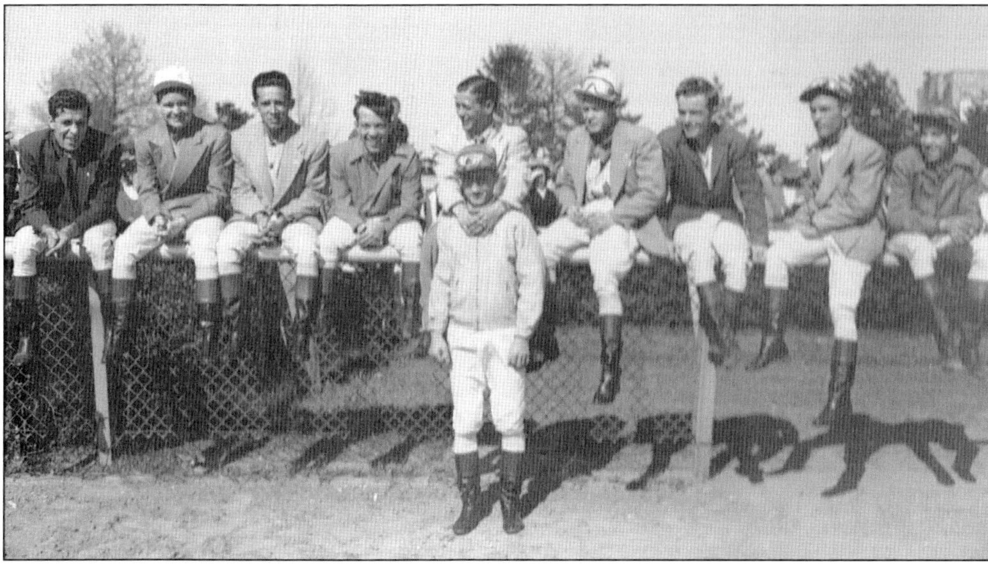

Small but Strong. Thoroughbred jockeys are gifted athletes, capable of guiding thousand-pound horses galloping at high speeds down a narrow track with other horses and riders in close proximity. Pictured here are jockeys who raced at Keeneland in 1949. They are, from left to right, Andy LoTurco, R. Nash, M.H. Gonzalez, Conn McCreary, E. LaBlanc (standing), an unidentified man sitting on the fence behind LaBlanc, D. Madden, R. Glidewell, R.L. Baird, and H. Featherstone.

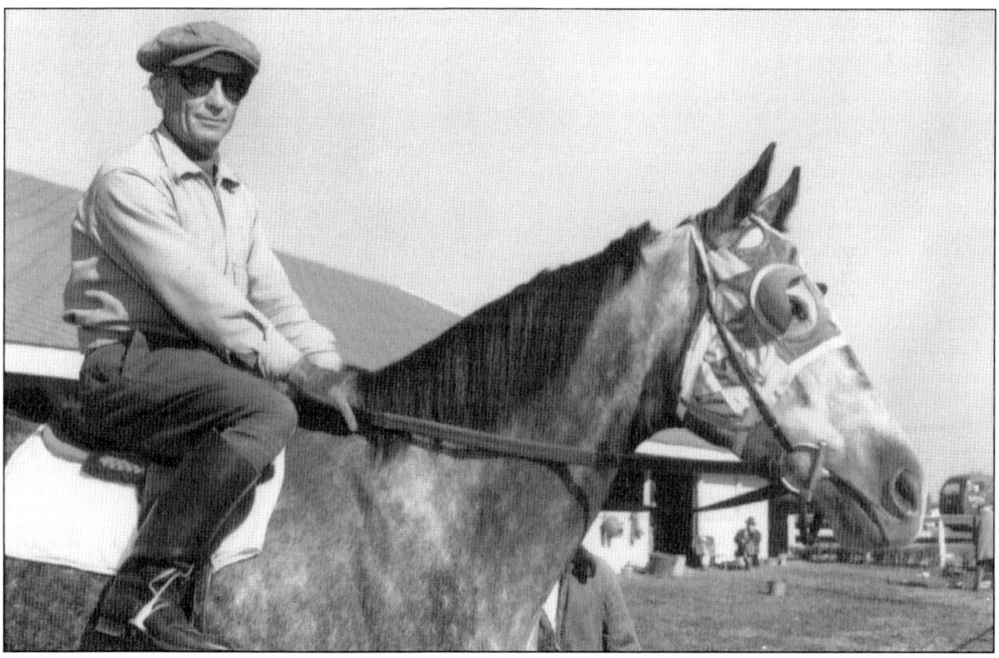

Goggles Inventor. They say that necessity is the mother of invention. When jockey James "Goggles" McCoy's left eye was injured while riding at old Latonia racetrack in Kentucky, it continued to bother him every time he rode, so he designed a pair of goggles using mesh taken from his screen door and eventually replaced that with shatter-proof glass. His design became the prototype for the goggles jockeys wear today.

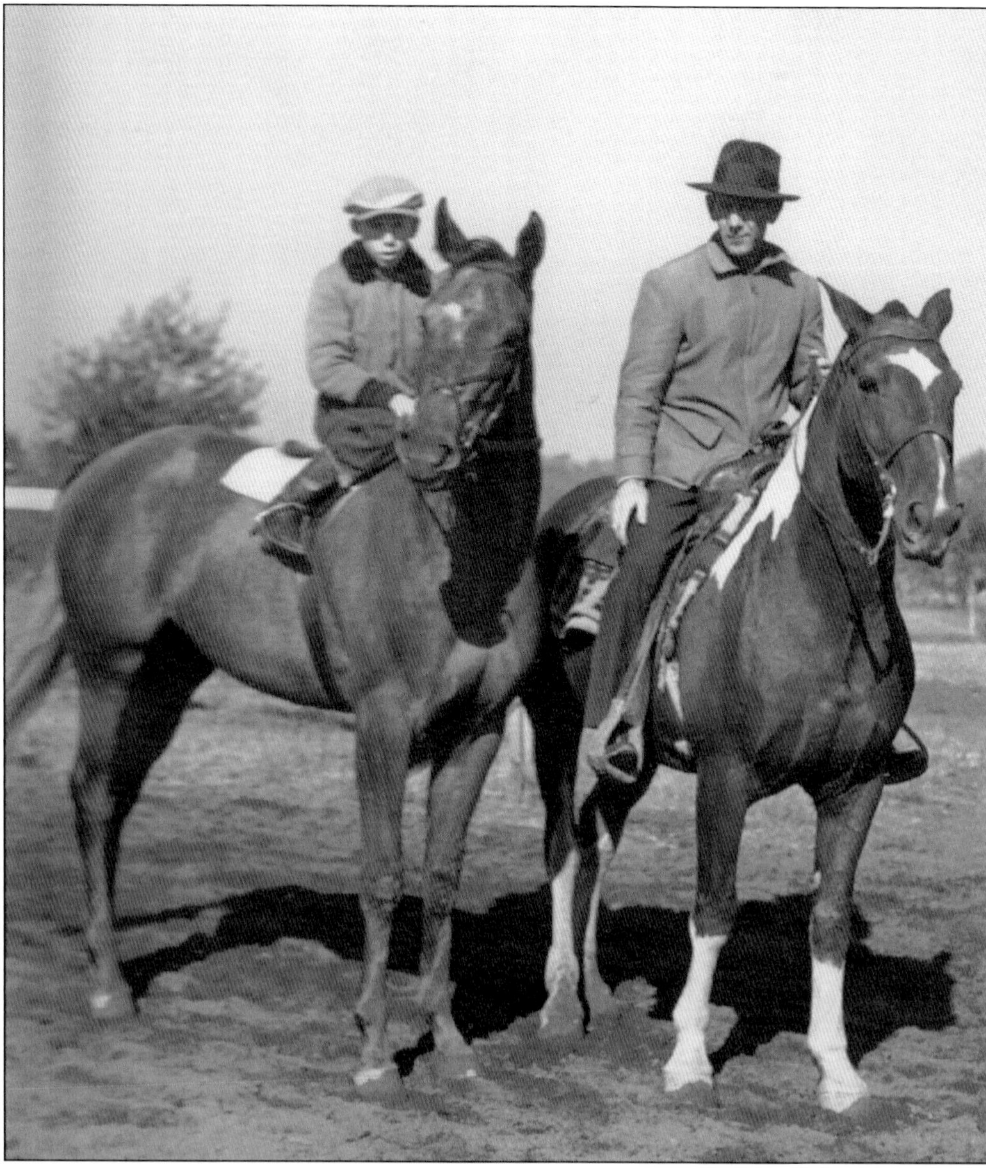

Starting Young. Don Brumfield, who went on to be a racing Hall of Fame jockey, is shown here aboard Menawa with his father, Edgar Brumfield. He was 15 years old and weighed 70 pounds when photographed here in 1953 according to the information in the Keeneland Library scrapbook. Don rode his first winner on August 2, 1954, at Monmouth Park. A native of Nicholasville, Kentucky, he raced most of his career at Kentucky racetracks. By the time he retired in 1989, he had ridden 33,222 mounts, including 4,573 winners—a 14 percent winning percentage. At the time of his retirement, he had won more races at Churchill Downs and Keeneland than any other jockey, although those records no longer stand.

Five

On the Backside

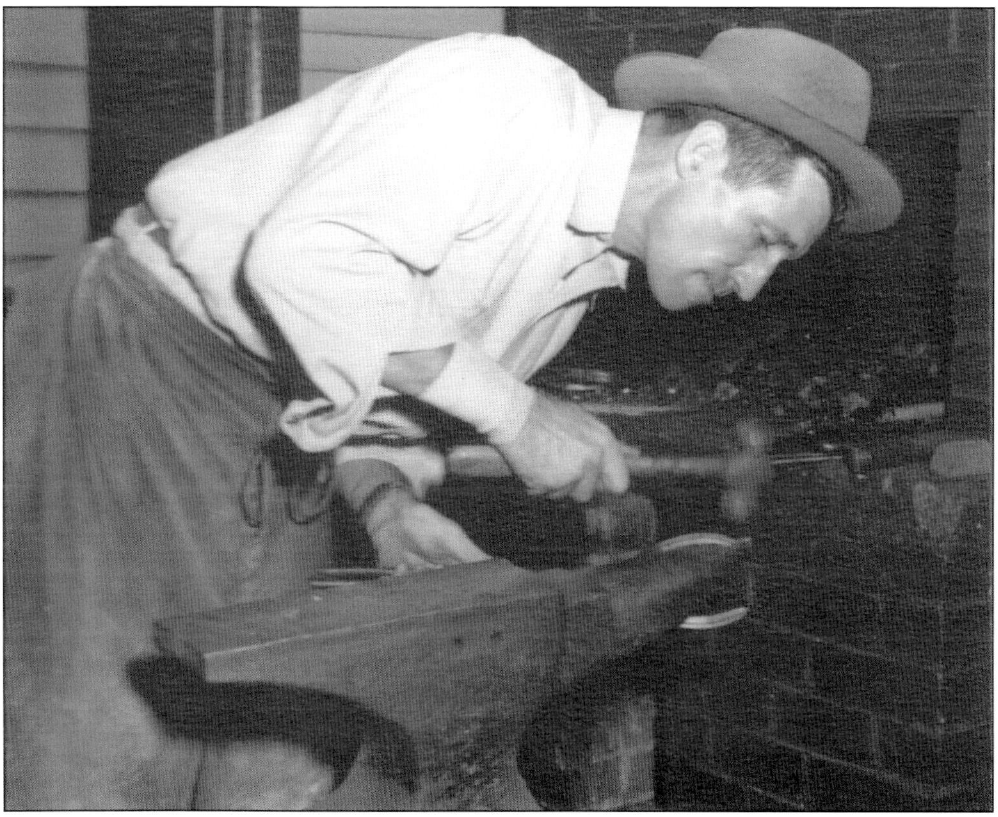

Precision Work. Blacksmiths like A. Porter Moynahan, shown in 1948 working on a horseshoe, are often seen on the backside at Keeneland. The backside of a racetrack is the area usually on the opposite side of the track from the grandstand that houses the barns where horses are stabled. Blacksmiths usually trim and file the hooves of horses in training and fit them with shoes about every four weeks.

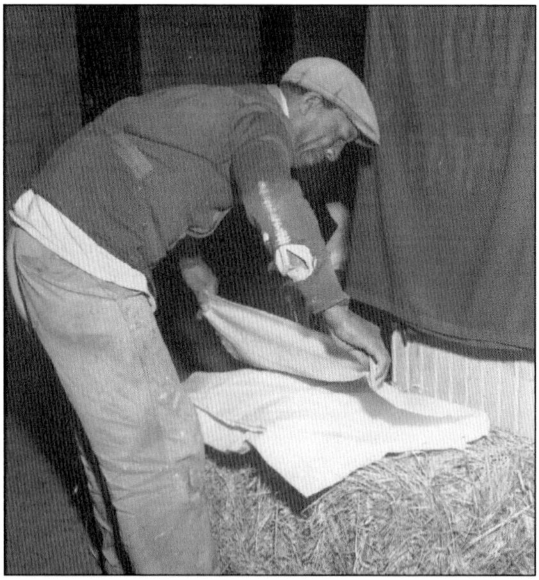

Folding Bandages. Grooms are in charge of keeping all the different pieces of tack and equipment used by the horses they care for clean and neat, as well as making sure the horses are comfortable. In this 1959 photograph, groom Charles Martin can be seen folding bandages, which are sometimes used as leg wraps that many horses in training wear as protection in the morning when they exercise.

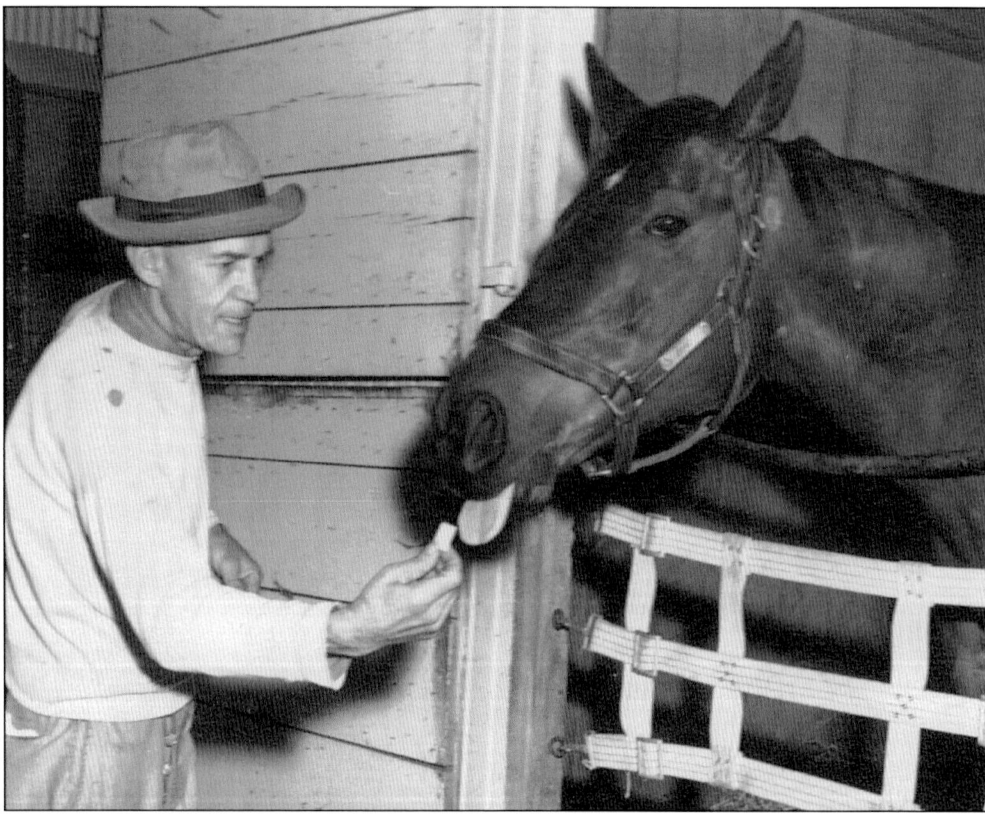

A Treat for Armed. An unidentified groom treats Armed to some sugar in 1949. The gelded son of Bull Lea was the 1947 Horse of the Year. When he ended his racing career in 1950, he was the leading money-winning gelding and had set or equaled nine track records in addition to beating Triple Crown winner Assault in a match race. He retired to Calumet Farm near Lexington, Kentucky.

IMPORTANT NUMBER. Racing Thoroughbreds now have a lip tattoo that consists of a letter indicating the year a horse was foaled, followed by four or five digits from the horse's Jockey Club identification number. Before lip tattoos, race officials had to use a horse's description to make sure that the right horse was running in a race. This 1952 photograph shows Side Prime's lip tattoo.

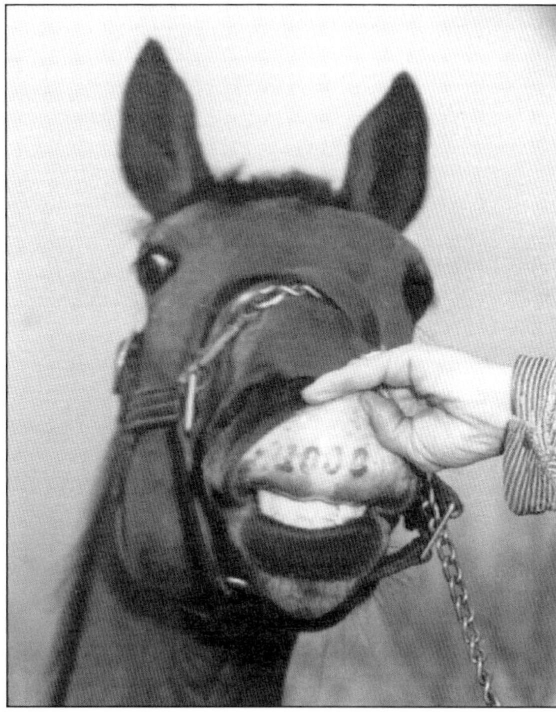

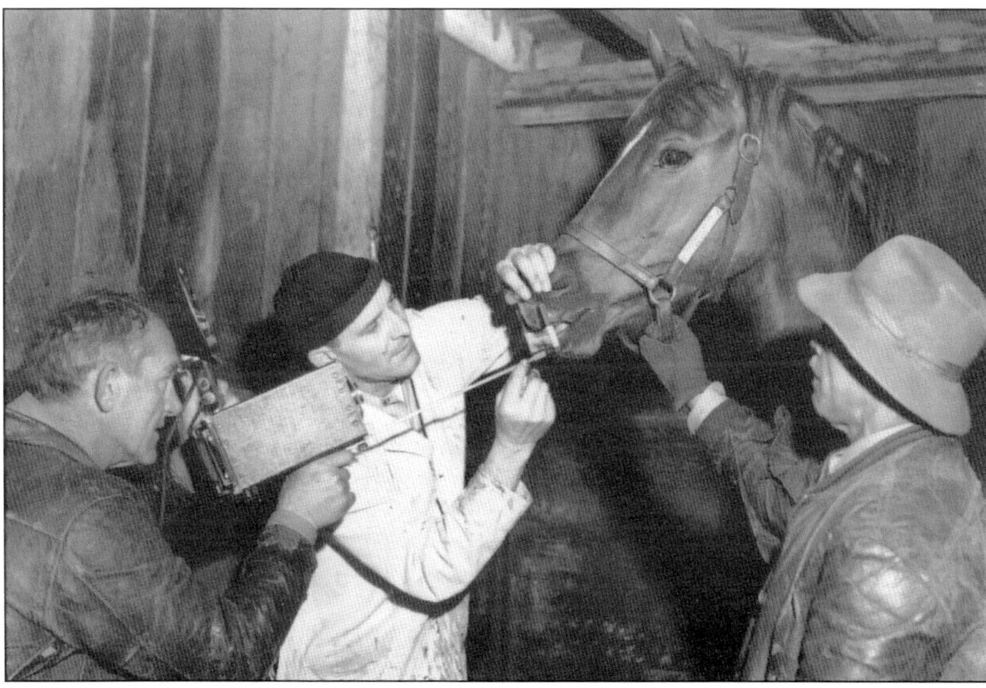

READY TO RACE. Thoroughbreds must have a lip tattoo before they can race. Tattoos are applied by a representative of the Thoroughbred Racing Protective Bureau, and horses have them checked by a horse identifier before each race. This 1952 image shows a photographic record being made of this horse's lip tattoo by C.A. White (with camera) while Al Parkel holds the horse's lip back; the groom is unidentified.

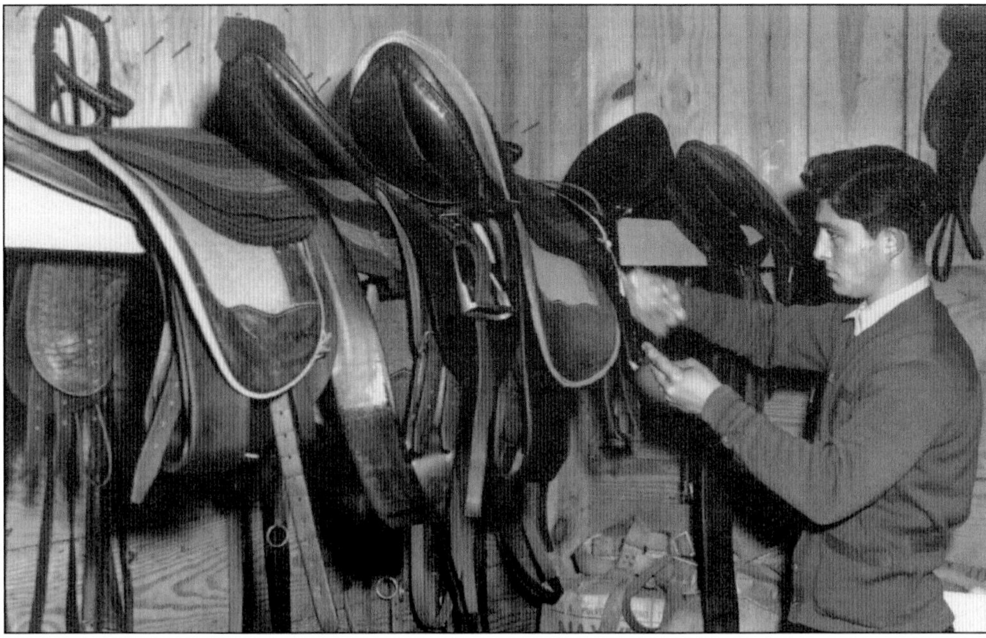

Cleaning Tack. This 1949 photograph shows Dan Hauer cleaning tack on the backside at Keeneland. Tack includes saddles and bridles used by all the stable's horses. The valuable items are often stored in one of the barn's tack rooms when they are not being used.

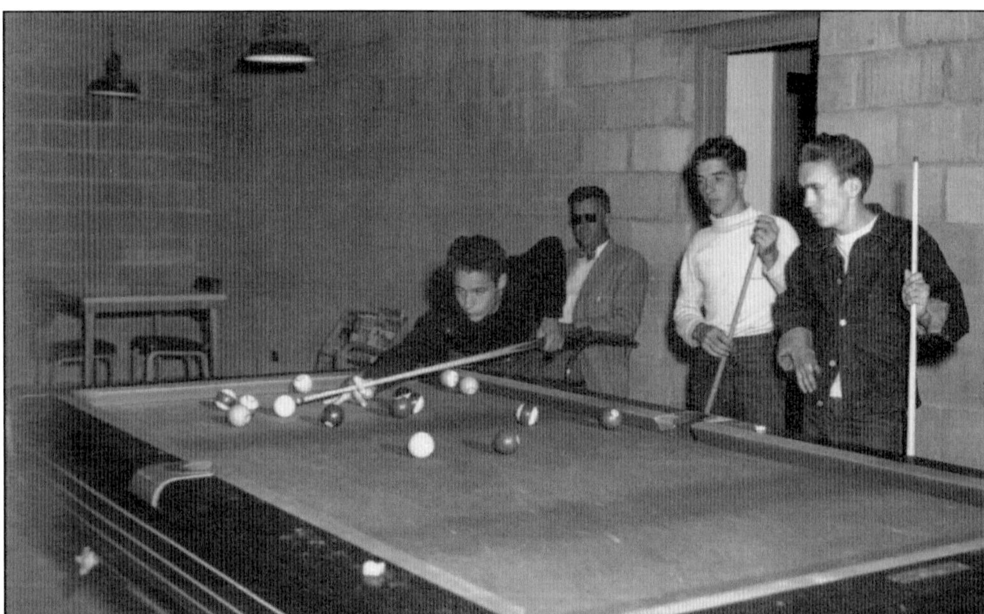

Not All Work. The backside at Keeneland quiets down in the evening, and backside residents can enjoy some time off like these unidentified young men in the stable recreation room playing pool in 1950.

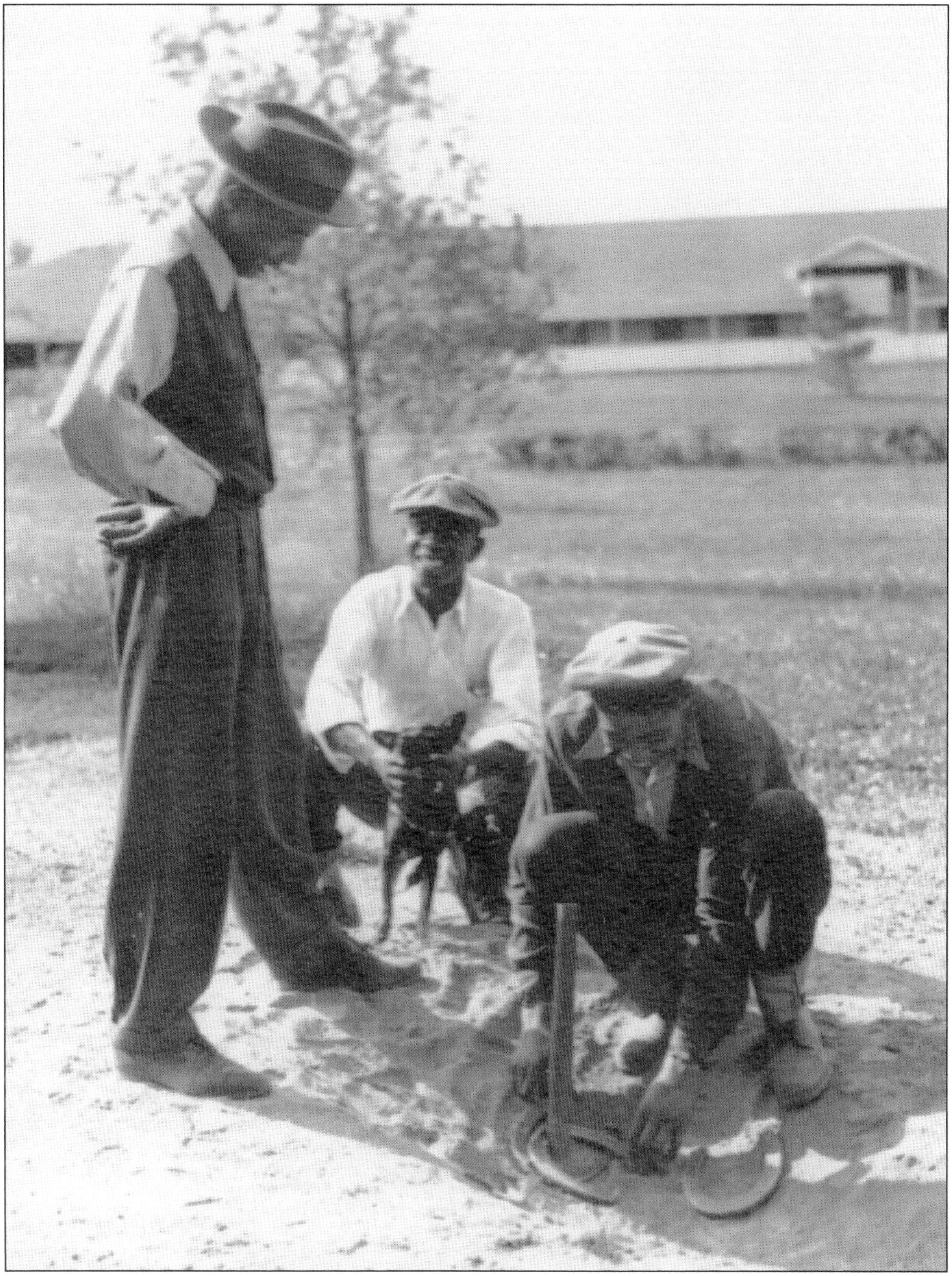

TIME TO RELAX. There are always extra horseshoes around on the backside, and that probably helped make pitching horseshoes a perfect game on a sunny afternoon in 1948 for, from left to right, Joe White, Charles Robinson with his dog Tippy, and Dan Wilson. Work on the backside at all racetracks starts before the sun comes up each morning and does not end until all the horses have been exercised, fed, watered, and settled down for the night. However, some of the photographs in the Keeneland Library scrapbooks were of scenes like these showing relaxed interludes during an otherwise busy day.

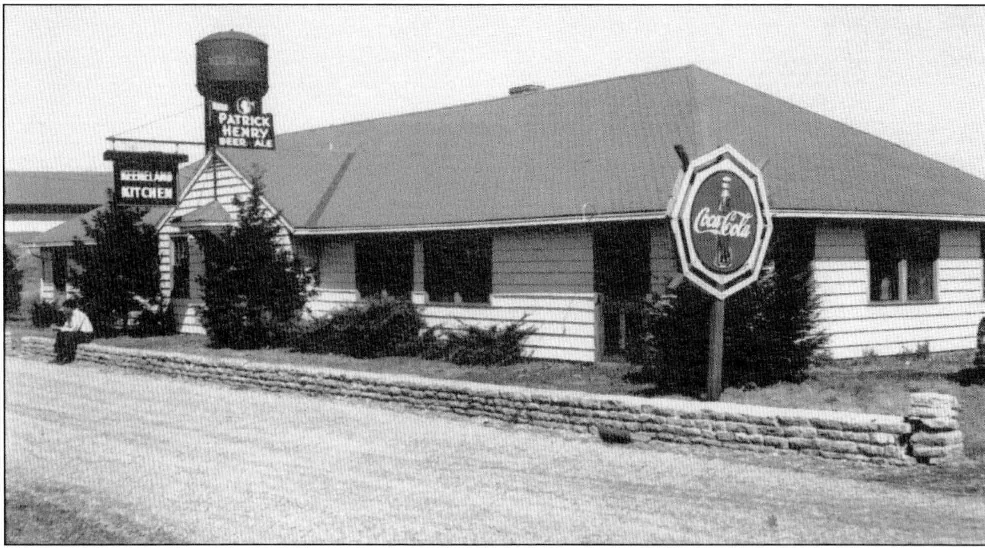

HOME OF GOOD FOOD. The track kitchen is an important part of life on the backside at Keeneland. It opens much earlier than most restaurants to accommodate all the backside residents who are up and working before the sun comes up. This photograph was taken in 1939.

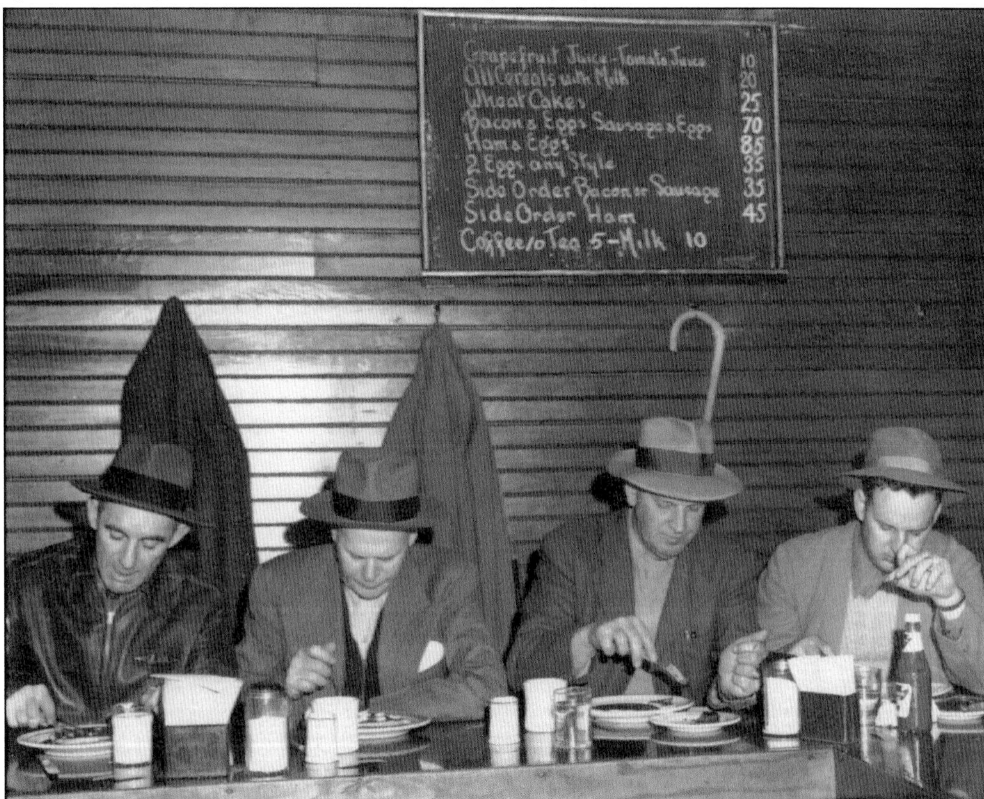

HEARTY BREAKFAST. According to the sign on the wall in the background of this 1950 photograph, patrons at the track kitchen could enjoy a full breakfast for less than a dollar. The men are, from left to right, Charles Gormley, H.C. Dobson, J. Price Sallee, and William Sallee.

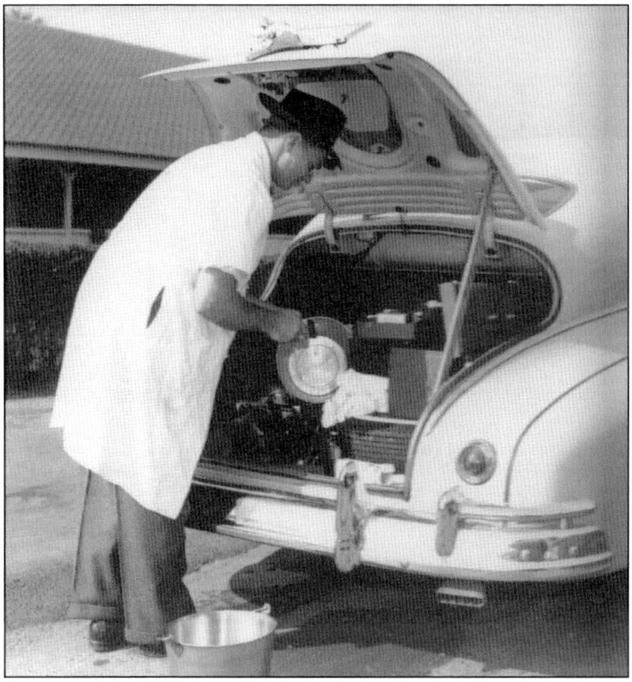

Travelling Office. Veterinarians are frequently seen on the backside. Since their patients cannot come to the office, they make barn calls and keep their car trunks well stocked with the necessary supplies. Dr. Arthur Davidson, seen here in 1948, became a partner in the prominent equine veterinary practice of Hagyard-Davidson-McGee Associates. The firm was founded in 1876 by Dr. Edward T. Hagyard, a graduate of Professor Dick's Veterinary College in Scotland.

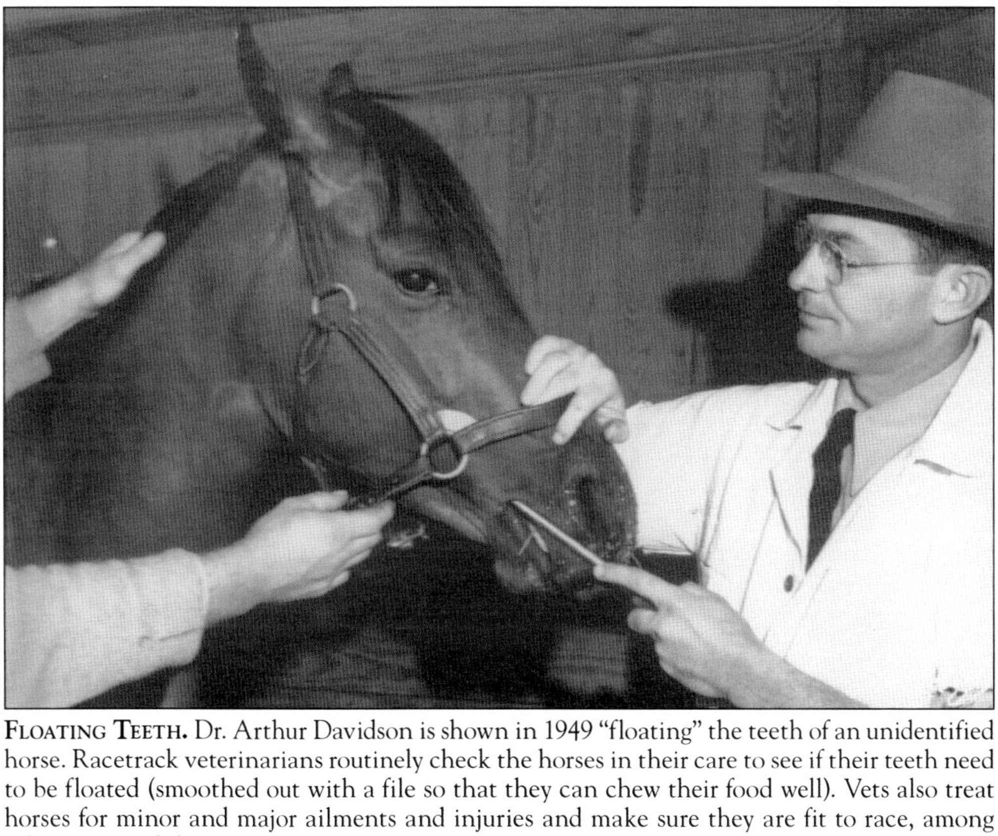

Floating Teeth. Dr. Arthur Davidson is shown in 1949 "floating" the teeth of an unidentified horse. Racetrack veterinarians routinely check the horses in their care to see if their teeth need to be floated (smoothed out with a file so that they can chew their food well). Vets also treat horses for minor and major ailments and injuries and make sure they are fit to race, among other responsibilities.

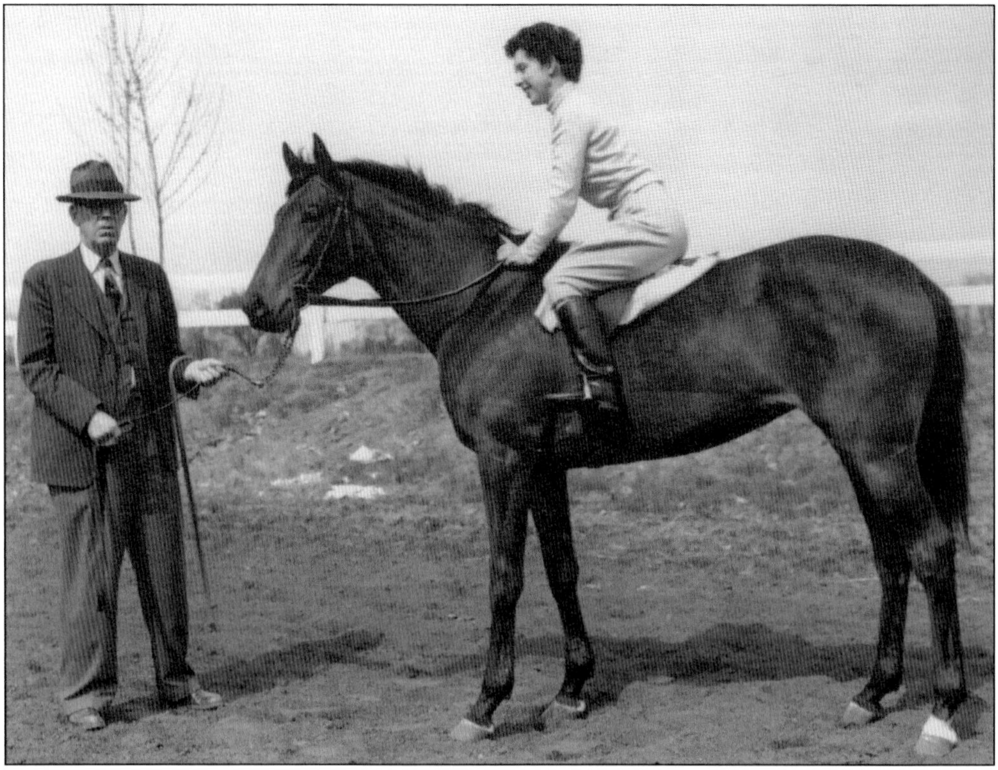

From Rider to Writer. This photograph, taken in 1952, is captioned, "Mary Jane Gallaher, up, Tom Young, holding." Gallaher went on to graduate from the School of Journalism at the University of North Carolina and became one of the first female turf writers. She worked at the *Thoroughbred Record* and wrote for other publications, including *Sports Illustrated,* the *Lexington Leader,* the *Courier-Journal,* and the *New York Times.*

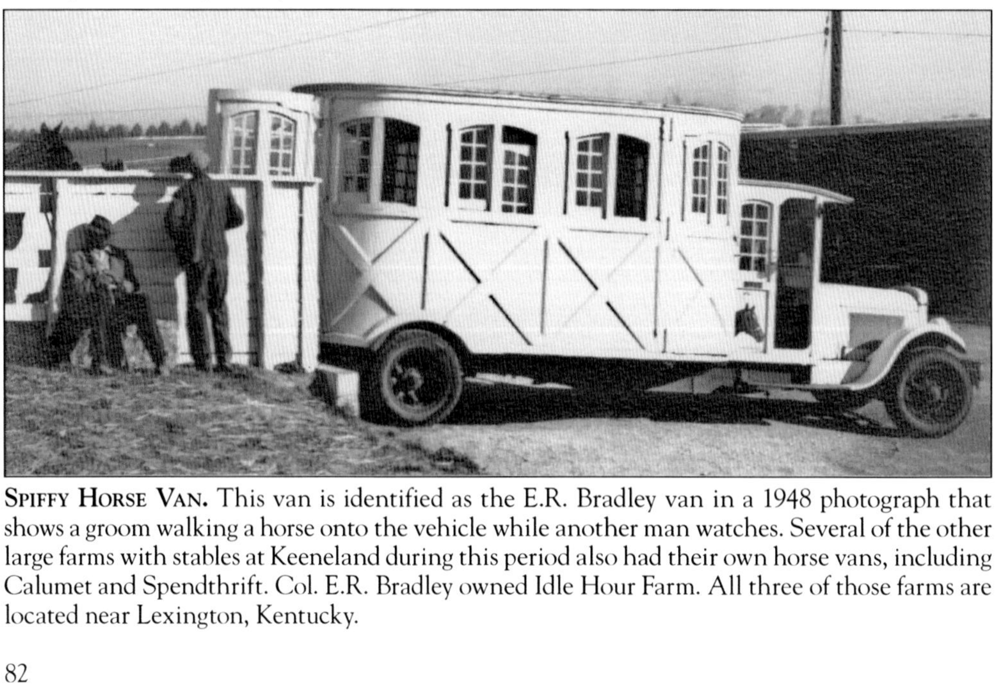

Spiffy Horse Van. This van is identified as the E.R. Bradley van in a 1948 photograph that shows a groom walking a horse onto the vehicle while another man watches. Several of the other large farms with stables at Keeneland during this period also had their own horse vans, including Calumet and Spendthrift. Col. E.R. Bradley owned Idle Hour Farm. All three of those farms are located near Lexington, Kentucky.

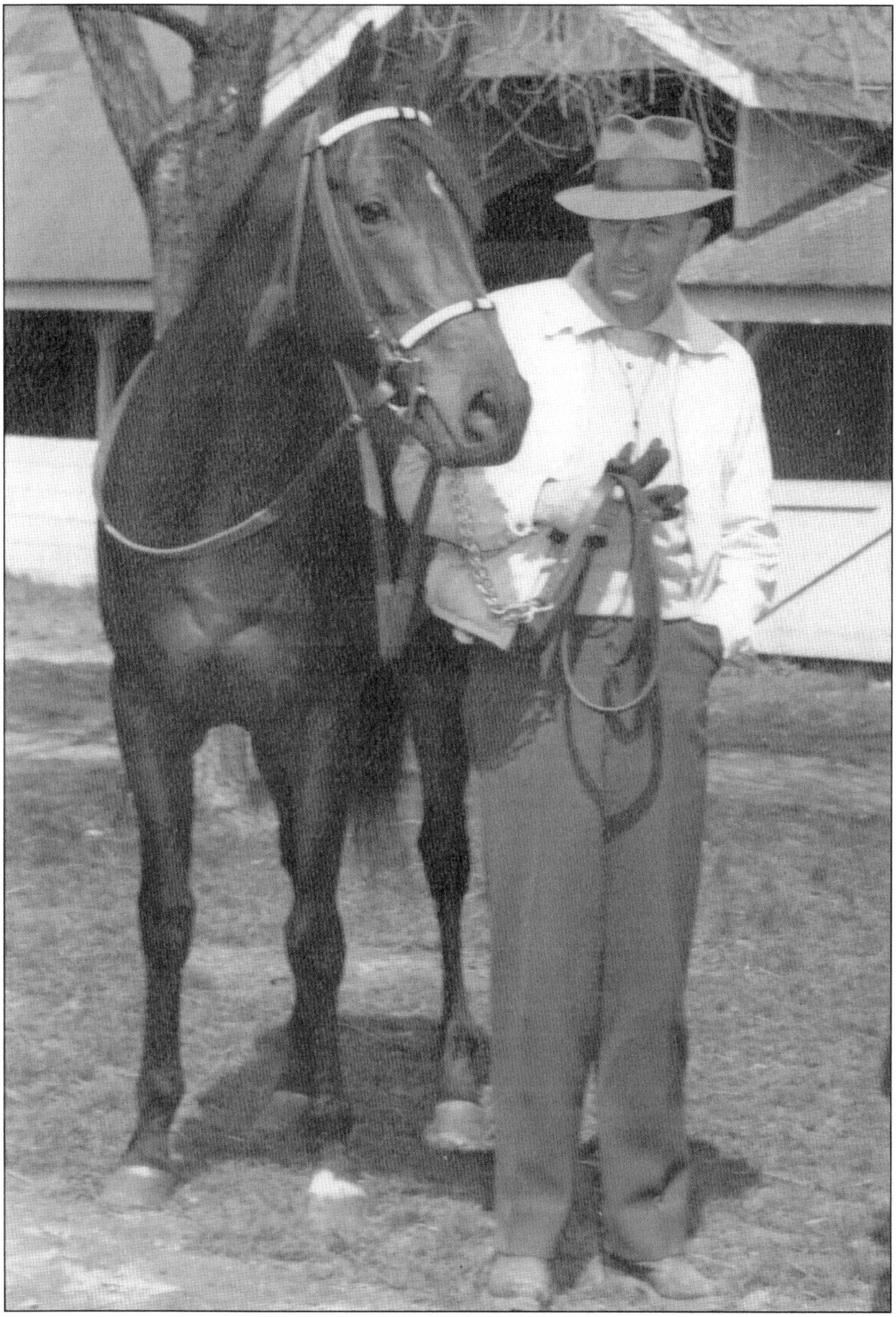

Eclipse Award–Winning Trainer. Although he spent most of his time on the West Coast, trainer Charlie Whittingham also trained horses at Keeneland. Whittingham won the Eclipse Award for Outstanding Trainer in 1971, 1982, and 1989 and was the leading North American trainer in annual earnings seven times. Whittingham also trained two Kentucky Derby winners: Ferdinand and Sunday Silence. He finished his career with 2,534 wins that paid more than $109 million in purses. He is seen here with Swift Sword in 1954.

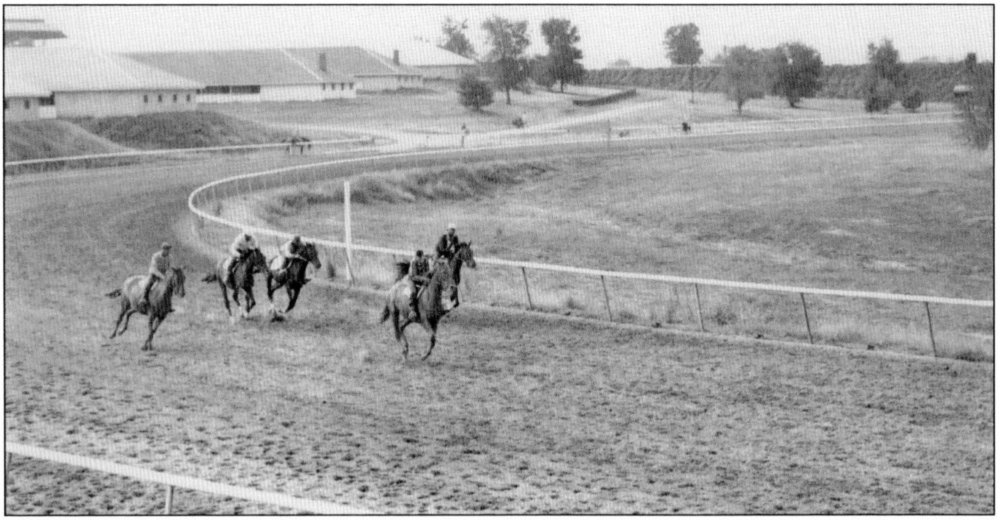

Enjoying New Training Track. Exercising horses stabled at a racetrack takes place in the early morning, and during busy periods the Keeneland track could be a hectic place. In 1955, a new training track was built, and this photograph was taken soon after it opened in September of that year. Both tracks are used now, but the main track is only available for horse workouts between 5:30 a.m. and 10:00 a.m.

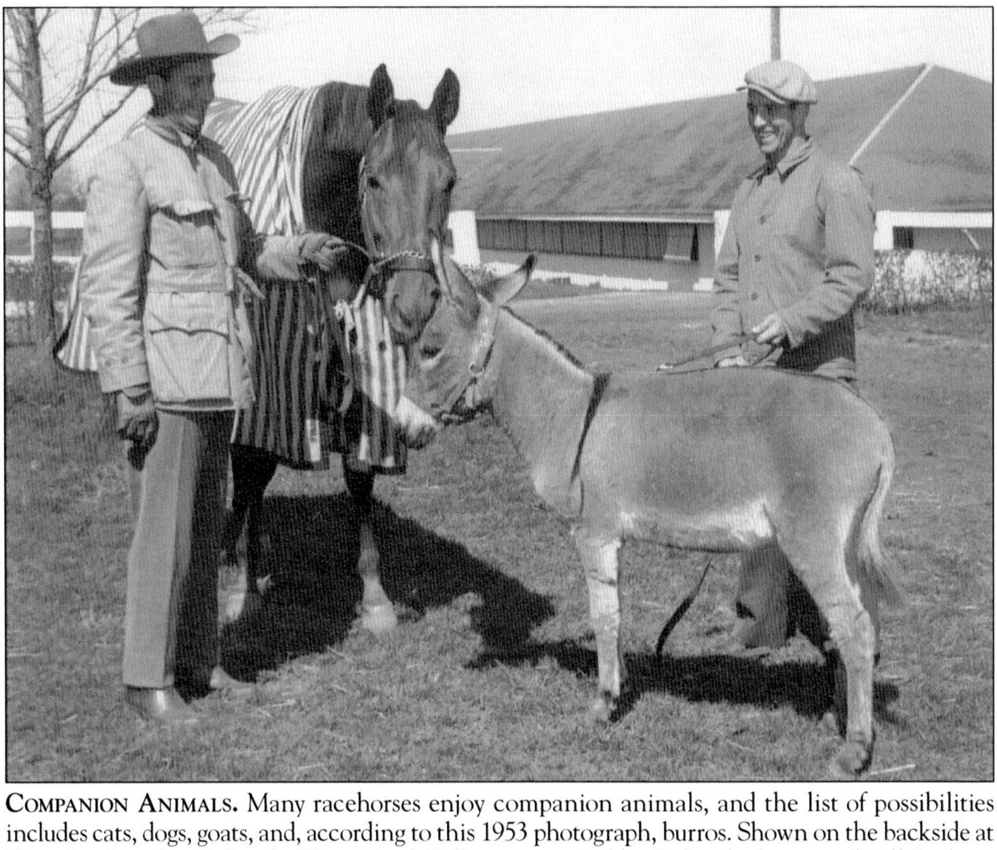

Companion Animals. Many racehorses enjoy companion animals, and the list of possibilities includes cats, dogs, goats, and, according to this 1953 photograph, burros. Shown on the backside at Keeneland are Joe Bolero holding Good Call accompanied by Pedro the burro and Bill Jordan.

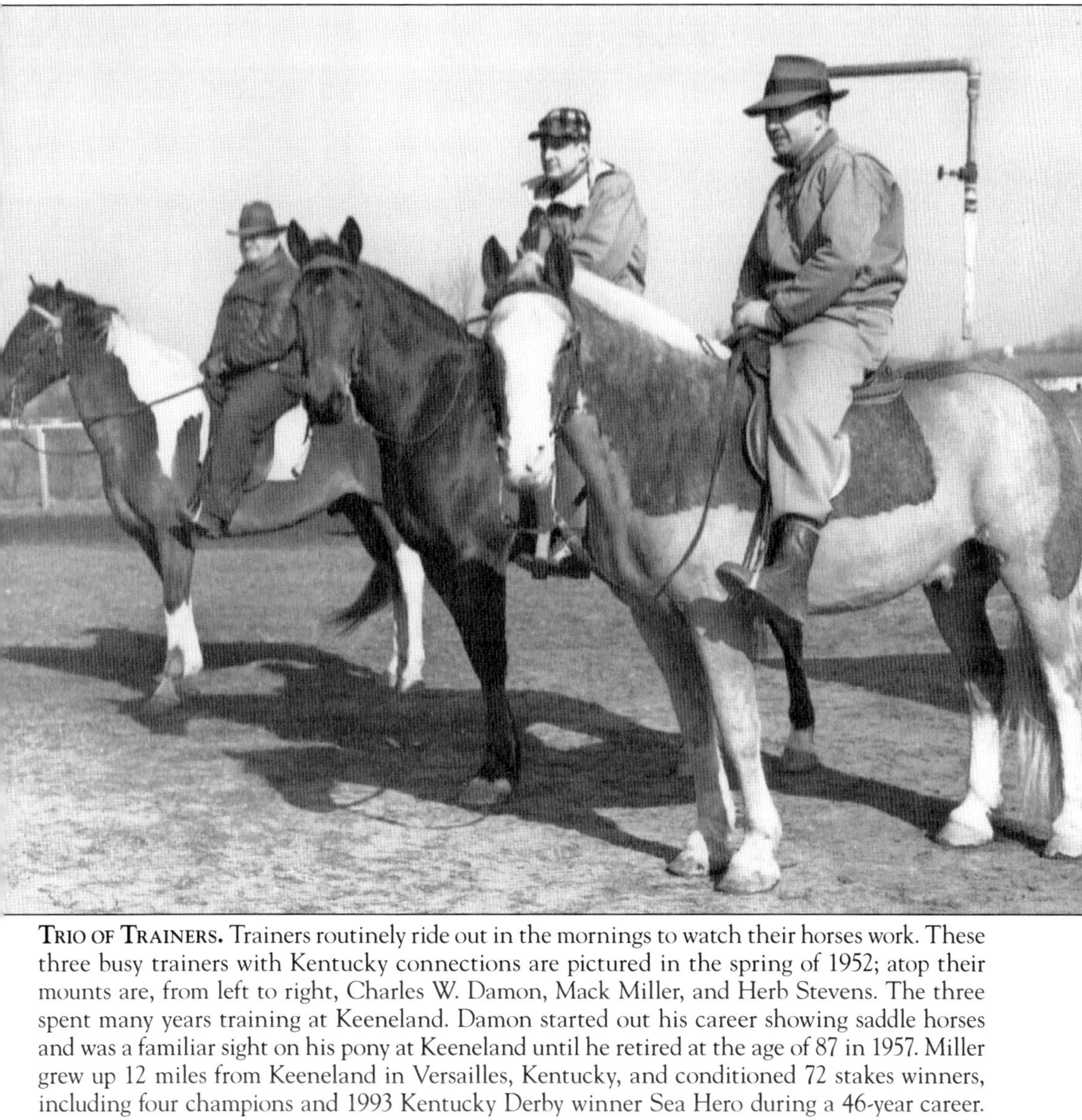

TRIO OF TRAINERS. Trainers routinely ride out in the mornings to watch their horses work. These three busy trainers with Kentucky connections are pictured in the spring of 1952; atop their mounts are, from left to right, Charles W. Damon, Mack Miller, and Herb Stevens. The three spent many years training at Keeneland. Damon started out his career showing saddle horses and was a familiar sight on his pony at Keeneland until he retired at the age of 87 in 1957. Miller grew up 12 miles from Keeneland in Versailles, Kentucky, and conditioned 72 stakes winners, including four champions and 1993 Kentucky Derby winner Sea Hero during a 46-year career. Stevens, another longtime trainer at Keeneland, trained champion two-year-old Rockhill Native, the 1980 Blue Grass Stakes winner.

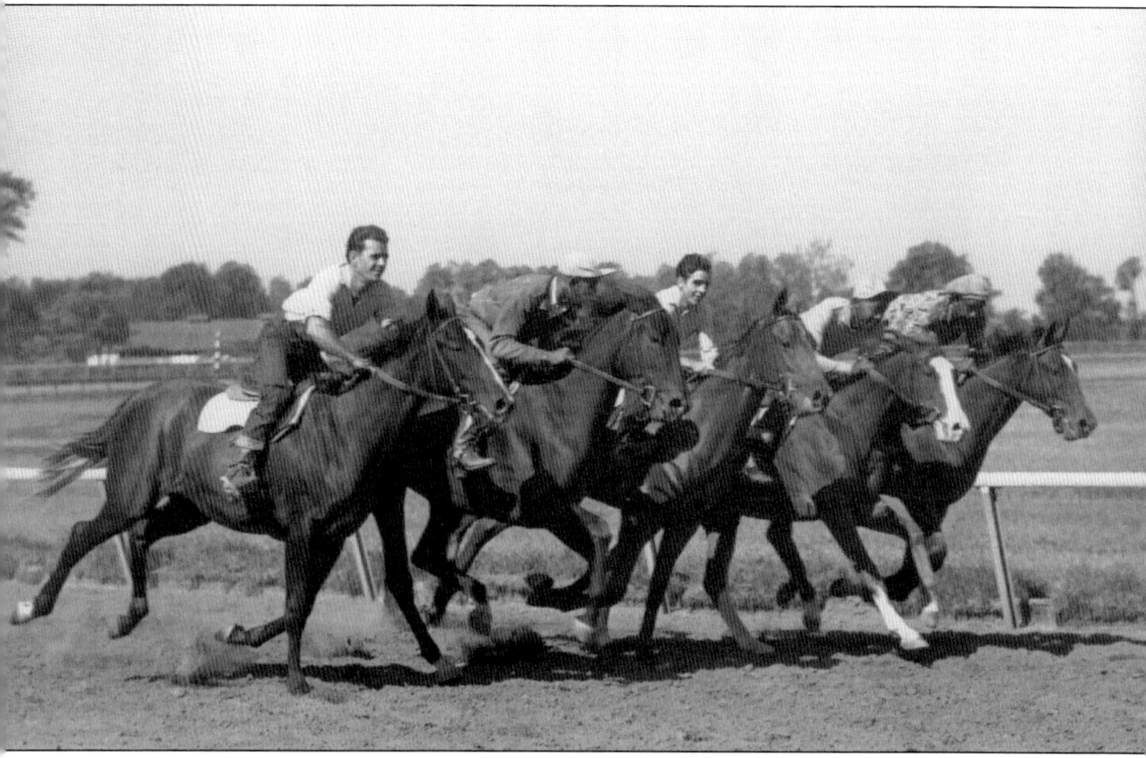

Early Morning Race. These exercise riders and their mounts are enjoying an early morning workout in 1952. Trainers sometimes work or "breeze" their horses, which is when the animals are allowed to run at race speed for a timed speed interval, usually from three to five furlongs (a furlong is equal to an eighth of a mile). They usually work three to seven days before a race and typically no more than once a week; these works are recorded by an official clocker. On most days, horses in training usually gallop during their morning workout. The distance they go is set by the trainer and averages about a mile and a half daily.

Six

AFTER WORLD WAR II

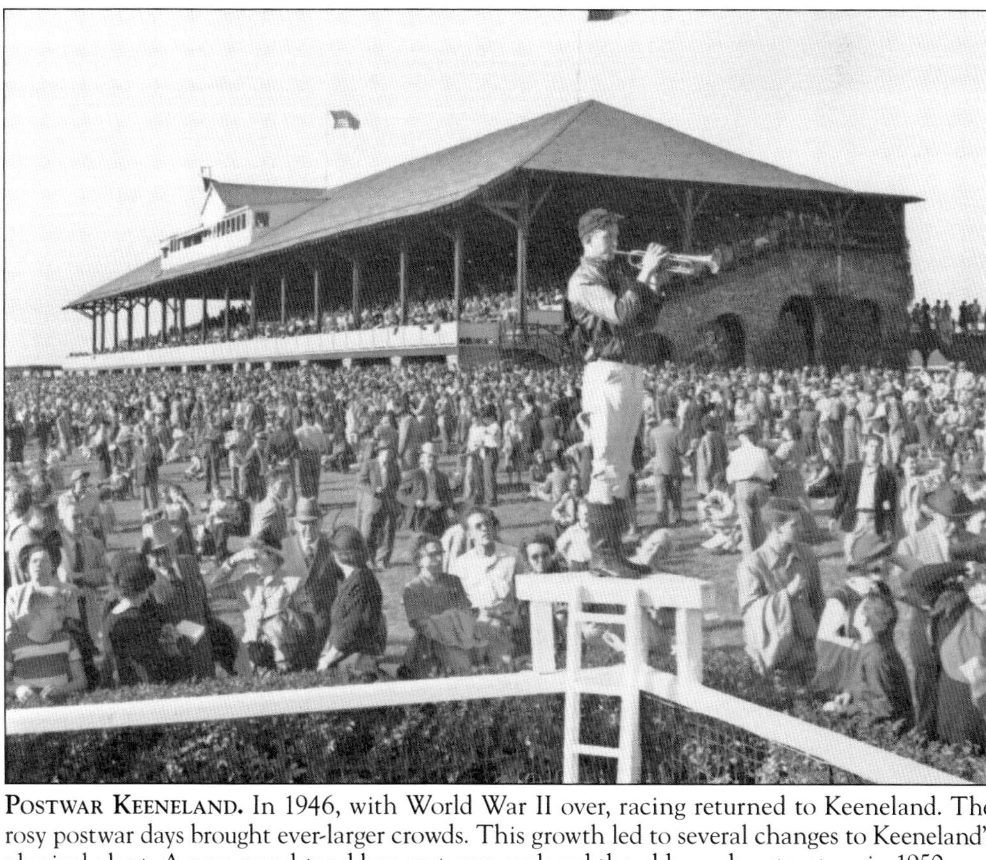

POSTWAR KEENELAND. In 1946, with World War II over, racing returned to Keeneland. The rosy postwar days brought ever-larger crowds. This growth led to several changes to Keeneland's physical plant. A new grandstand box-seat area replaced the old wooden structure in 1950, and an enlarged grandstand was built in 1953. Bugler Cline Duff is shown here in 1950 with the grandstand and new box-seat area behind him.

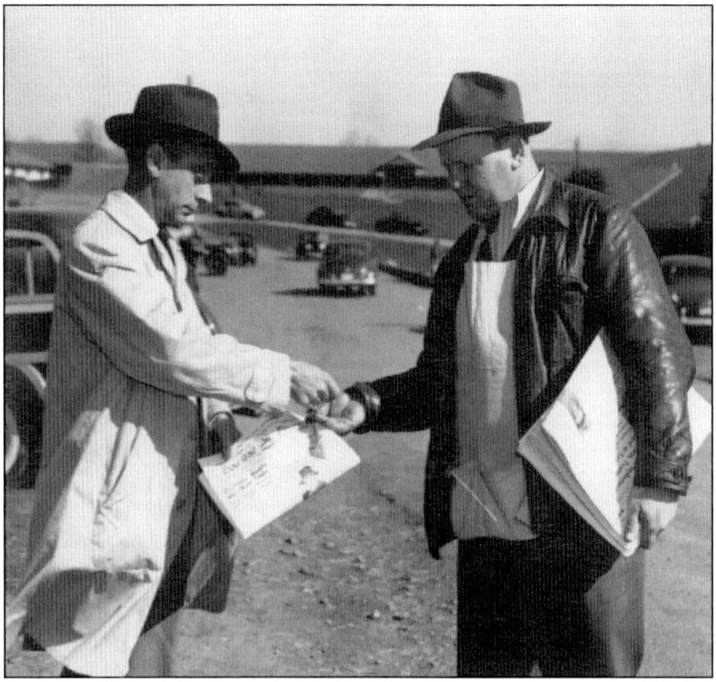

Current Racing News. Harold Ware, Calumet Farm's stable agent, is shown buying a copy of the *Daily Racing Form* from an unknown vendor in 1949. The *Racing Form* carries information on the current day's races taking place at tracks around the country, as well as past performance information. The publication has been in business since 1894. The *Racing Form's* archives were donated to the Keeneland Library in 2000.

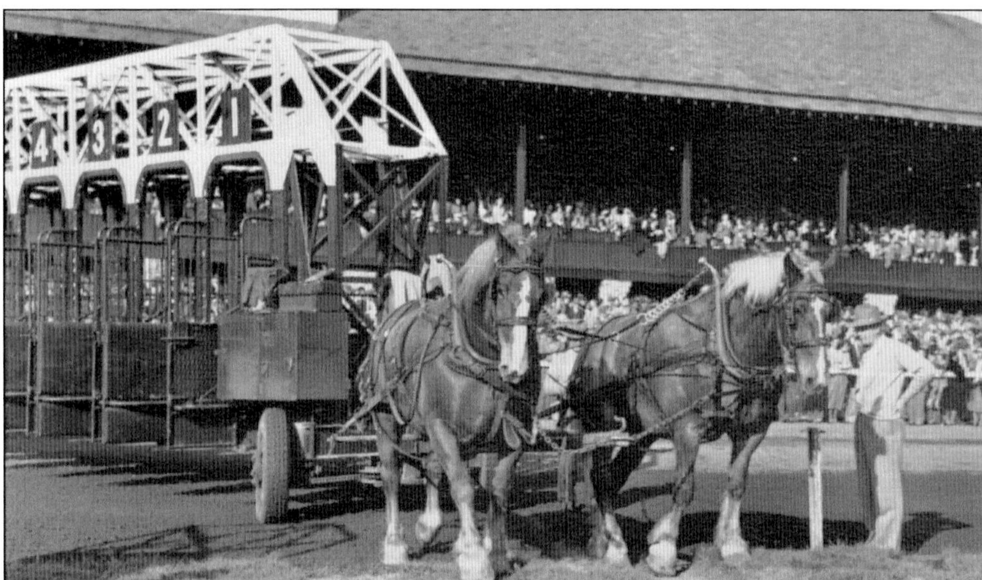

Work Horses. These horses were not on the track to race but to pull the starting gate on and off the track. That worked fine, until one day when the horses refused to move the starting gate off the track after the race had begun. Race goers jumped the rail to help move the gate before the racehorses came back around—a tractor was used to move the starting gate after that.

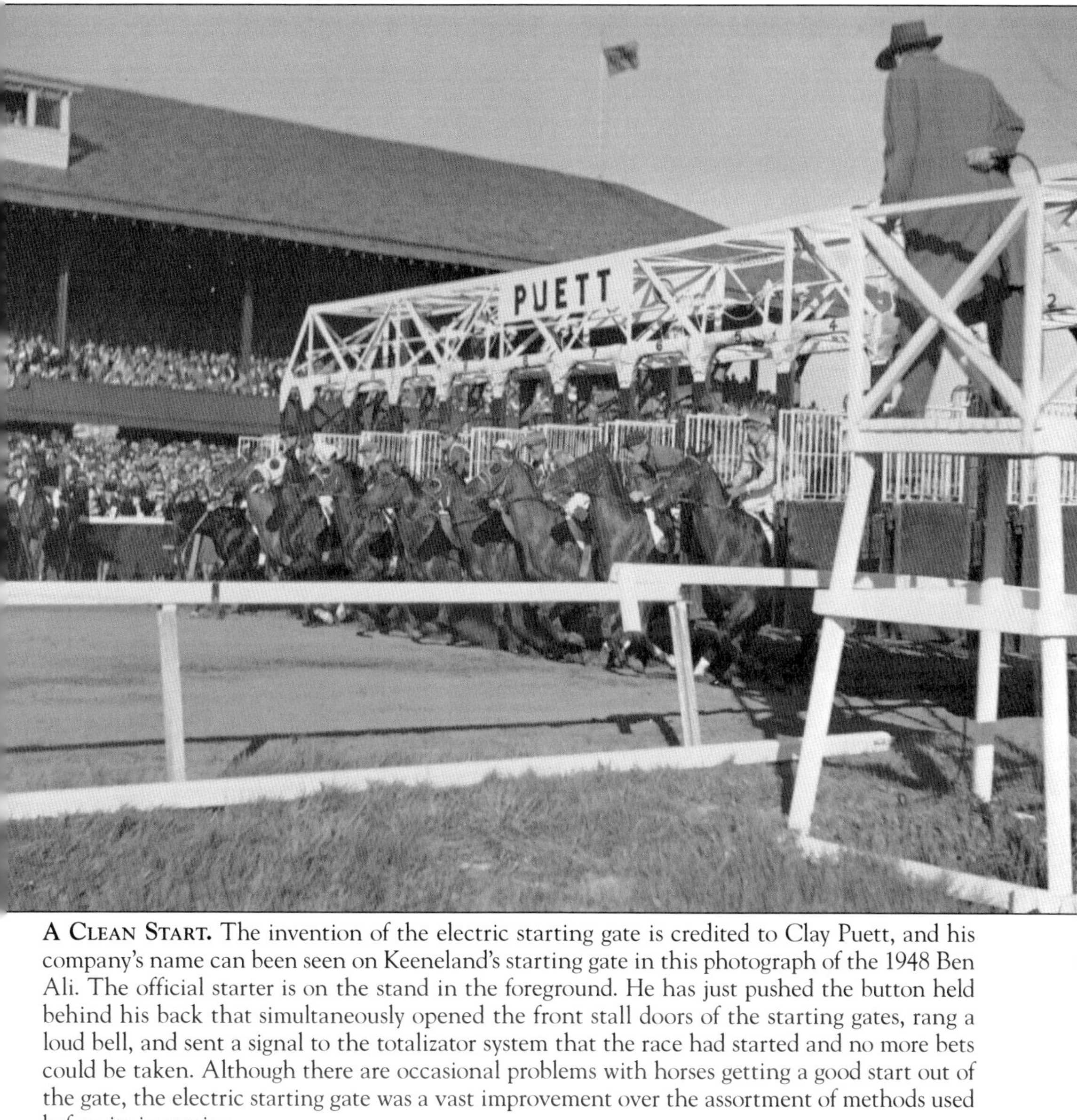

A Clean Start. The invention of the electric starting gate is credited to Clay Puett, and his company's name can been seen on Keeneland's starting gate in this photograph of the 1948 Ben Ali. The official starter is on the stand in the foreground. He has just pushed the button held behind his back that simultaneously opened the front stall doors of the starting gates, rang a loud bell, and sent a signal to the totalizator system that the race had started and no more bets could be taken. Although there are occasional problems with horses getting a good start out of the gate, the electric starting gate was a vast improvement over the assortment of methods used before its invention.

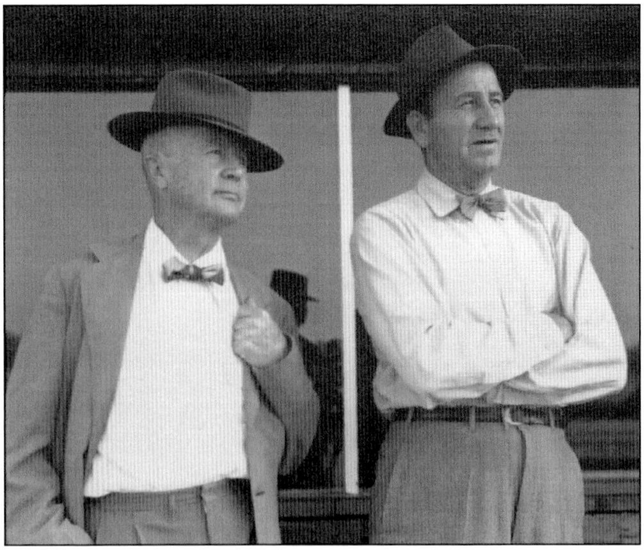

Sharp Eyes. Longtime Keeneland Association officers Brownell Combs (left) and A.B. Gay look very interested in what is happening on the track in this 1949 photograph. Gay was elected as first vice president and Combs was selected as secretary of the first Keeneland Association board. Both men continued in those offices for many years and were outstanding Thoroughbred owners and breeders. Combs owned Myrtlewood Farm and Belair Farm, and Gay owned Lanark Farm.

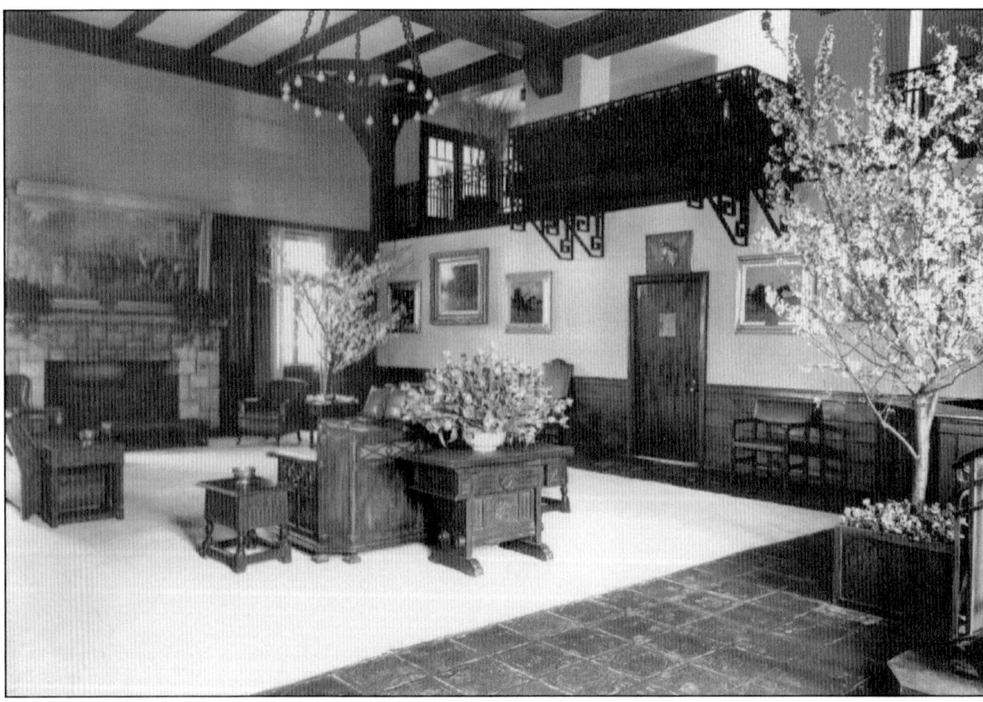

Feels Like Home. The main reception room of the Keeneland Clubhouse, seen here in 1950, has changed very little over the years. It started out as a space that evoked a living room of a beautiful Southern home with fresh flowers and comfortable chairs. That ambience can still be felt today. Famed interior designer Billy Baldwin decorated the clubhouse in the mid-1950s, updating the materials but retaining the look.

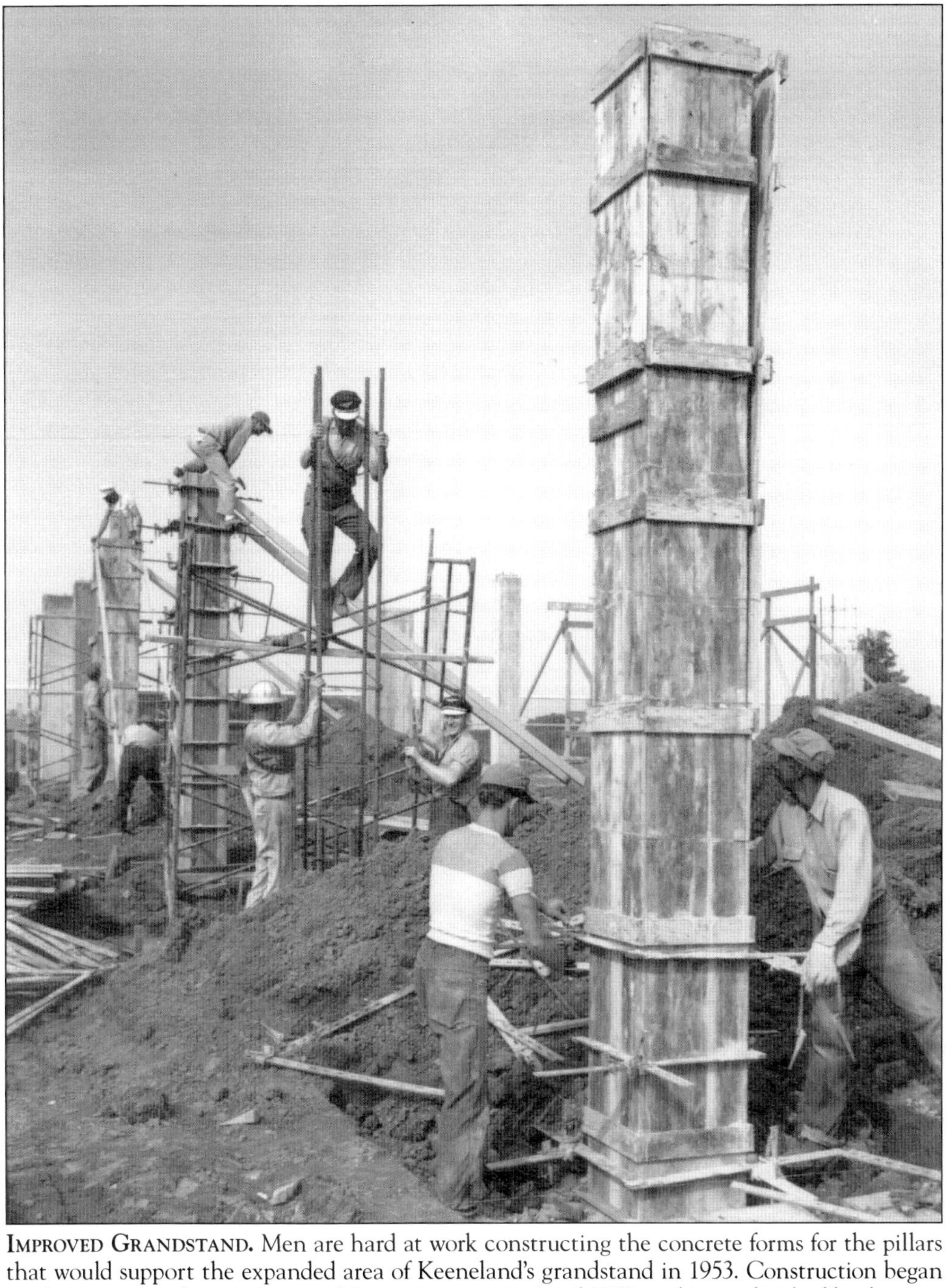

IMPROVED GRANDSTAND. Men are hard at work constructing the concrete forms for the pillars that would support the expanded area of Keeneland's grandstand in 1953. Construction began on the project at the conclusion of the spring meet in April 1953, and it was finished by the time the fall meet began in October. The addition of 1,542 seats brought the total capacity to 3,489, including the box seats. It was designed by Robert McMeekin, the central Kentucky architect who designed the original Keeneland buildings. The new structure also allowed room for a grandstand restaurant that could seat 384 people.

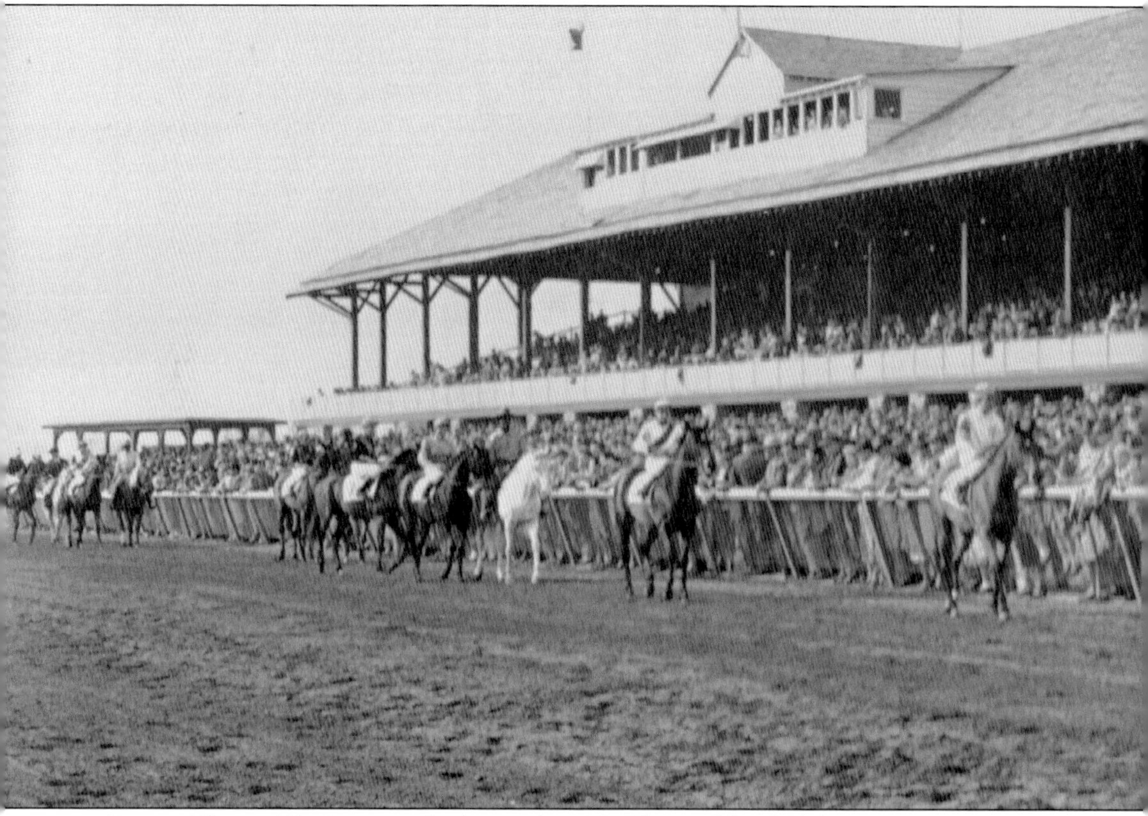

Packed House. The horses and riders in the 1951 Thoroughbred Club Dinner Purse post parade move slowly past a packed grandstand area in 1951. Some of the horses in the post parade are accompanied by an outrider, and some are not depending on individual preferences. The Thoroughbred Club Dinner Purse was run as an allowance race each spring from 1944 to 1989, with the exception of 1945. Until 1985, the race was restricted to horses owned by members of

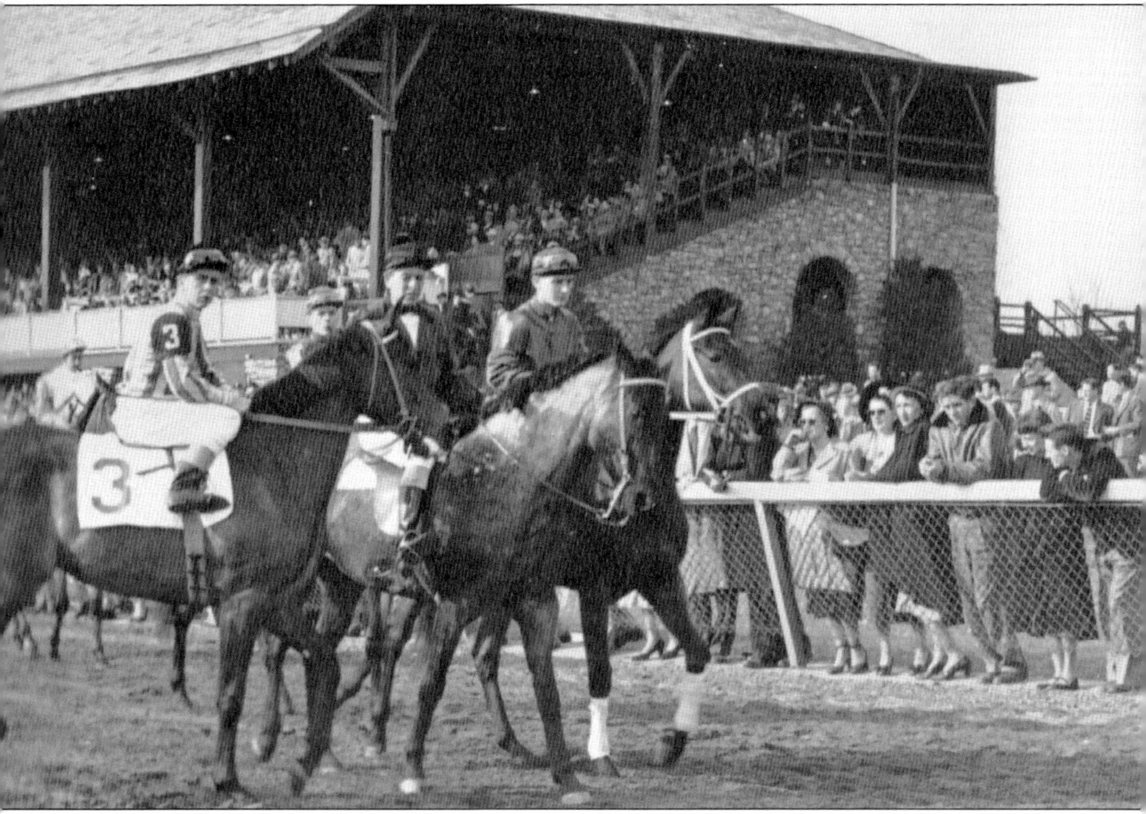

the Thoroughbred Club of America, which is headquartered in Lexington, Kentucky. In the foreground of the photograph and on the front cover of this book are no. 3 Miss Break, ridden by Ken Church and accompanied by an outrider, and another horse and jockey. Miss Break went on to win this race, which was held on April 19, 1951, on the Headley Course, which is about a half-mile long.

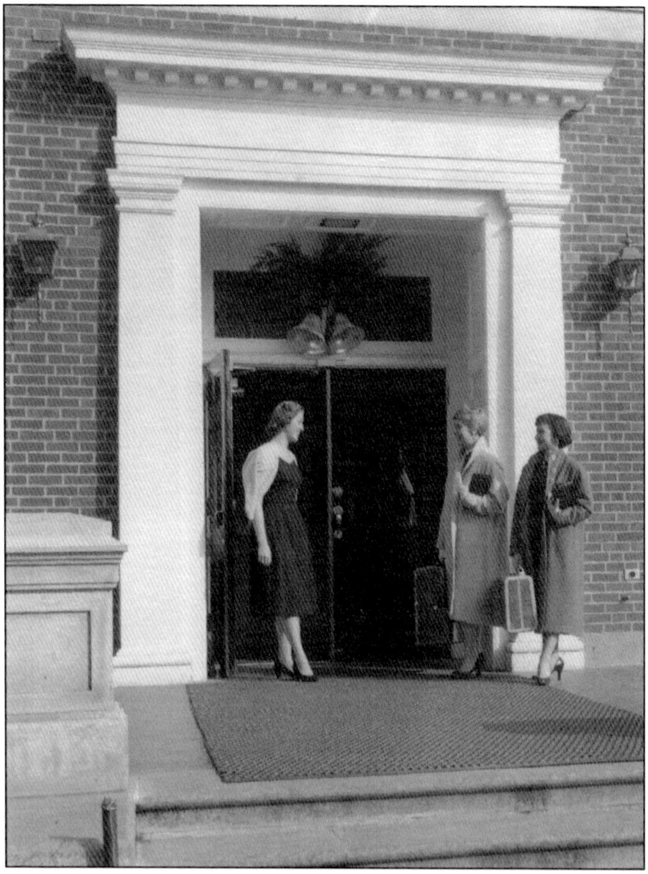

Keeneland Hall. In 1953, the Keeneland Foundation donated $200,000 to the University of Kentucky to build a new women's dormitory. This photograph, taken in the spring of 1955, shows three of the young ladies who were residents of the new dorm. Pictured from left to right are Angela Riggs, Joan Reeves, and Joyce Hood. Also, in 1955, Keeneland donated $10,000 to furnish Salk anti-polio vaccine for Lexington-area pre-school children.

Stands Out in a Crowd. Hoikuieez, a spotted mule, was easy to spot in a crowd of Thoroughbreds. Outriders provide their own mounts, often stabling more than one horse at Keeneland during race meets. This photograph was taken in 1951.

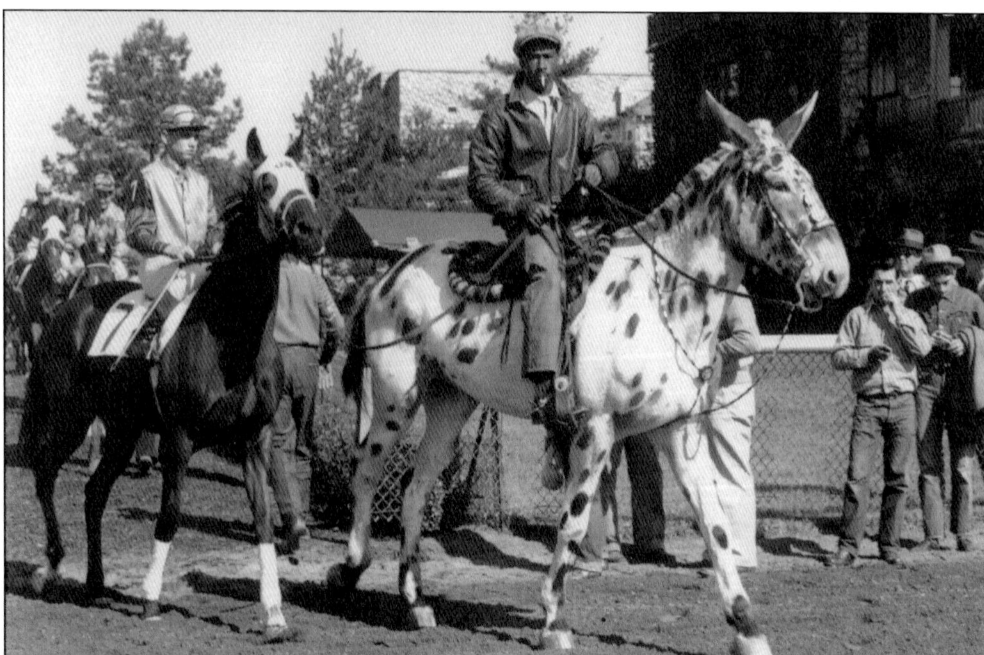

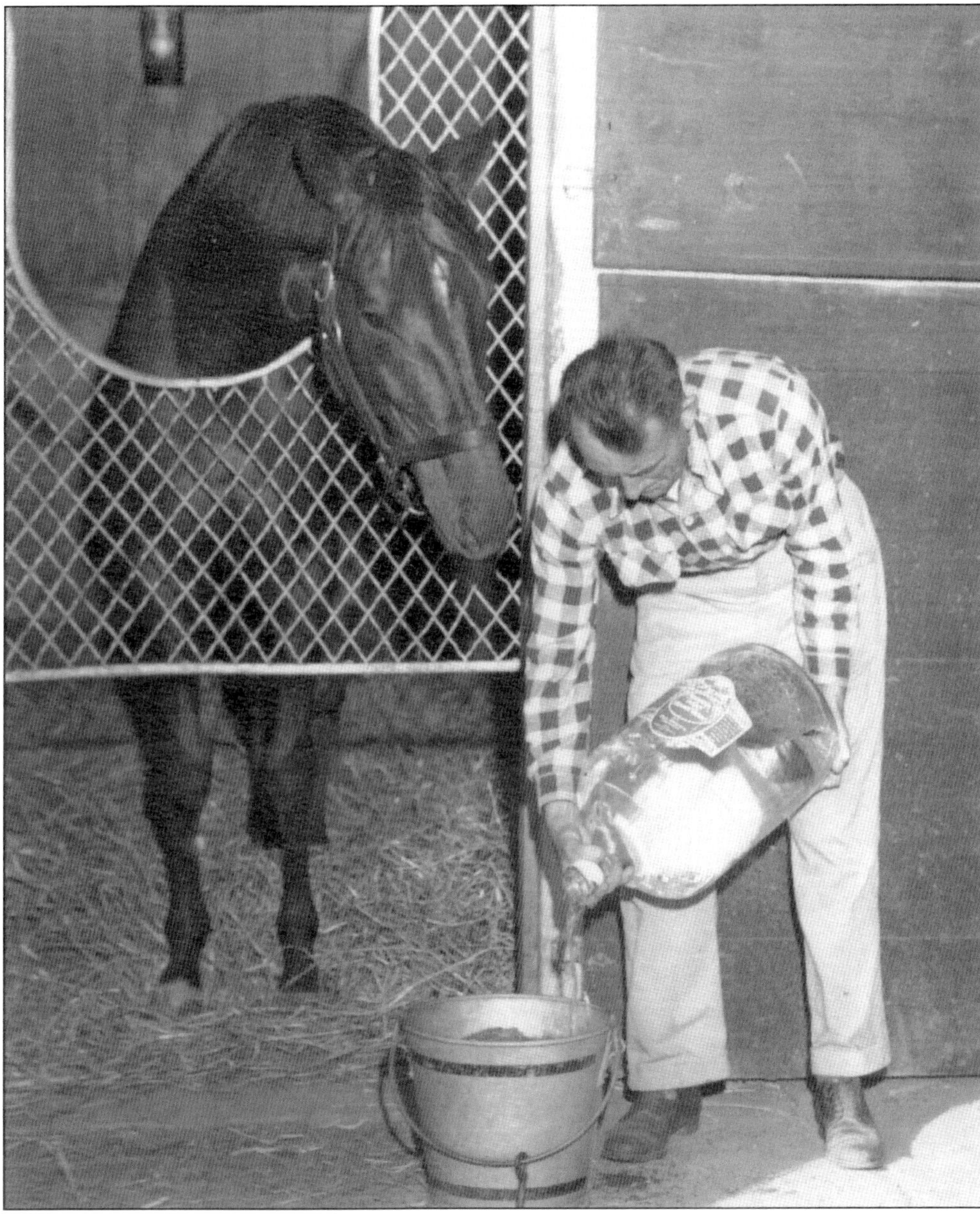

PICKY CHAMPION. Nashua was trained by "Sunny Jim" Fitzsimmons and ridden by jockey Eddie Arcaro. As a two-year-old in 1954, Nashua won six of eight starts and was named champion two-year-old. The following year, he won 10 out of 12 starts, including the Preakness and the Belmont. He finished second to Swaps in the 1955 Kentucky Derby but avenged the loss later that year in a match race. Nashua was at Keeneland in 1956 for his last public appearance under tack before he was retired to stud. He was galloped around the track by Arcaro in front of the admiring crowd. Nashua is seen here supervising his groom Al Robertson as he pours Nashua's favorite Mountain Valley Water into his water bucket.

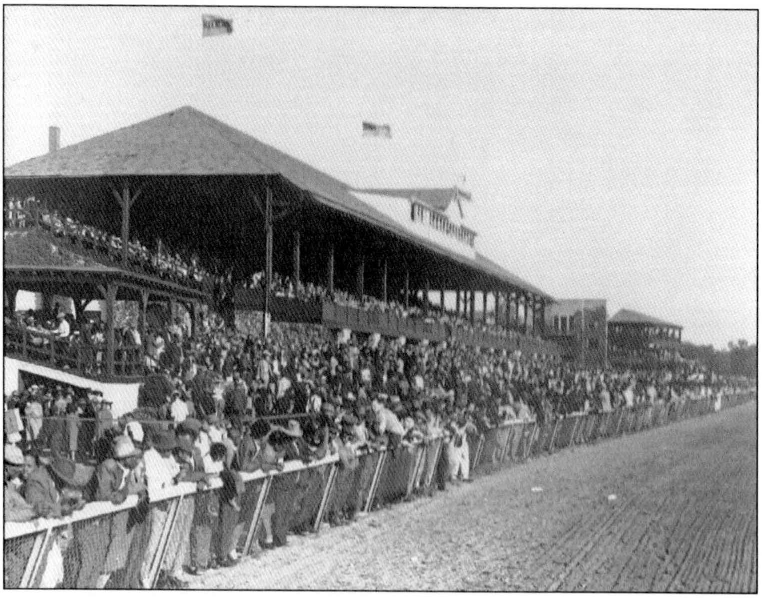

Anticipation. A big crowd waits impatiently for the horses to come into sight before a race in the late 1940s at Keeneland. The "colored" grandstand, seen in the left foreground, was a busy place this day but was torn down in 1953 when racial barriers to track attendance were removed.

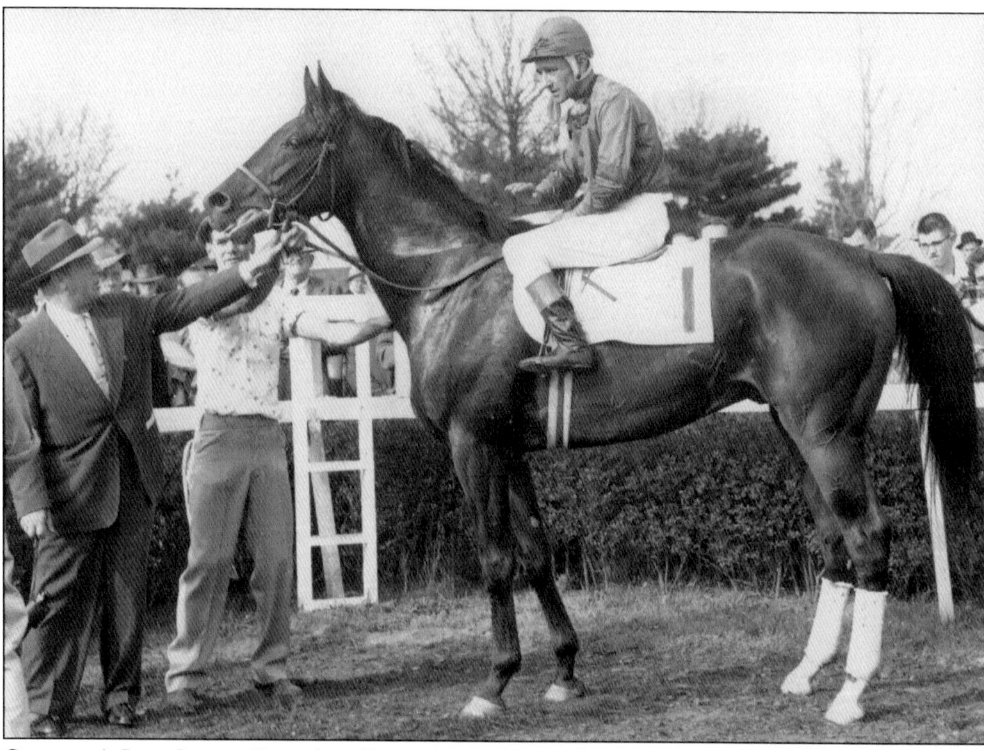

Calumet's Iron Liege. Considered by many as a "second-stringer" in Calumet's impressive stable of stars in 1957, Iron Liege was a winner after a Special Race in April. Eighteen days later, he was the long-shot winner of the Kentucky Derby, defeating among others future Hall of Fame horses Round Table, Bold Ruler, and Gallant Man. Jimmy Jones was his trainer, Dave Erb was his jockey at Keeneland, and Bill Hartack rode him in the Derby.

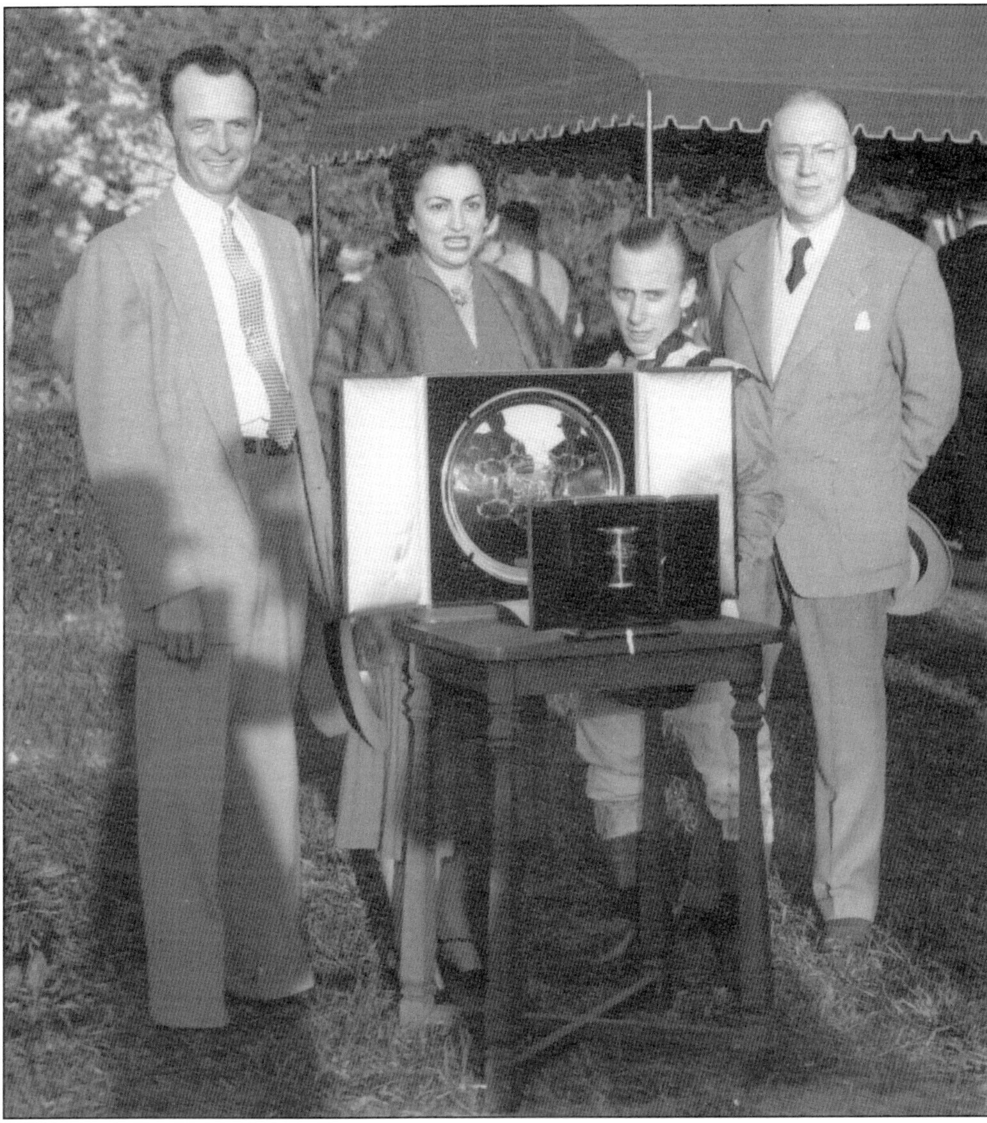

Happy Owner-Trainer. Woodford C. "Woody" Stephens and his wife accept the trophy for Brother Tex's win in the 1954 Breeders' Futurity from Keeneland president Guy Huguelet (far right) with jockey Pete Anderson looking on. Stephens was Brother Tex's owner and trainer. The Breeders' Futurity was first run at the Kentucky Association track from 1910 to 1930 before moving to Latonia in northern Kentucky for two years. It was revived at Keeneland in 1938 and has been held there every year since, with the exception of the three years during World War II when it was held at Churchill Downs as part of Keeneland's meets there. Stephens was born in Stanton, Kentucky, and started his racetrack career as a jockey at age 16. He began training in 1936 and continued until he died in 1998, just a few days short of his 85th birthday. In his career, he had 1,937 winners (including three Blue Grass Stakes winners and five consecutive Belmont Stakes winners) who earned more than $53 million.

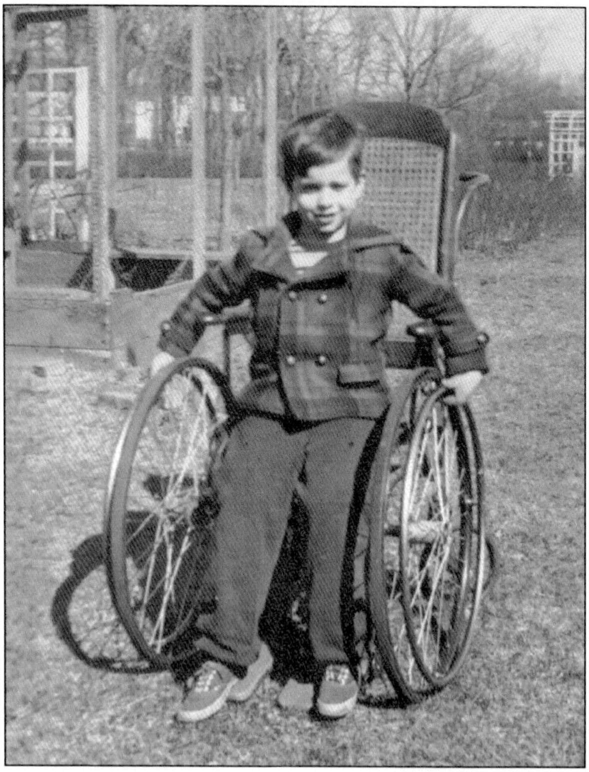

Wheelchair-Bound for Now. Young Tommy Clinch is seen here in a wheelchair. A polio victim from Brooklyn, New York, Clinch had to use the wheelchair because he could not walk from the age of three when he was stricken with polio. He took his next steps at age 11 and developed his leg muscles by swimming, and he always wanted to be a jockey.

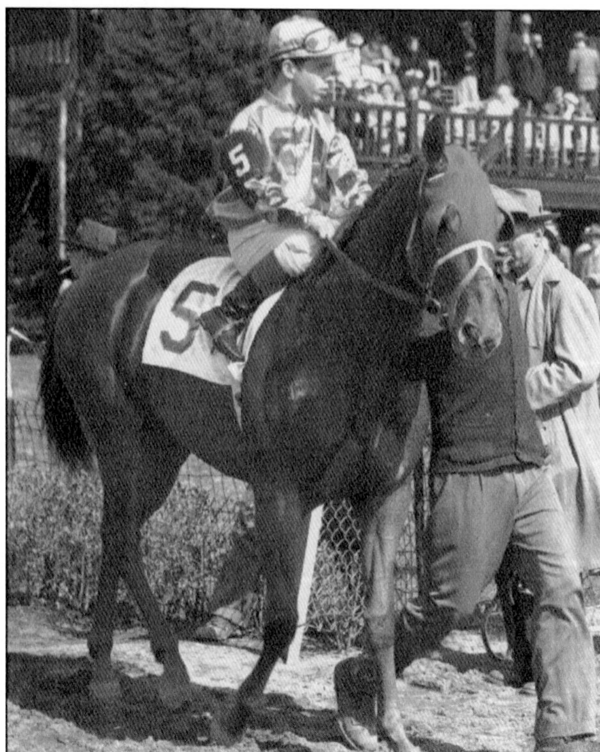

First Race. Tommy "Brooklyn" Clinch fulfilled his dream to be a jockey with help from Big Brothers of America and High Hope Farm near Lexington, Kentucky. The formerly wheelchair-bound young man is shown here at Keeneland in 1953 on his first mount, L'Amour. Later that year, Clinch won his first race at Randall Park in Ohio on Elaine Ruth, owned by Douglas M. Davis Jr. of High Hope Farm.

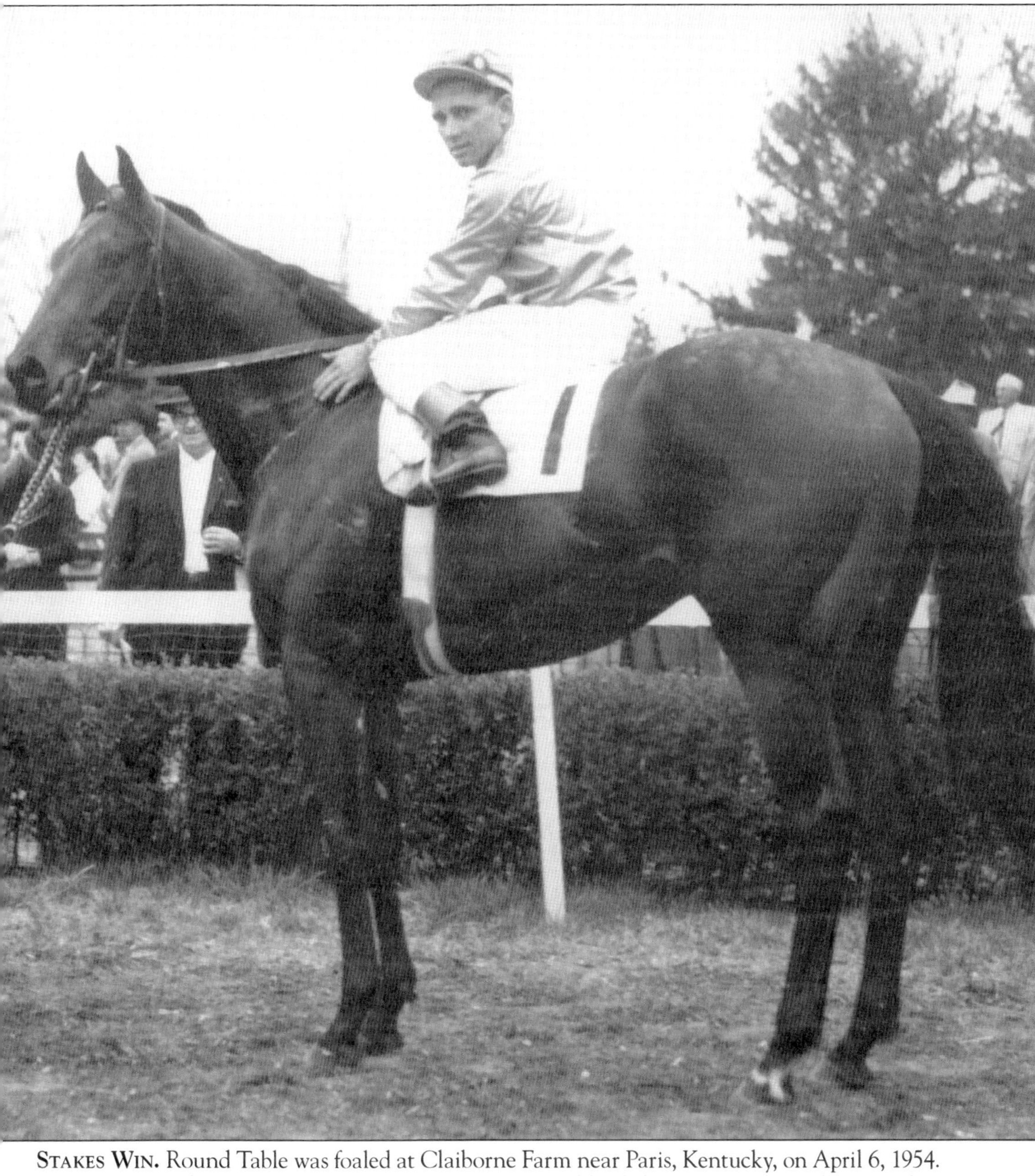

Stakes Win. Round Table was foaled at Claiborne Farm near Paris, Kentucky, on April 6, 1954. Bold Ruler was born on the same day at Claiborne, and both horses went on to be named as Horse of the Year during their careers. This 1957 photograph shows two-year-old Round Table with jockey Steve Brooks after he won the Lafayette Stakes. He was owned at that point in his career by Claiborne Farm, but partway through his three-year-old season, he was sold to Travis Kerr and finished his racing career under the Kerr Stable colors. As part of the sales agreement, Kerr agreed that Round Table would return to Claiborne to stand at stud.

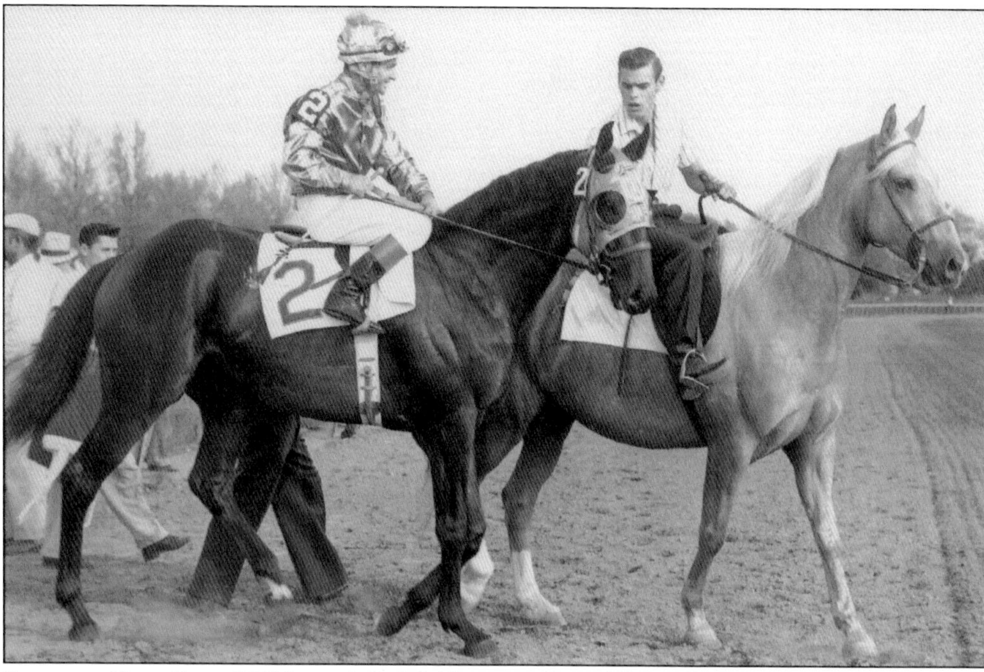

READY TO RUN. Round Table, with Ralph Neves in the saddle, walked onto the track before the 1957 Blue Grass Stakes looking like the champion he was. He won 11 consecutive races at three years of age, earning more than $600,000. He topped that at age four by winning $662,780 and was named 1958 Horse of the Year. He raced at five years of age and added $413,380 in winnings for a total of $1,749,869.

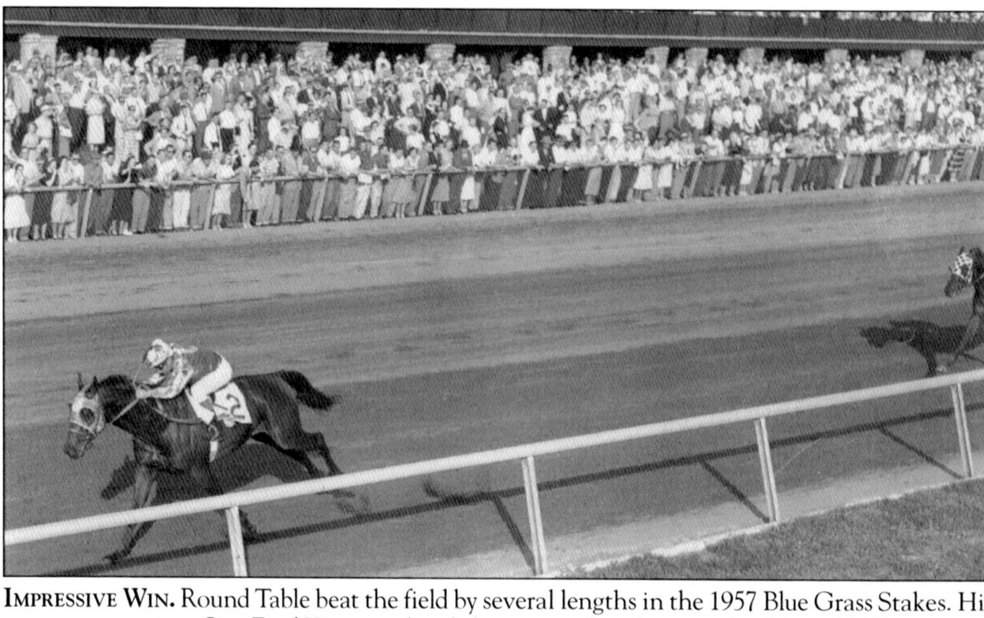

IMPRESSIVE WIN. Round Table beat the field by several lengths in the 1957 Blue Grass Stakes. His nearest competitor, One-Eyed King, can barely be seen in this photograph of Round Table running easily down the stretch. Round Table was five for five at Keeneland, including three stakes wins. He retired from the racetrack to Claiborne Farm and became one of the most important sires of the 20th century, producing 20.6 percent stakes winners.

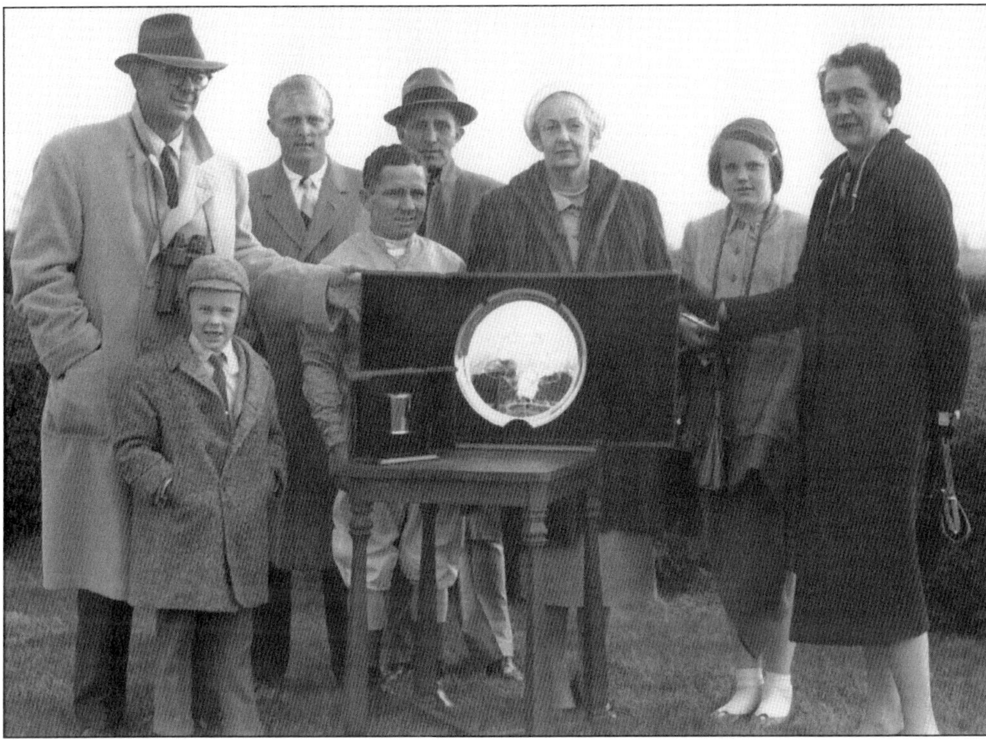

A Family Affair. A.B. "Bull" Hancock (far left), owner of Claiborne Farm in Paris, Kentucky, is joined here by, from left to right, his eight-year-old son Seth, LeRoy Jolley, Steve Brooks, Moody Jolley, wife Waddell Hancock, daughter Clay Hancock, and Mrs. Charles Thomas in accepting a Keeneland gold julep cup and tray after Claiborne's colt Bandit won the 1957 Phoenix Stakes. Currently, Claiborne Farm has won more Keeneland stakes than any other owner.

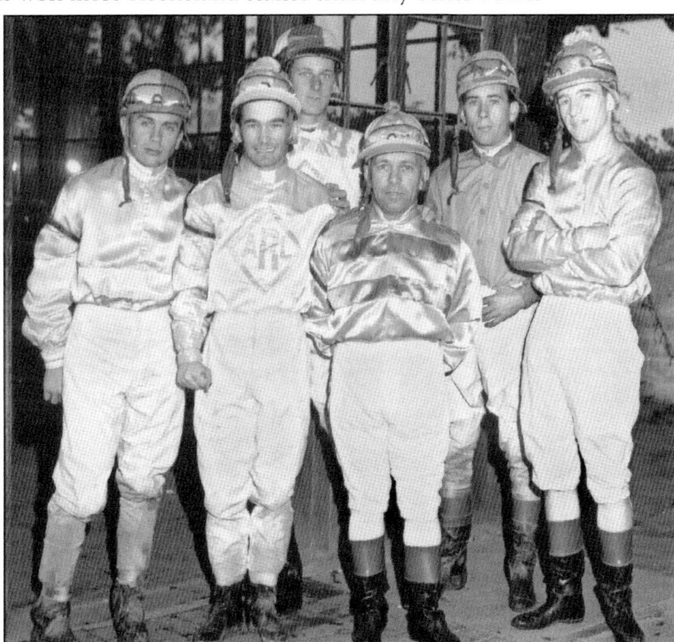

1957 Spinster Jockeys. This group includes several jockeys who enjoyed much success at Keeneland. From left to right are Ken Church, William "Bill" Shoemaker, John Heckmann, Conn McCreary, Robert Ussery, and L. Hausmann. Church won the 1957 Spinster on Bornastar, and they won again the following year. Heckmann was the leading rider at Keeneland during the 1950s in terms of meets won: he took 5 out of 20.

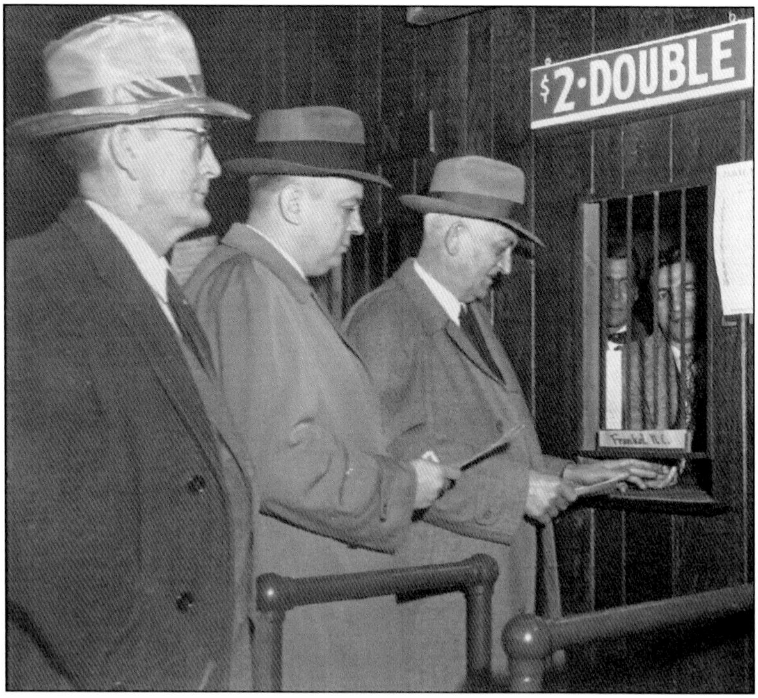

First Daily Double. What is known today as exotic wagering did not appear at Keeneland until 1958 when William Cummins (first at window) bought the first daily-double ticket at the spring meet. Introduced in North America in 1931, the wager required the bettor to pick the winner of the first two races of the day. In line behind Cummins are Fred Poplin and B.J. Santen. Tony Cerra is the teller.

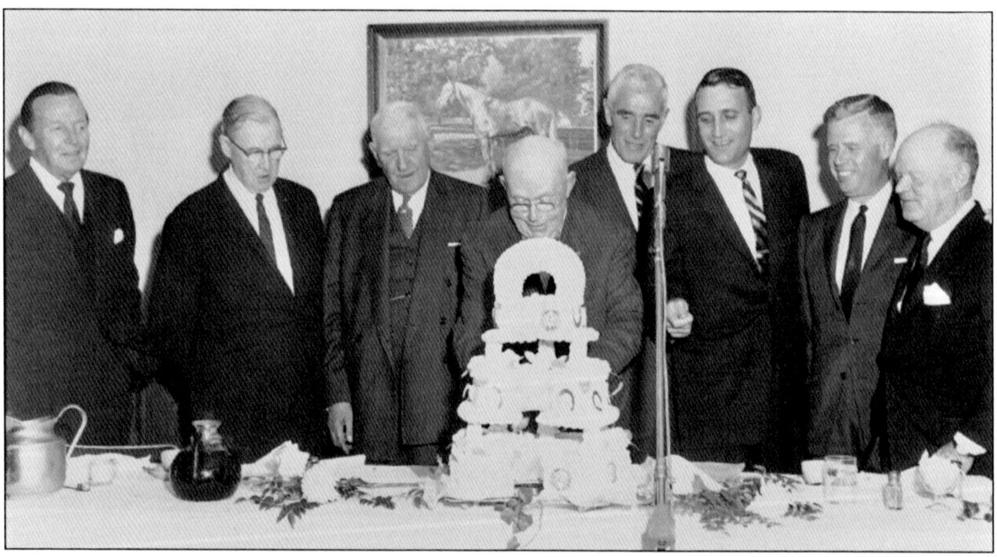

Keeneland's Silver Anniversary. The Keeneland Association celebrated its 25th anniversary with cake and a good bit of pride of accomplishment in 1960. Seen at the cake-cutting ceremony are, from left to right, Arnold Hanger, William Courtney, Thomas Piatt, Hal Price Headley wielding the knife, Louis L. Haggin II, J.B. Faulconer, W.T. Bishop, and Duval Headley. In 25 short years, Keeneland had become a Kentucky tradition and Thoroughbred landmark.

Seven

Keeneland Horse Sales

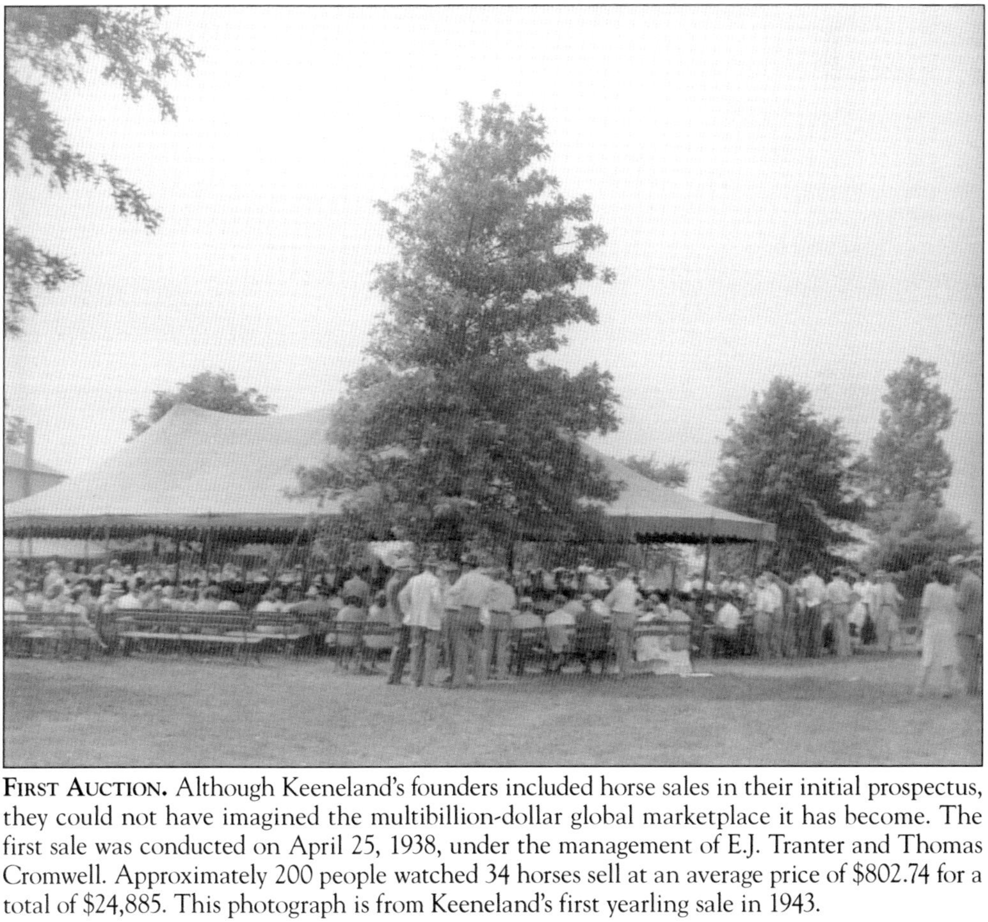

First Auction. Although Keeneland's founders included horse sales in their initial prospectus, they could not have imagined the multibillion-dollar global marketplace it has become. The first sale was conducted on April 25, 1938, under the management of E.J. Tranter and Thomas Cromwell. Approximately 200 people watched 34 horses sell at an average price of $802.74 for a total of $24,885. This photograph is from Keeneland's first yearling sale in 1943.

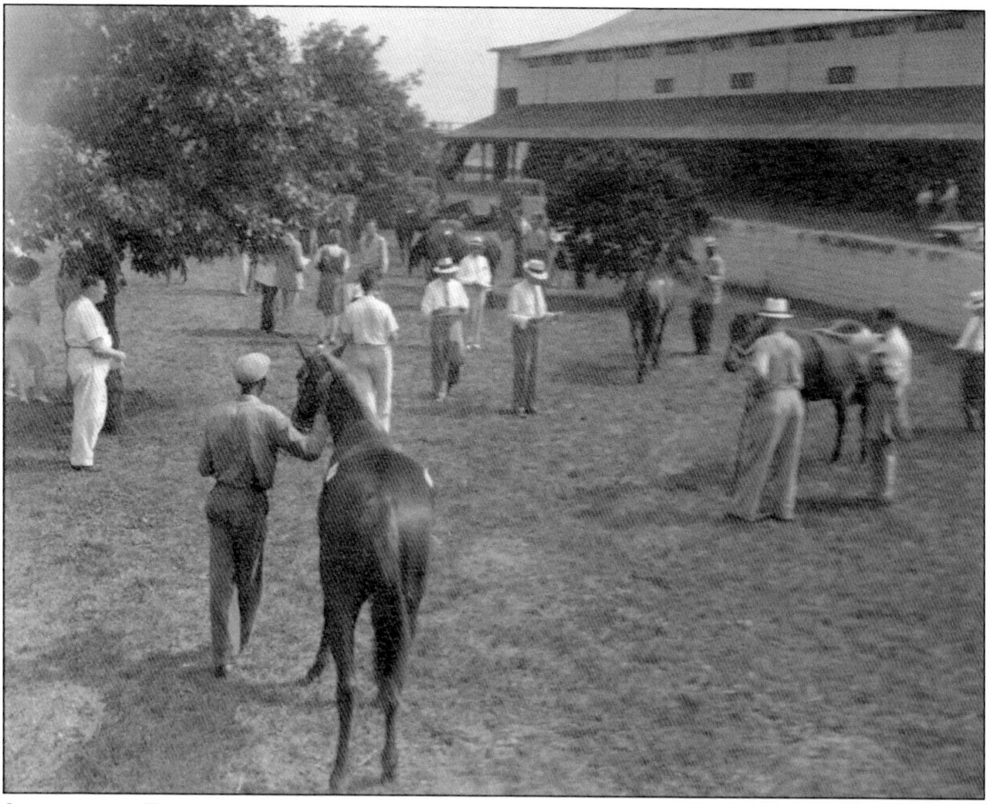

SUMMERTIME TRADITION. Before World War II, Kentucky's Thoroughbred breeders sent their best yearlings by rail to Saratoga Springs, New York, each summer to be sold at Fasig-Tipton's famous sale. But because of wartime restrictions on rail transportation, for three days in August of 1943 breeders sold their crop under a tent in Keeneland's paddock. The sale was conducted by Fasig-Tipton and consisted of an afternoon session and a cooler evening session.

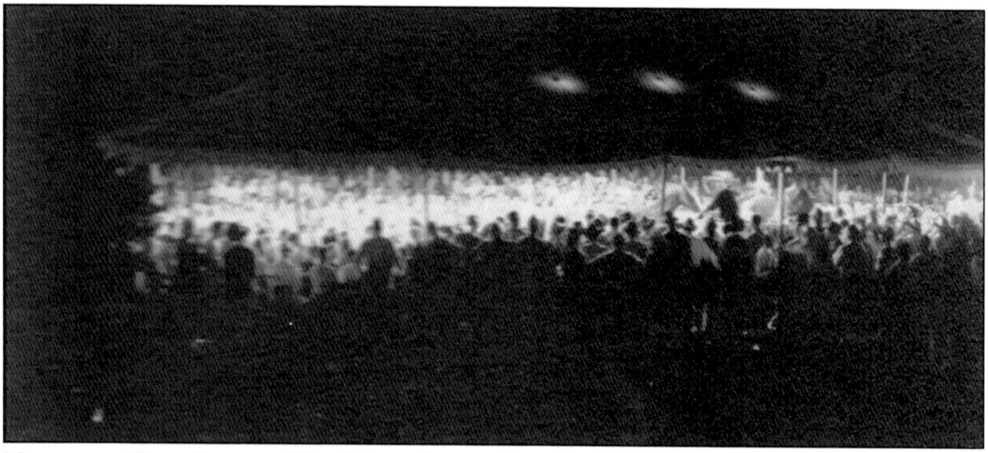

NIGHTTIME TENT SESSION. The 312 yearlings sold at Keeneland in 1943 brought an average of $2,980. It was reported that the average was almost three times that of the Saratoga sale the year before. The highest price paid for a yearling was $66,000. Floridian Fred W. Hooper attended his first horse auction that week and paid $10,000 for a Sir Gallahad III colt he named Hoop Jr., who won the Kentucky Derby in 1945.

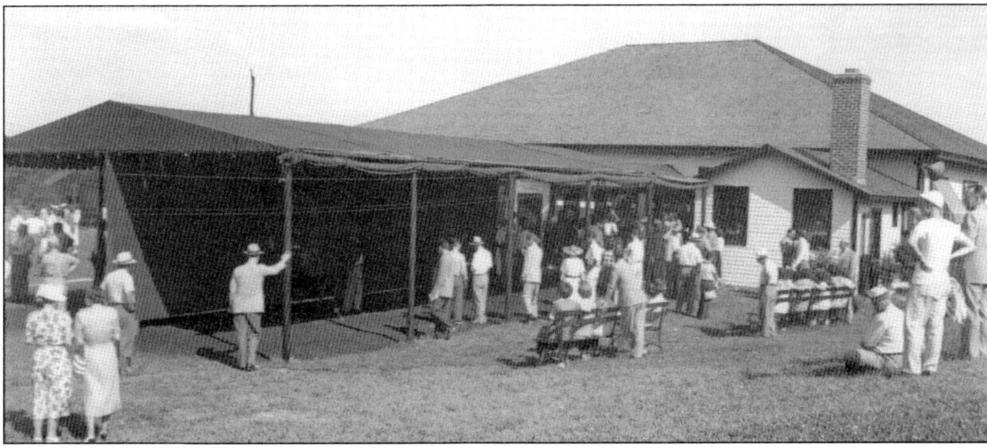

First Sales Pavilion. After the success of the 1943 sale, some Kentucky breeders, led by Claiborne Farm's Arthur B. Hancock and Hal Price Headley, decided to continue selling their yearlings at Keeneland on a permanent basis. After Fasig-Tipton decided not to continue its partnership with Keeneland, the Breeders' Sales Company was formed in 1944. The new co-op purchased an old Fasig-Tipton sales pavilion, pictured here in 1950, and had it rebuilt at Keeneland.

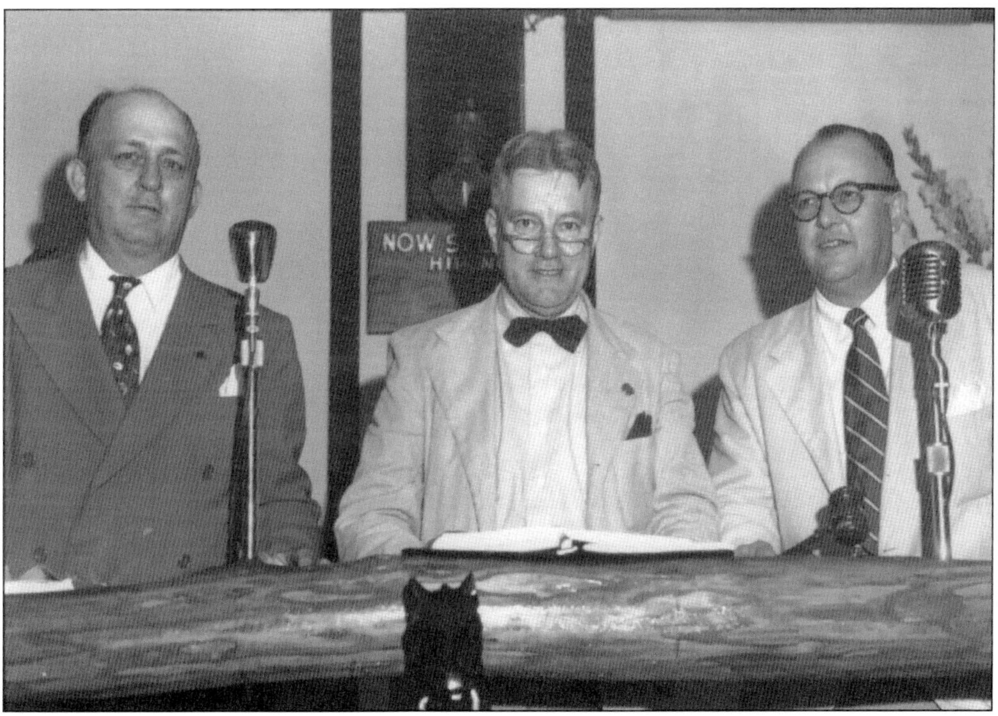

Auction Trio. In 1950, these three men, Doc Bond (left), Humphrey Finney (center), and George Swinebroad, directed the auctions, which had already become the industry's standard. Swinebroad joined the Breeders' Sales Company when it was founded in 1944 and was Keeneland's first director of auctions until his death in 1975. Finney became Fasig-Tipton's long-serving president and, later, chairman. Doc Bond continued to work with Keeneland for years.

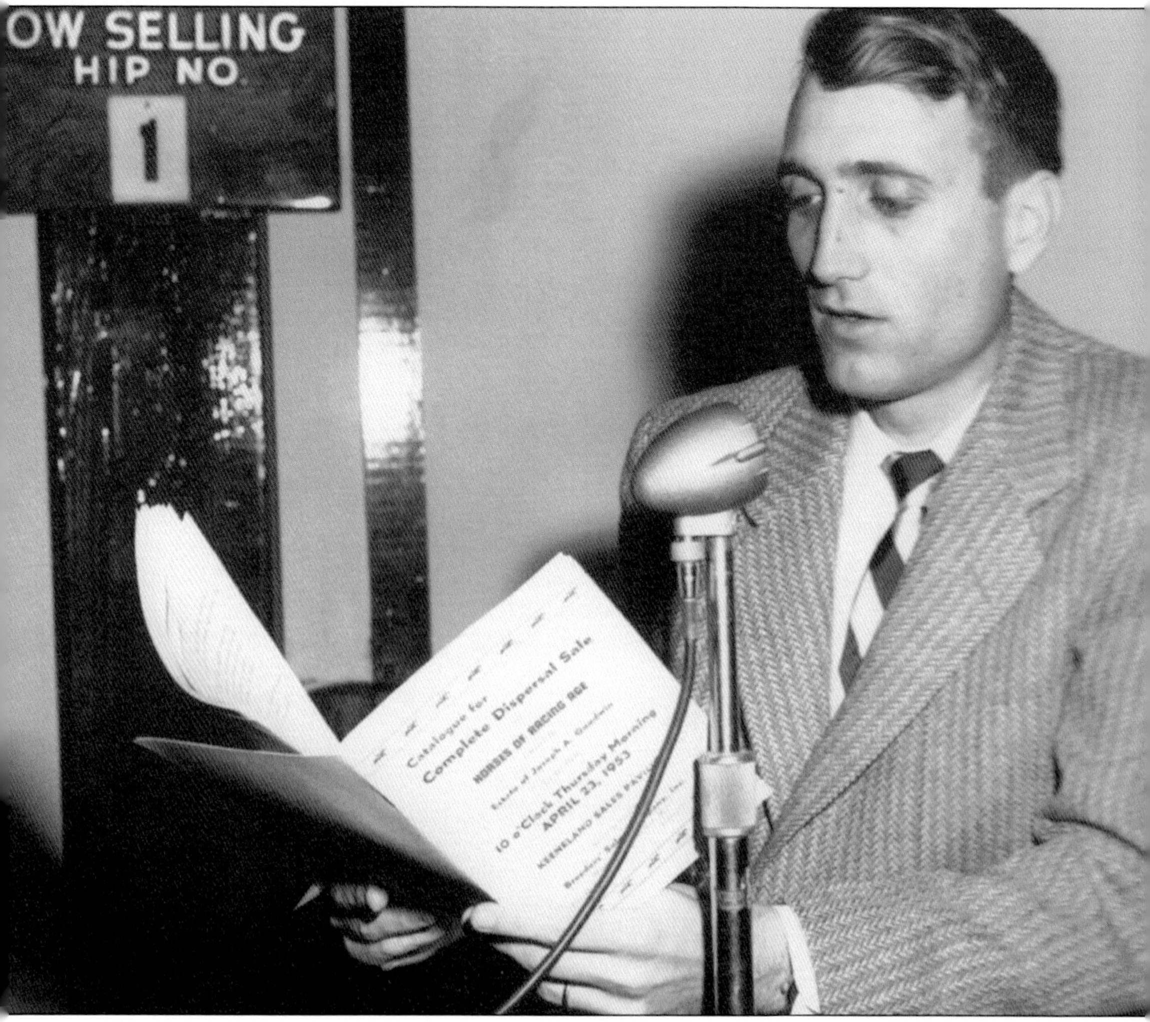

Sales Announcer. James Bailey "J.B." Faulconer, seen here in 1953, began his connection with the Breeders' Sales Company, later known as Keeneland Sales, as a pedigree announcer. In the early 1950s, he was the announcer for University of Kentucky basketball and football games for Lexington's WLAP Radio. During World War II, he was a decorated Army officer in the Pacific and later served as commanding general of Kentucky's 100th Army Reserve Division from 1969 to 1973. Faulconer left the radio business in 1955 to become the public relations director at Keeneland until 1971. As president of the Turf Publicists of America, he was credited with the creation of the Eclipse Awards, established in 1971.

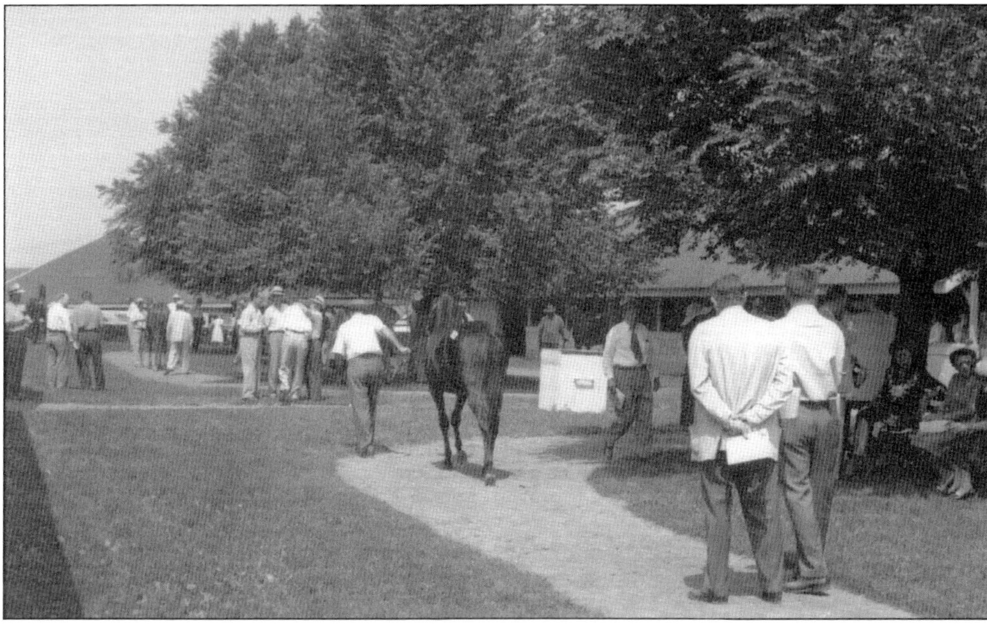

Spendthrift at Keeneland. This 1953 image shows a summertime process that continues to this day at Keeneland. Prospective yearling buyers wander through the barn area with sale catalogs in hand asking to see certain prospects and perhaps accepting a cold drink from the hospitable consignors. The barn area shown here contained horses consigned by Spendthrift Farm, one of Keeneland's oldest and most successful sellers.

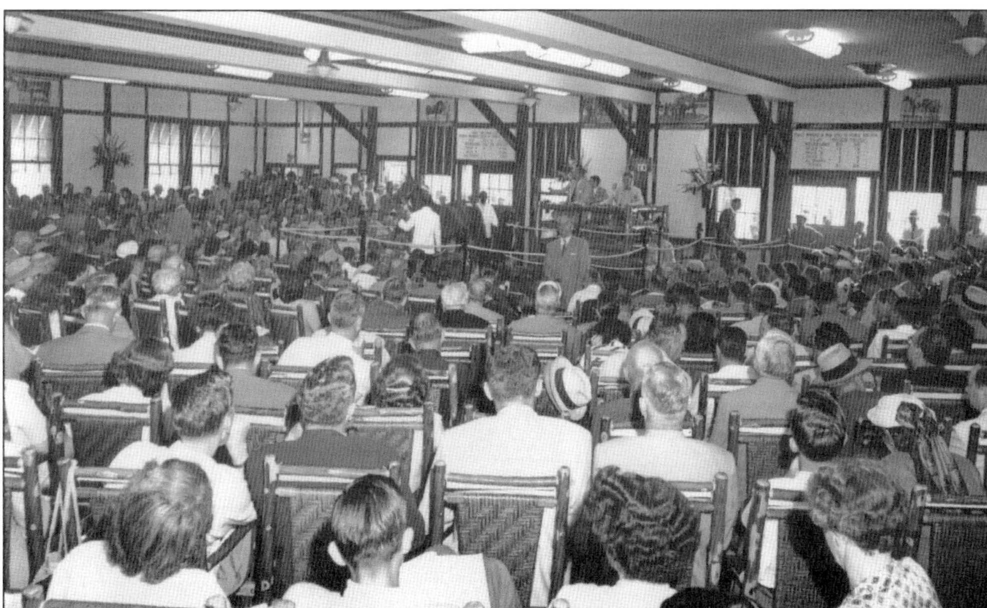

1950 Sales Ring. Keeneland's Breeders' Sales Company continued its steady growth in popularity and average sales price through the 1950s. This 1950 photograph shows a large crowd seated in the cane-back chairs that were used at the sales in its early years. In 1952, all three winners of the 1954 Triple Crown races—Determine (Kentucky Derby), Hasty Road (Preakness) and High Gun (Belmont Stakes)—were sold at Keeneland.

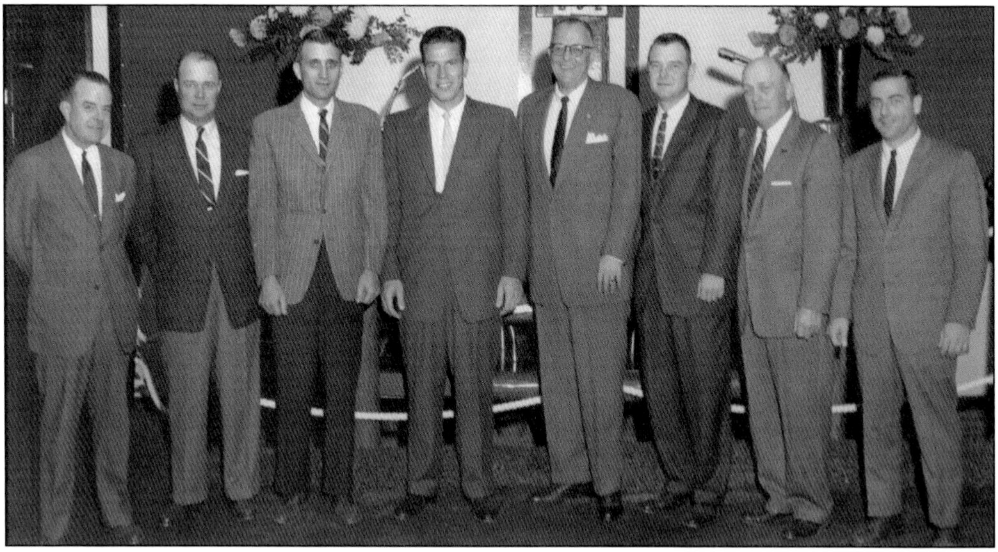

1957 SALES TEAM. The Breeders' Sales auctioneers in 1957 included, from left to right, J. T. Denton, J. L. Teater, J. B. Faulconer, Tom Caldwell, George Swinebroad, Carl Garner, Doc Bond, and Laddy Dance.

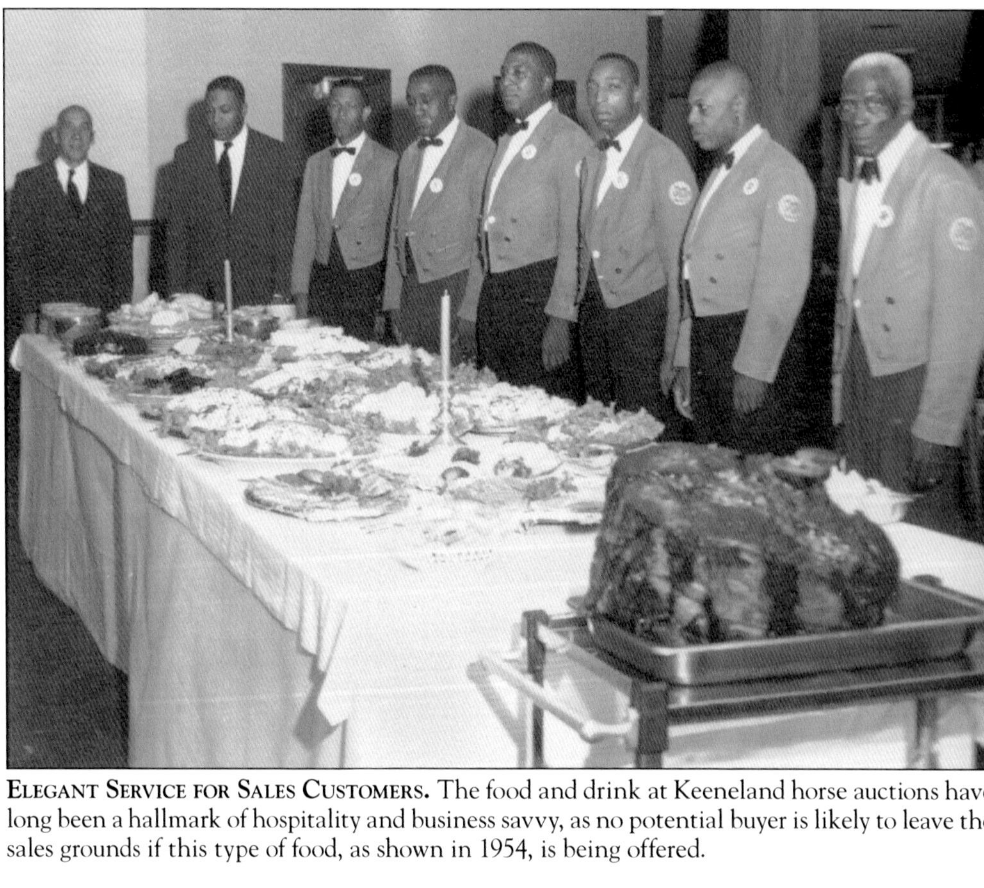

ELEGANT SERVICE FOR SALES CUSTOMERS. The food and drink at Keeneland horse auctions have long been a hallmark of hospitality and business savvy, as no potential buyer is likely to leave the sales grounds if this type of food, as shown in 1954, is being offered.

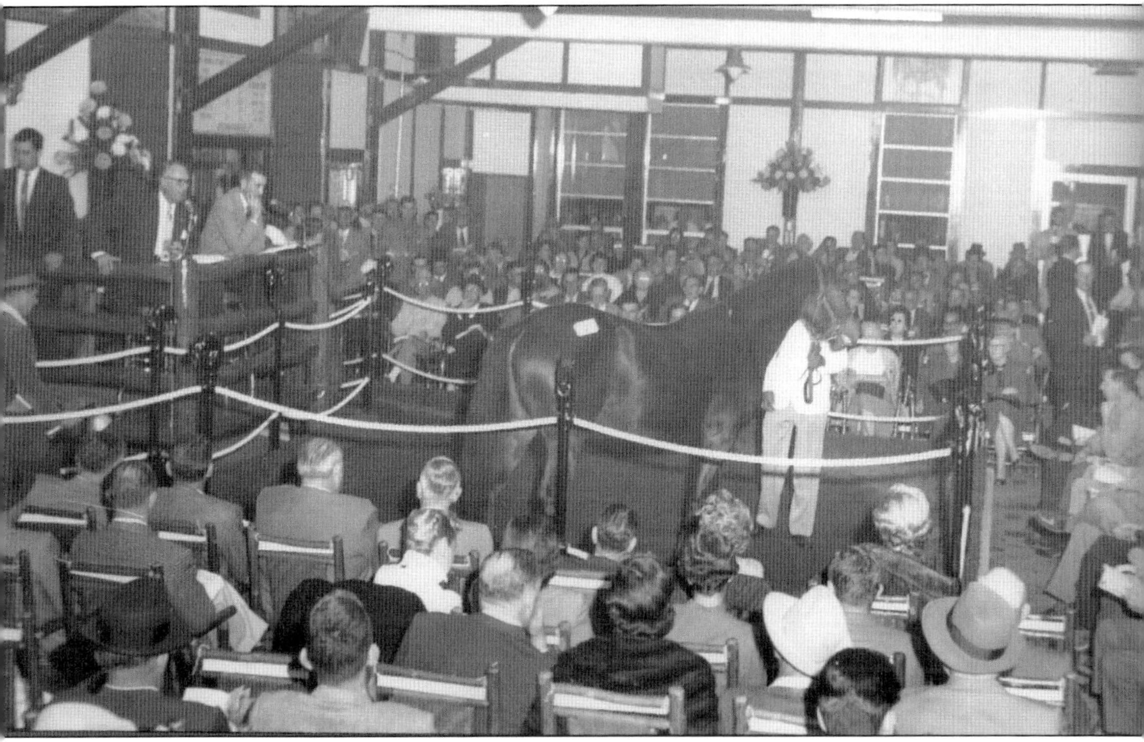

Future Champion Filly. This photograph shows a bay filly by Royal Charger out of Tige O'My Heart in the sales ring. The filly was bred and consigned to the 1956 summer yearling sales by Leslie Combs II and John W. Hanes. She sold for $63,000, a record for a yearling filly, to Mrs. Charles Ulrich Bay, who named her Idun after the Norse goddess of eternal youth. Idun, trained by future Hall of Fame trainer Sherrill W. Ward and ridden by another Hall of Famer, Bill Hartack, was named champion two-year-old filly in 1957 after being undefeated in eight races and winning a record $220,995. She went on to be named champion three-year-old filly in 1958, finishing her career with a total of 17 wins out of 30 starts, earning $392,490. Selling horses such as Idun did much to establish Keeneland as the premier Thoroughbred marketplace in the world.

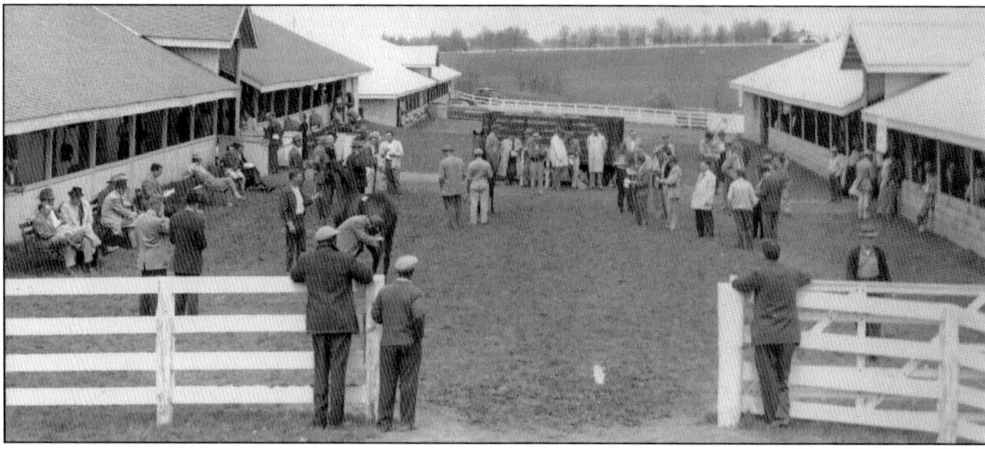

Horses-in-Training Sale. Keeneland's first sales were primarily for yearlings, but they soon provided other types of sales for the racing and breeding industry. Auctions are usually conducted by age and by purpose. Yearling sales are held in late summer and early fall, mares and weanlings (breeding stock) are sold in late fall, and two-year-olds in training are shown and sold in April, as depicted in this 1958 photograph.

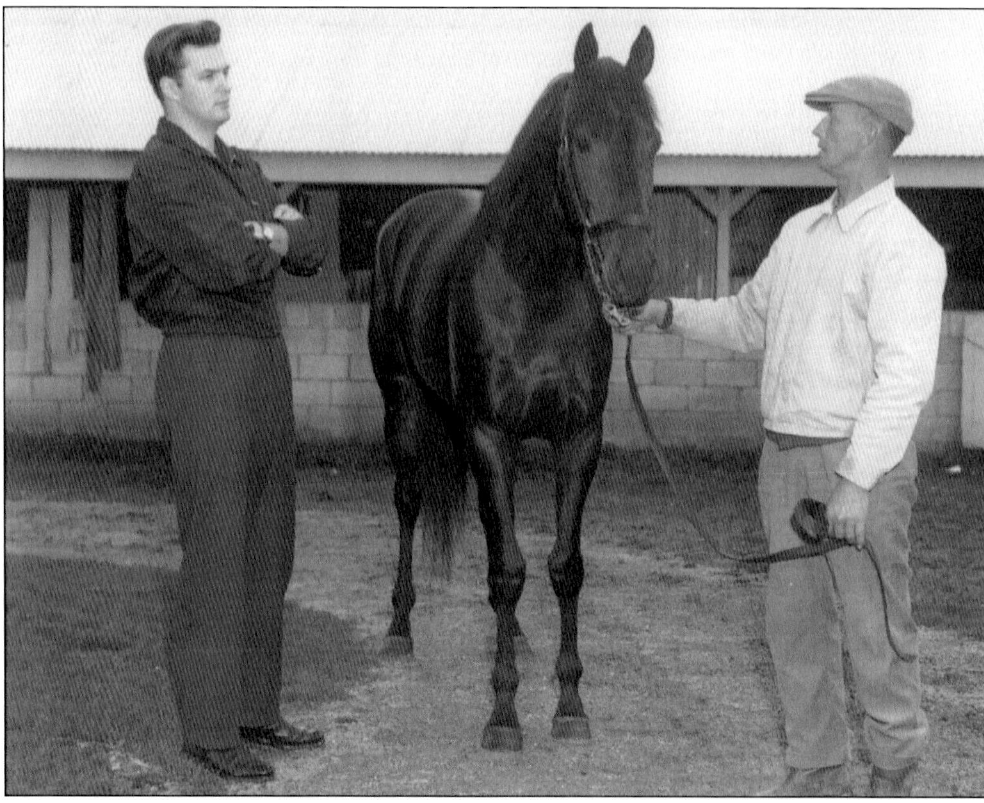

Young Preston Madden. When this photograph was taken outside one of Keeneland's sales barns in 1959, Preston Madden (left) was struggling to rebuild one of Lexington's premier Thoroughbred breeding farms, Hamburg Place. His grandfather John E. Madden had been one of the industry's greatest breeders. His grandson Preston brought the farm back by breeding and selling such great horses as Alysheba in 1984.

Eight

Unusual Events and Extreme Weather

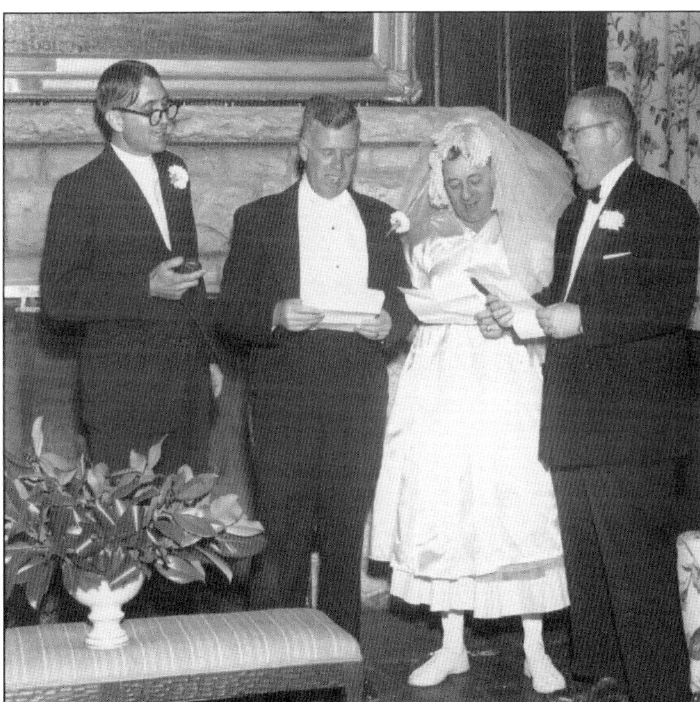

Womanless Wedding. This humorous ceremony happened in 1959 and included members of the Keeneland staff. From left to right are J.B. Faulconer, director of public relations (preacher); W.T. Bishop, general manager (father of the bride); Joe Kramer (bride); and Frank Werner, assistant general manager (groom). It took place on Betty Hodgkins's last day of work before her wedding to Louis Lee Haggin III; Hodgkins was Bishop's secretary.

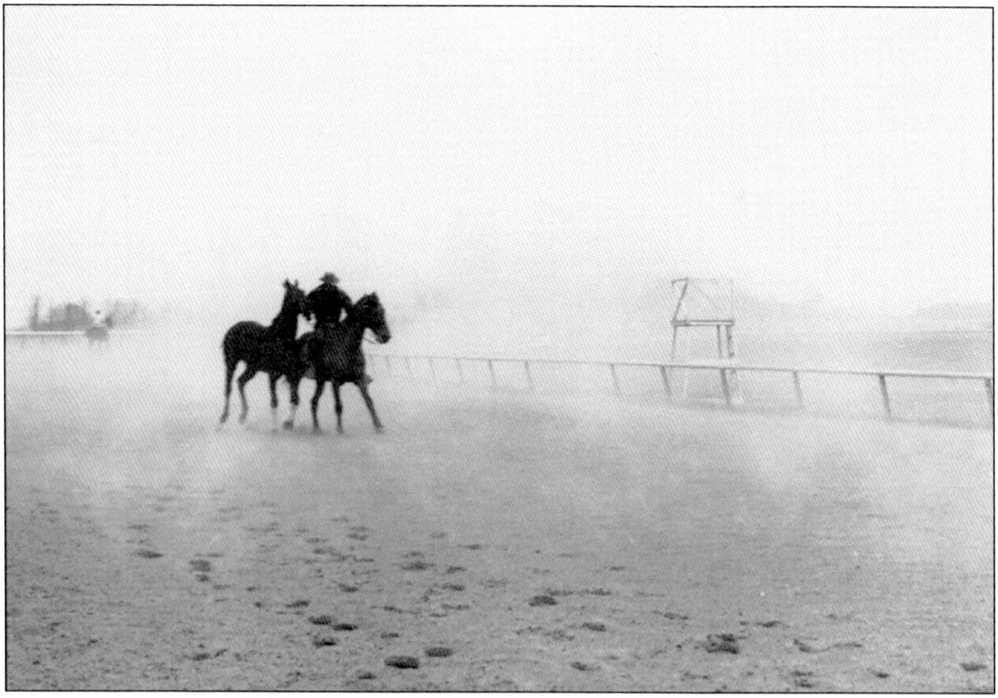

Blowing in the Wind. Getting out on the track to exercise was no fun for horses or riders on this windy day in 1950. The 60-mile-per-hour winds removed more than 400 tons of sand from the track. Working on the backside is no place for anyone not totally committed to maintaining the horses in their care, as they require lots of work, no matter what the weather is like.

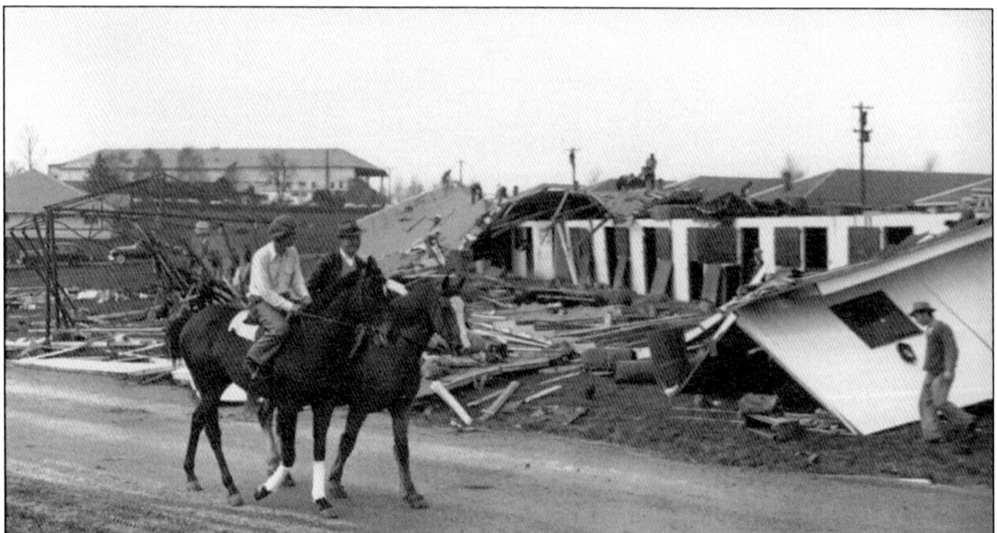

Fatal Windstorm. There was a violent windstorm on the afternoon of April 8, the opening day of the spring meet in 1948. The twister destroyed barns on the backside at Keeneland less than 12 hours before the meet's first race, killing one groom and injuring others. The horses escaped with minor injuries. Keeneland spring meets are held in April, which can be an extreme weather month in Kentucky.

Unusual Way to Arrive. There have been quite a few unusual arrivals at Keeneland through the years, but perhaps none was more spectacular than when a group of soldiers parachuted into the center field at Keeneland in 1950 on Armed Forces Day at the track. Keeneland has made a practice through the years of honoring military personnel.

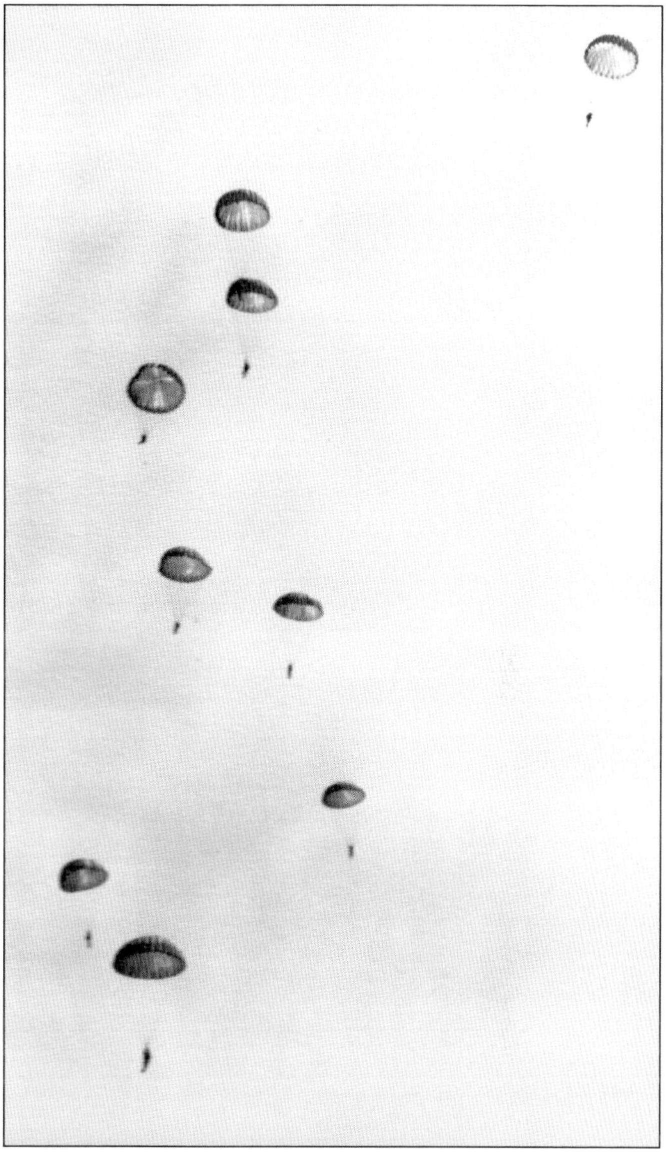

Armed Forces Day. These troopers from the 11th Airborne Division, based at Fort Campbell, Kentucky, parachuted into the infield on Keeneland's Armed Forces Day on May 20, 1950. Since it was May, there was no racing at Keeneland that day, but if there had been the track would have been a busy place best reached by parachute. After World War II, meets continually broke attendance and handle records.

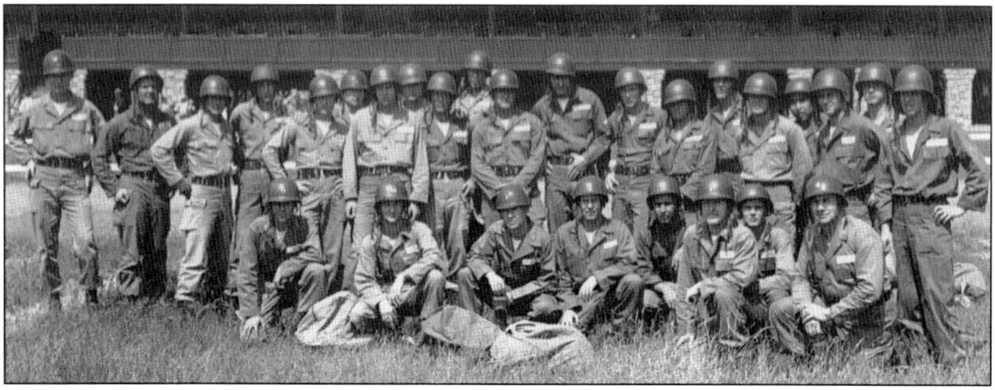

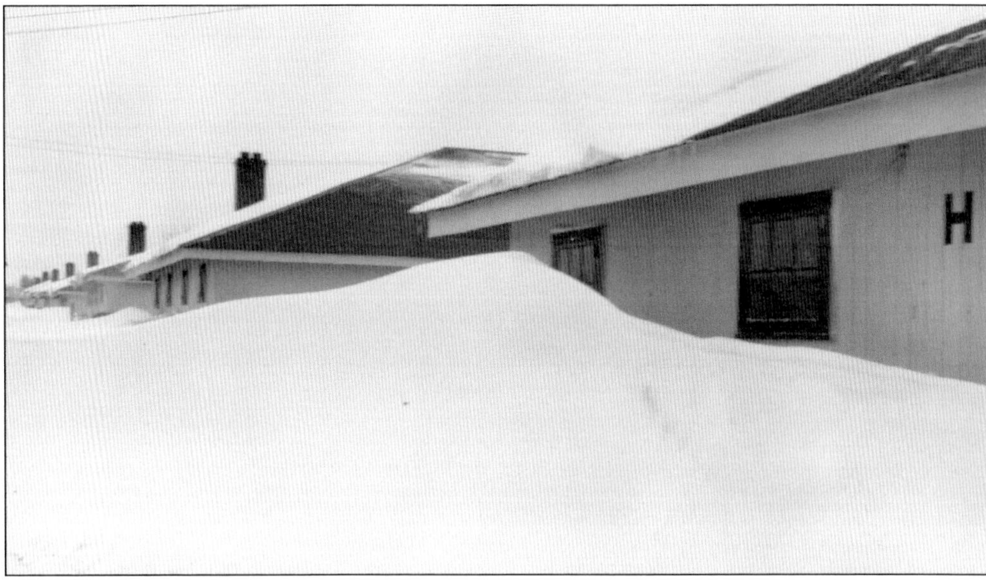

More Than Enough Snow. Although there are some people who enjoy snow, major snowstorms like this one in 1950 disrupt the daily routines of the humans and horses that live year-round on the backside at Keeneland.

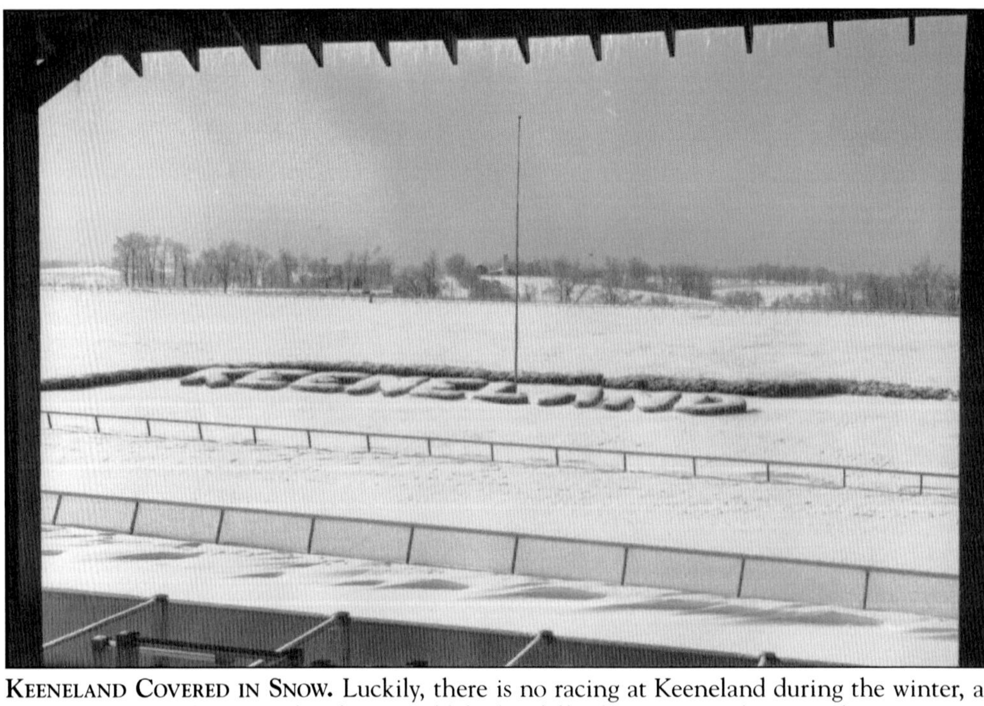

Keeneland Covered in Snow. Luckily, there is no racing at Keeneland during the winter, as even the hardiest horses and jockeys would find it difficult to race in these conditions. A 1951 snowstorm covered the clipped hedges spelling out Keeneland in front of the flagpole.

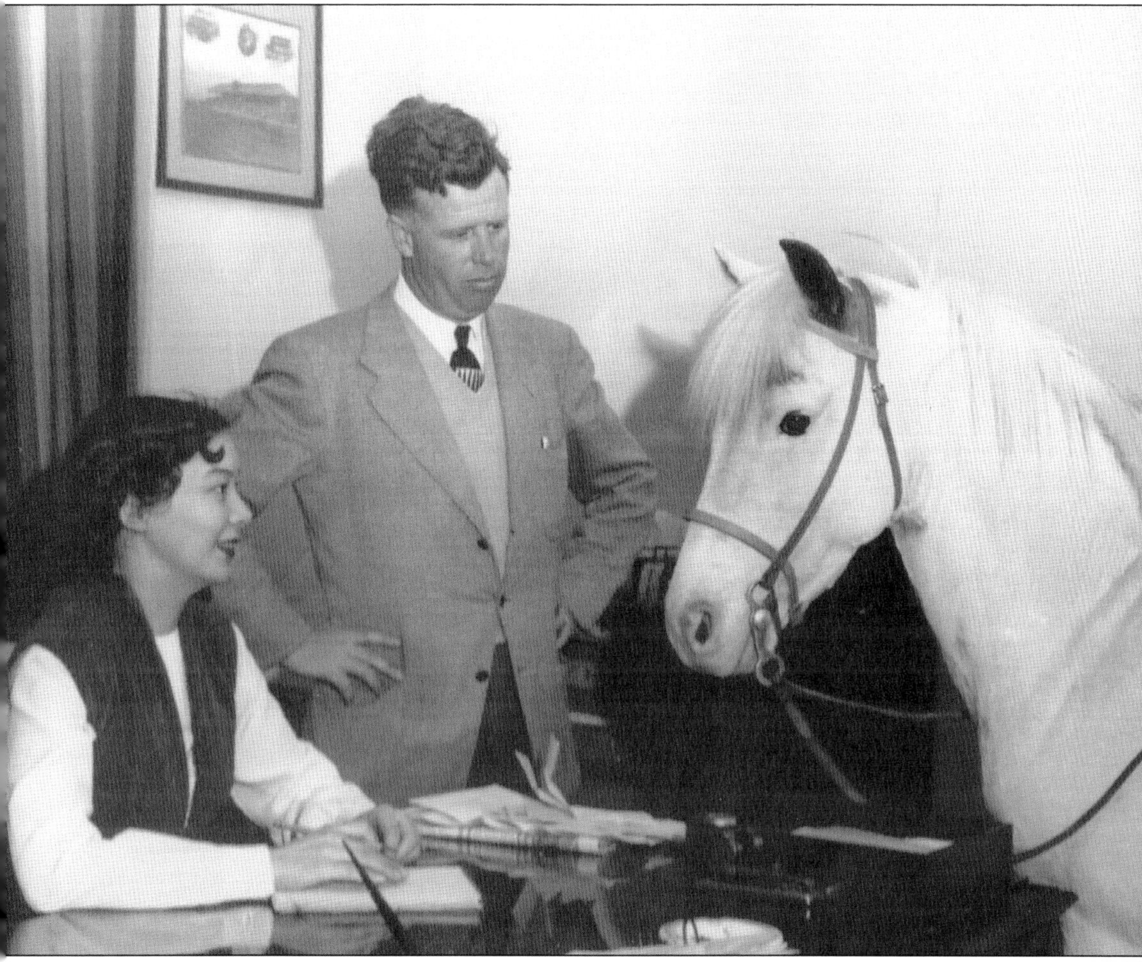

May I Have a Stall, Please? That was the caption for this photograph in the Keeneland Library's scrapbook, and the polite pony is identified as Tony. Standing is Keeneland general manager W.T. Bishop, and seated is his assistant, Karen Rains. This photograph was taken in 1951 after Bishop returned from serving in the armed services during World War II. He was Keeneland's first employee, hired by Hal Price Headley as general manager in 1936.

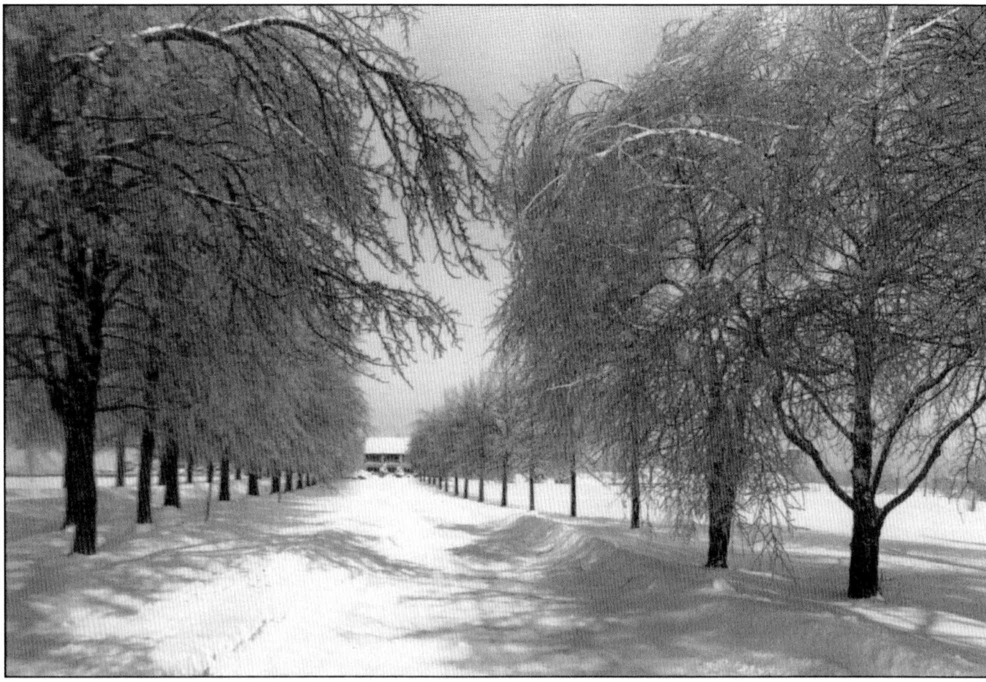

WINTER WONDERLAND. Heavy snow accumulations make it difficult for people and horses to get around. However, the thick blanket of white that covered the roads, fields, trees, and buildings at Keeneland when this photograph was taken in 1951 added a hushed beauty to the scene.

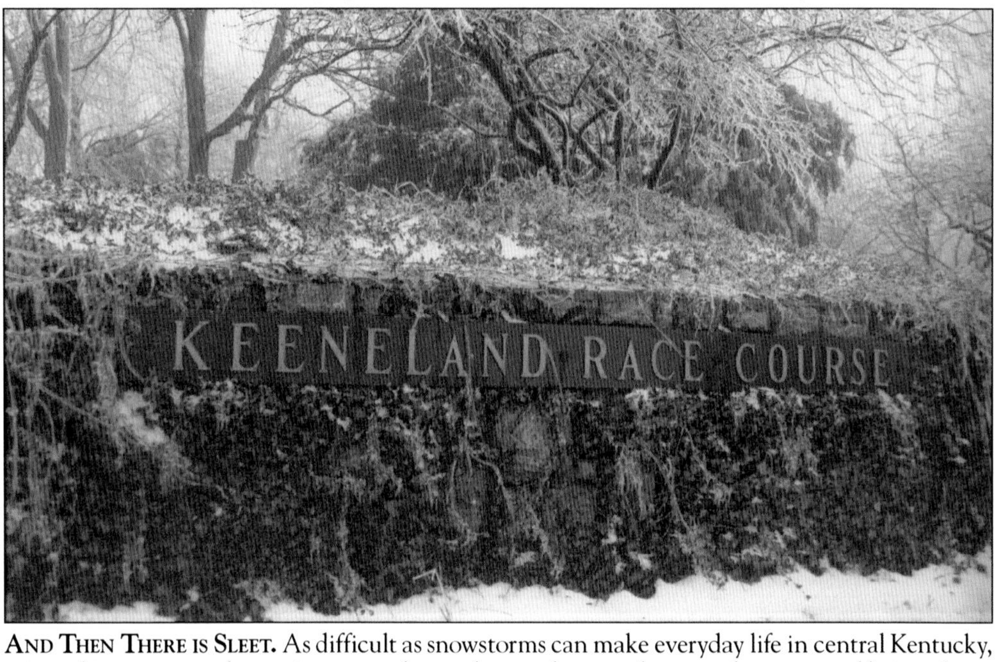

AND THEN THERE IS SLEET. As difficult as snowstorms can make everyday life in central Kentucky, it is nothing compared to an ice storm that makes roads a treacherous adventure and brings down tree limbs and power lines. It is easy to imagine that sleet is the least favorite form of winter precipitation. A coating of ice can be seen on all the trees behind the Keeneland Race Course sign after an ice storm in March 1953.

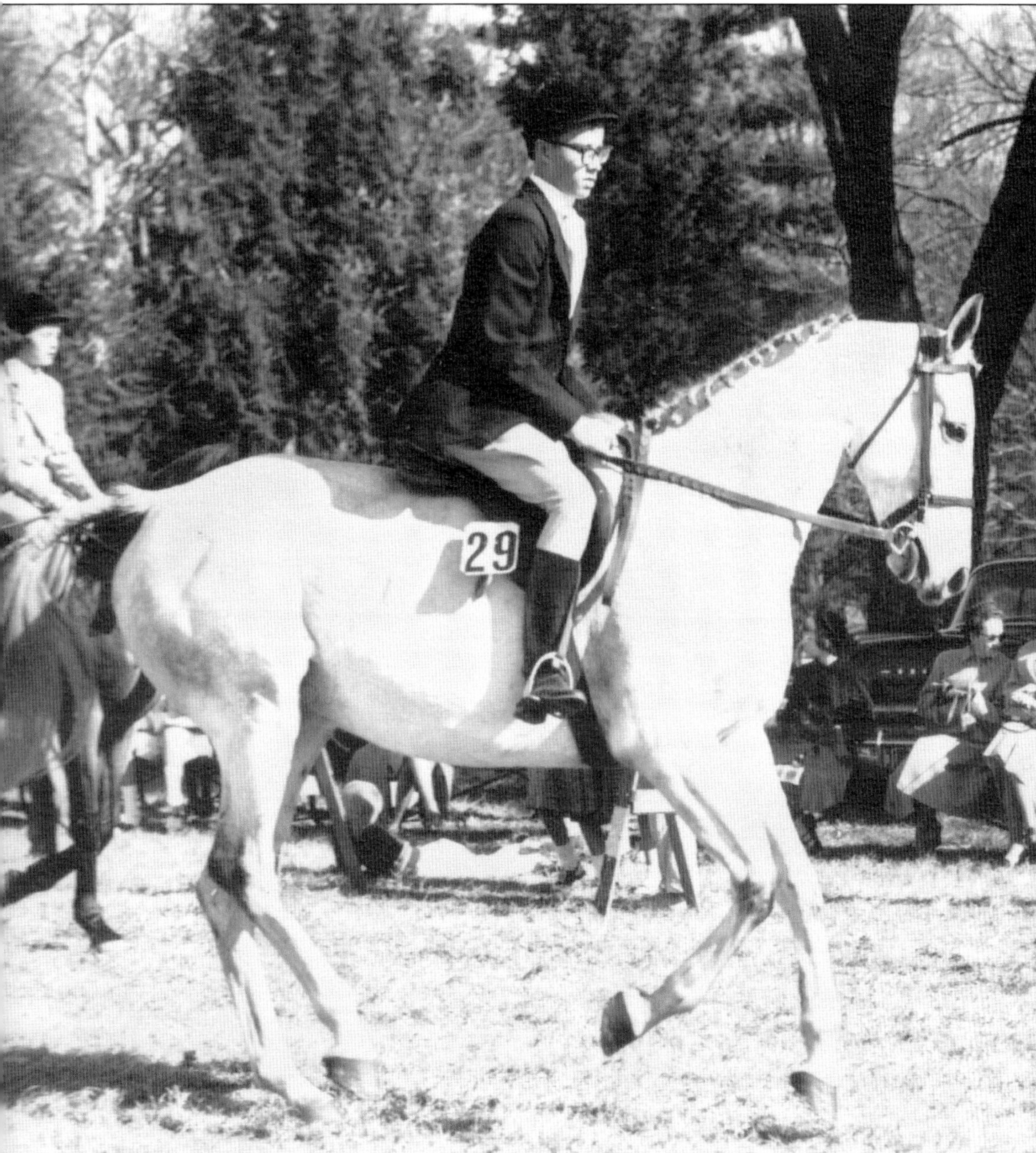

Keeneland Pony Club. The Keeneland Pony Club was founded in 1958, which is when this photograph was taken of one of the original members, W.T. "Buddy" Bishop III, son of Keeneland's first general manager, W.T. Bishop. Buddy went on to be a longtime member of the Keeneland board of directors and was named as a Keeneland trustee in 2005. Pony club members compete in several different events and earn points to go on to the national championship. Even though it now meets at Masterson Station Park in Lexington, the club is still named the Keeneland Pony Club.

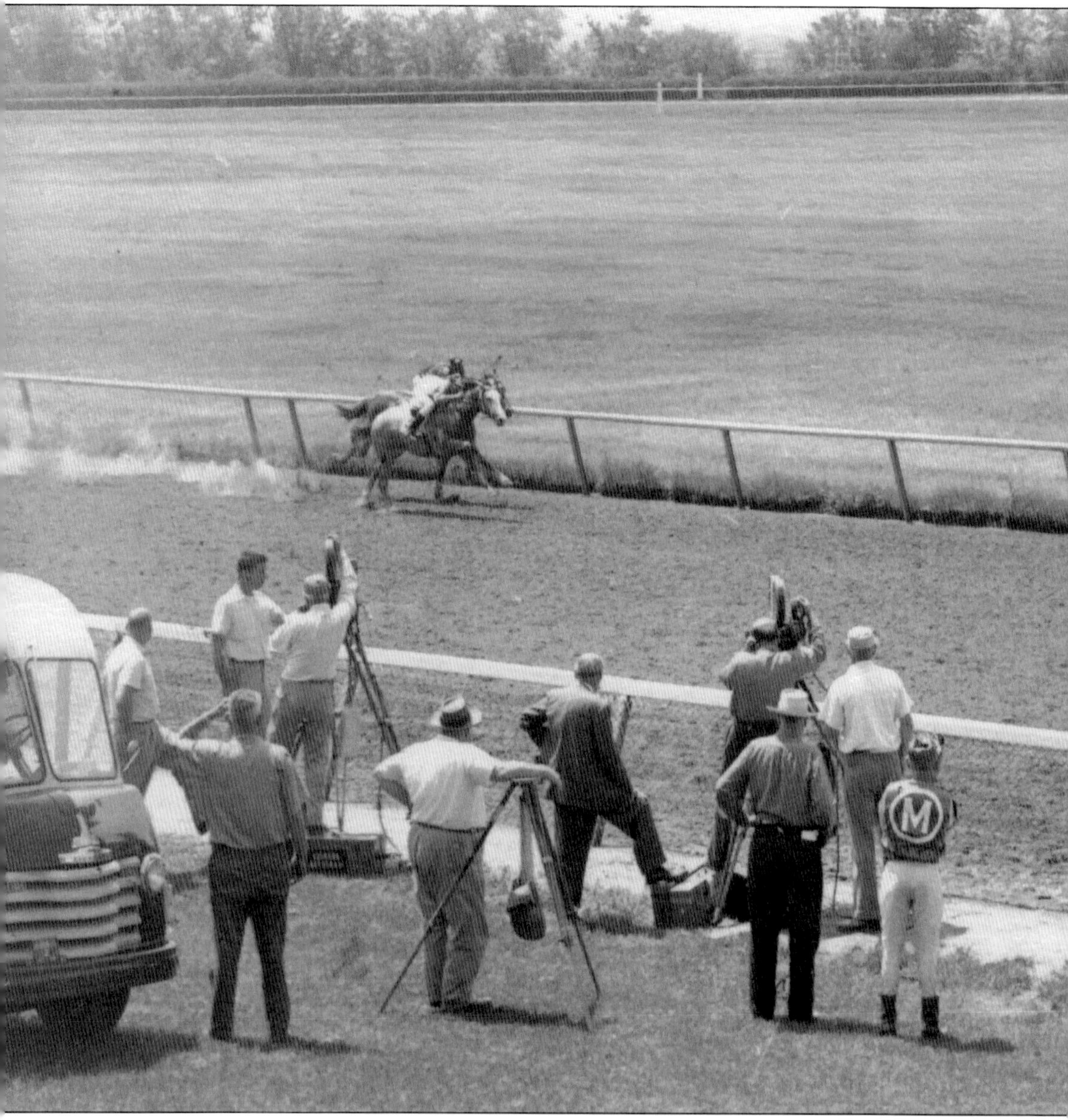

Movie Magic. Some of the outdoor scenes for the movie *Glory* were filmed at Keeneland in 1955. The movie was based on a novel by Calumet Farm's Gene Markey, and the movie premiere was held in Lexington on January 11, 1956. More recently, racetrack scenes from the 2002 movie *Seabiscuit* were filmed at Keeneland, utilizing hundreds of central Kentuckians as extras dressed in 1930s-era clothing. The *Seabiscuit* filmmakers modified Keeneland's finish-line marker so that it looked like Pimlico's 1939 finish pole. Keeneland officials liked the look so much, they kept it that way after the movie was filmed.

Nine

Keeneland Library

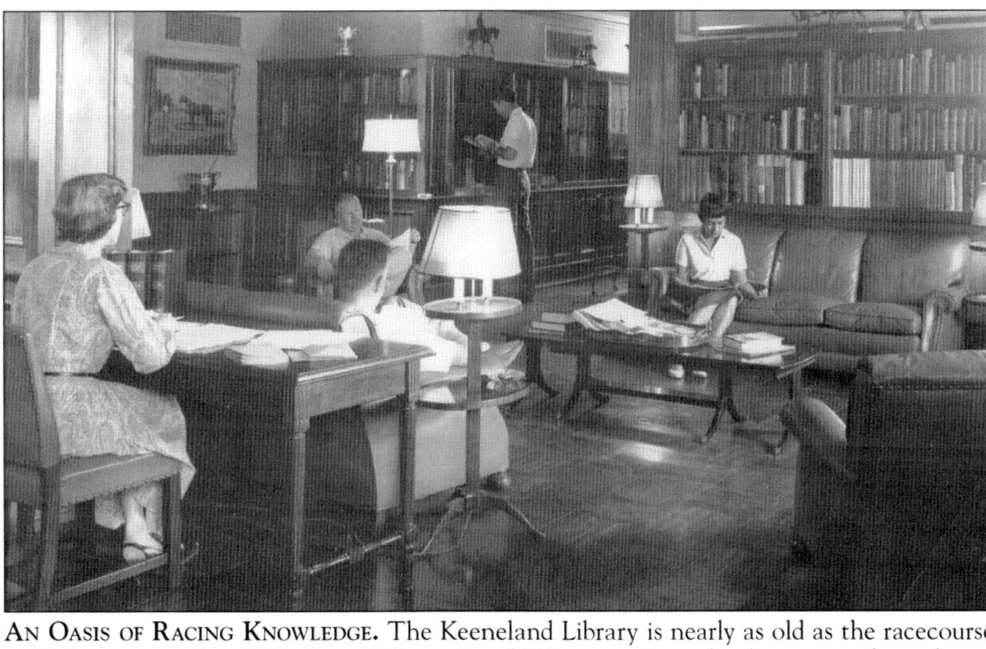

An Oasis of Racing Knowledge. The Keeneland Library is nearly as old as the racecourse itself. It was started in 1939 when William Arnold Hanger, a Keeneland trustee and member of its board of directors, donated a collection of nearly 2,300 books on Thoroughbred racing and breeding. The first library, seen here in 1958, was located on the second floor of the clubhouse. Today, it has its own 10,000-square-foot building.

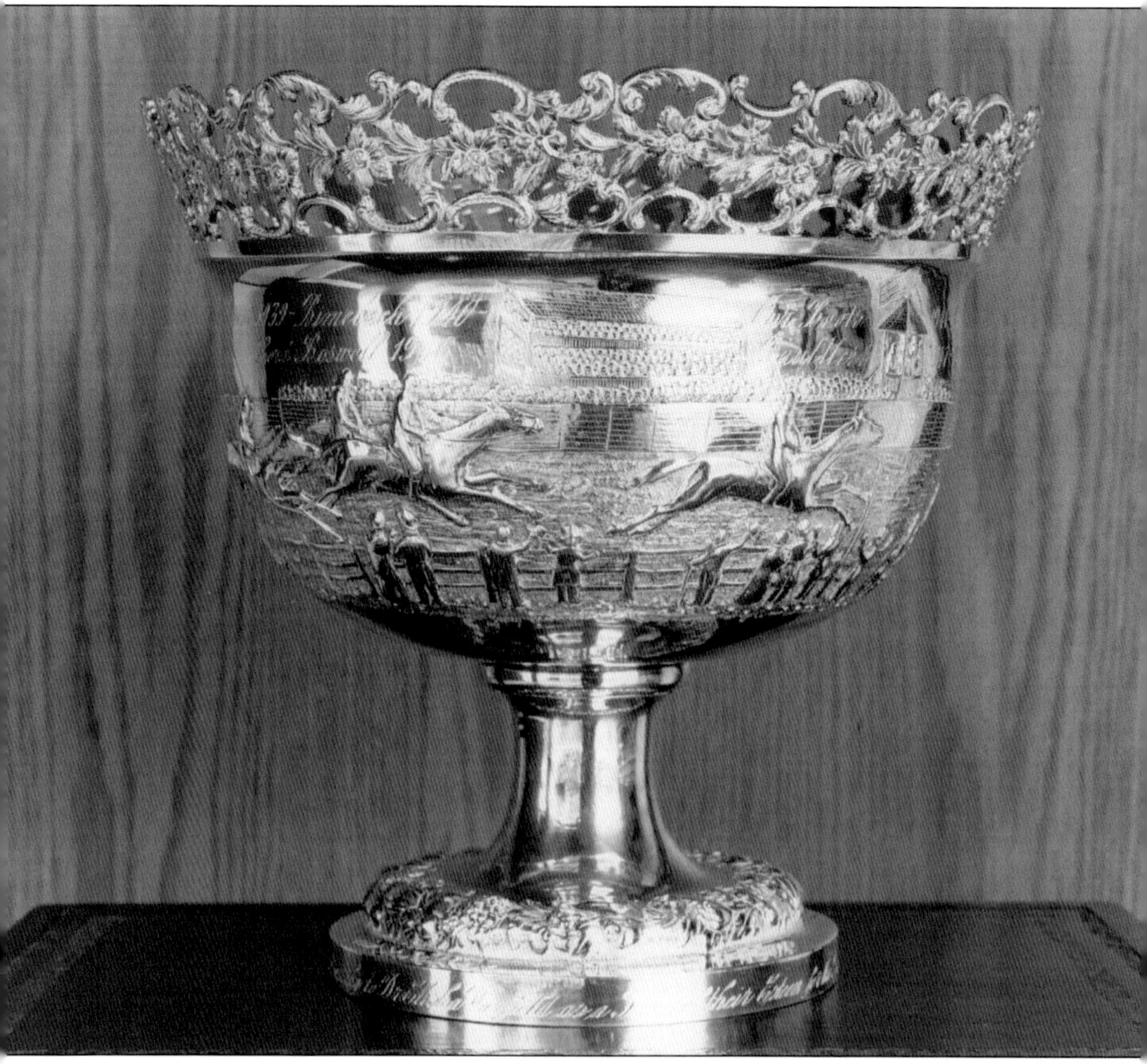

LEXINGTON BOWL. Keeneland has a wonderful collection of racing trophies, including the impressive Lexington Bowl. Made in 1854 by the Lexington firm of Garner and Winchester, the silver bowl was presented to Dr. Elisha Warfield, the breeder of Lexington, by admiring local citizens. The 15-inch-tall bowl depicts a horse race with a packed grandstand and a rail of cheering fans. The rim is decorated with flowers and scrolls. It was passed down to his daughter Mary Jay, wife of the famous abolitionist Cassius Marcellus Clay, and stayed in the Clay family for years. It was purchased in 1937 by "three nationally known sportsmen," who wished to remain anonymous, to be used as a commemorative trophy for Keeneland's Blue Grass Stakes. It was retired in 1952, and today Keeneland awards a gold julep cup to the winning owner of each graded stakes race.

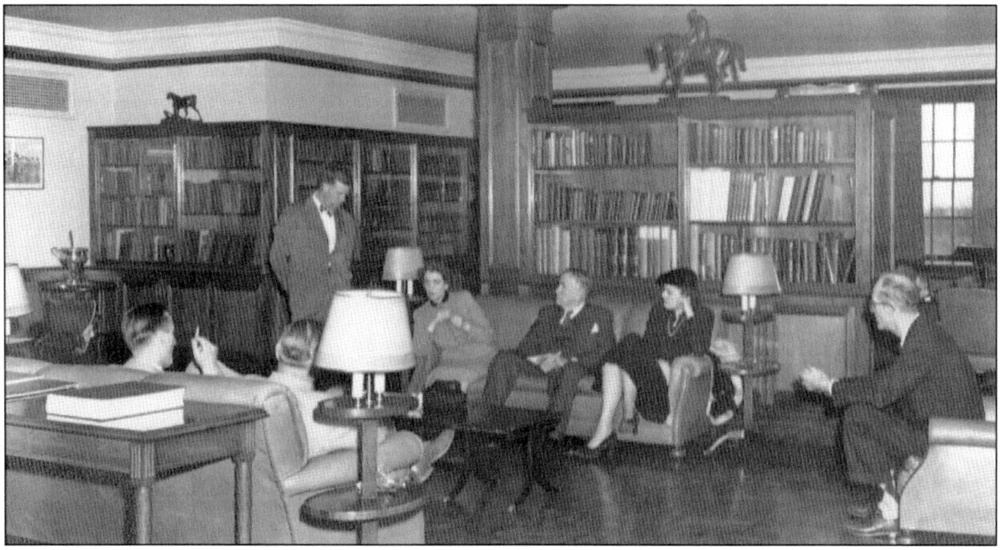

The Veep Makes a Visit. Keeneland general manager W.T. Bishop (standing) and librarian Amelia Buckley (far left on couch) hosted a gathering in the library for Vice Pres. Alben Barkley and Mrs. Barkley (center and right on couch) in 1950. Before serving as Harry Truman's vice president, Barkley represented Kentucky in the house and senate for a total of 38 years.

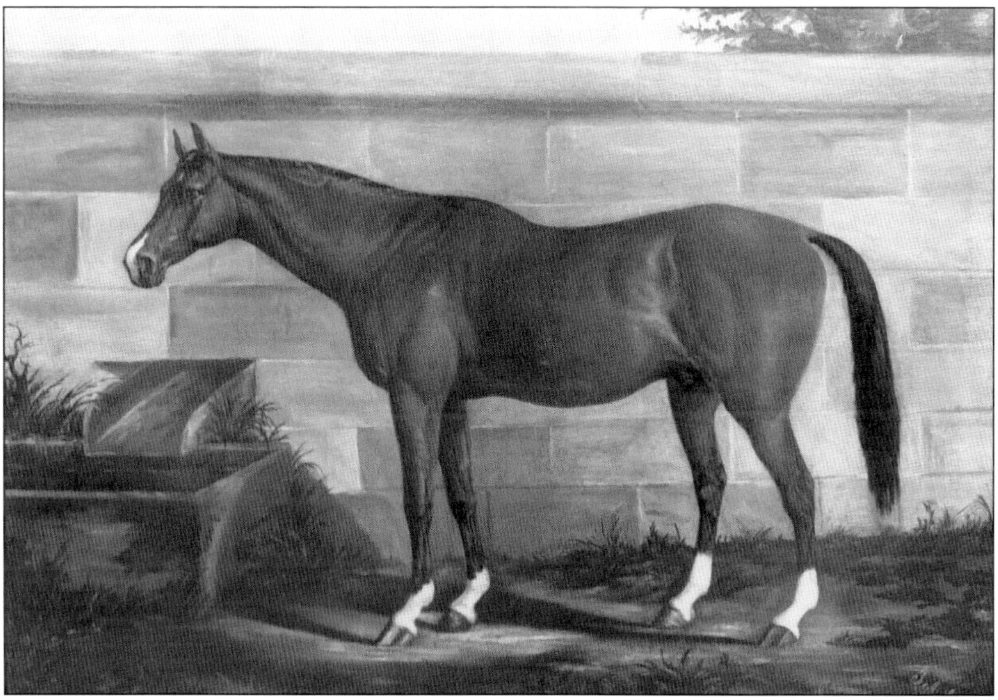

Horse, Town, and Logo. This painting of the horse Lexington was painted by Thomas J. Scott, a student of the renowned turf artist Edward Troye, in the 1860s and is one of many equine paintings in the Keeneland collection. Troye's image of Lexington, with the horse tinted blue, is currently being used by the Lexington Kentucky Convention and Visitors' Center on countless signs and ads promoting the area. Lexington was one of the first Thoroughbreds inducted into the racing Hall of Fame.

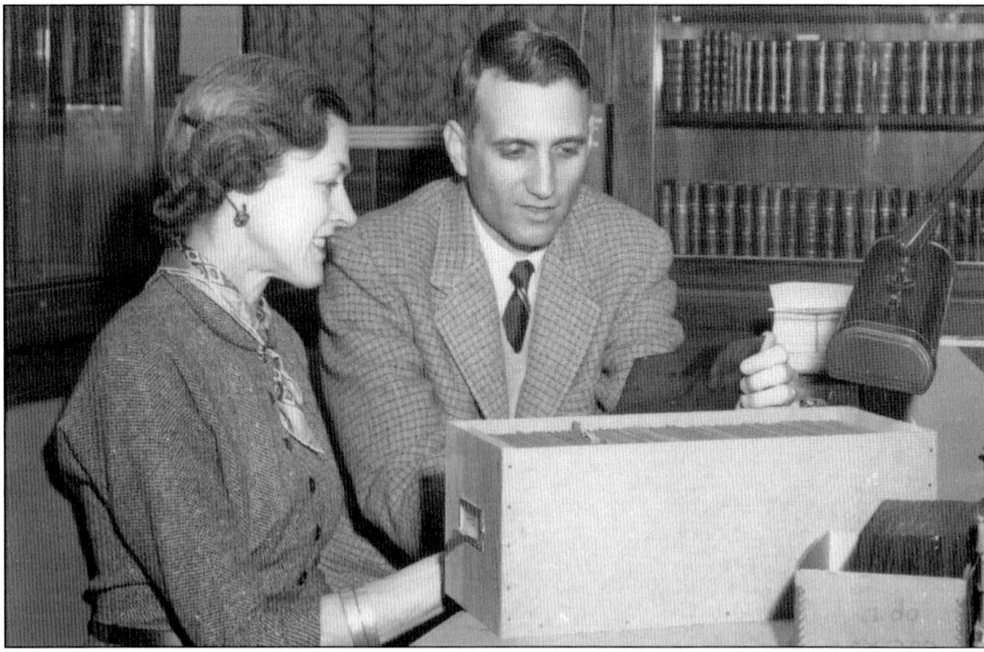

Librarian and P.R. Director. Keeneland's first librarian, Amelia Buckley, is credited with setting the standards of professionalism and hospitality still found in the library's staff. Publicity director J.B. Faulconer was responsible for recording much of Keeneland's early history. They are seen together in this 1955 photograph.

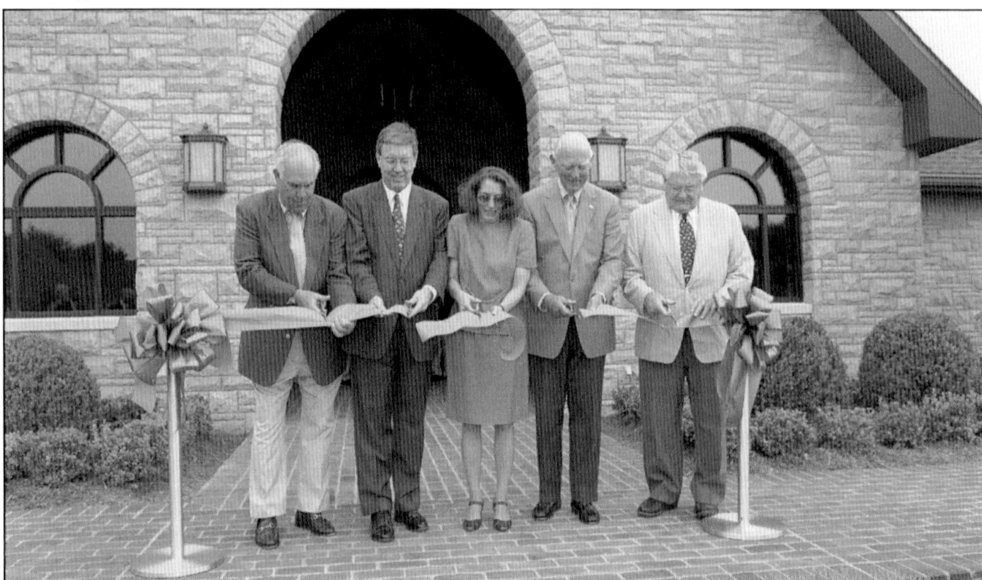

New Library. As the Keeneland Library continued to grow, it was obvious it would require a larger home. The ribbon-cutting ceremony for the new 10,000-square-foot stone library building is seen here in July 2002. Pictured from left to right are trustee Louis L. Haggin III, president Nick Nicholson, librarian Cathy Schenck, chairman emeritus James "Ted" Bassett, and trustee Charles Nuckols. Besides containing the complete *Daily Racing Form* archives and more than 10,000 books on racing, the library houses nearly 250,000 photographs and videos.

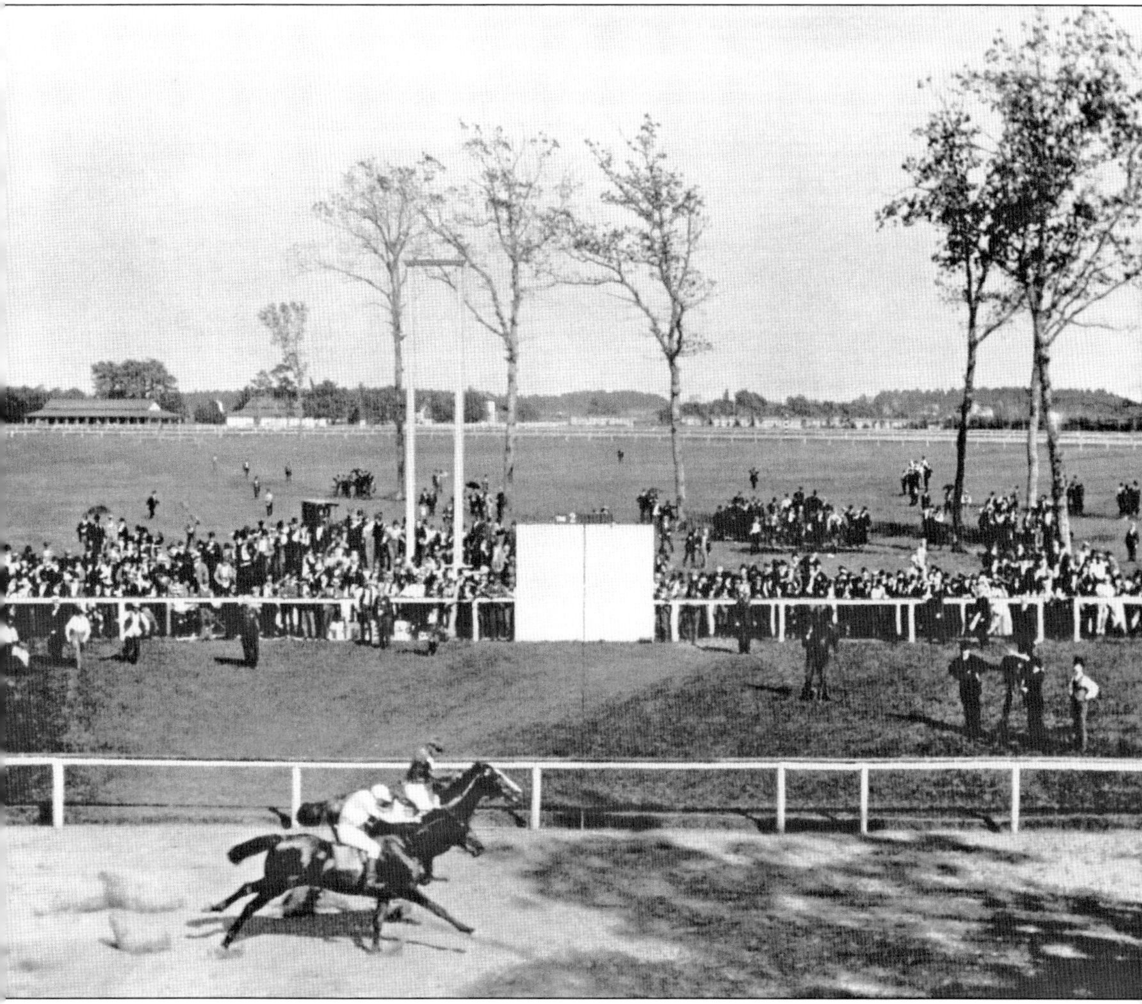

Famous 1890 Match Race. Salvator, ridden by Isaac Murphy, set an American record of two minutes and five seconds in a one-and-one-fourth-mile match race against Tenny in June 1890 at the Coney Island Jockey Club in New York. Salvator, who is in the racing Hall of Fame, was bred by Daniel Swigert of Elmendorf Farm and owned by James Ben Ali Haggin. The white screen seen at the finish line was designed to assist the finish judges and timers make an accurate call. The photograph is part of the 3,500-image John C. Hemment Collection at the Keeneland Library. It records nearly every major Thoroughbred-racing event that occurred in New York from 1890 through 1910. The total number of photographs at the library is approximately 250,000—the largest such collection of American turf photographs anywhere.

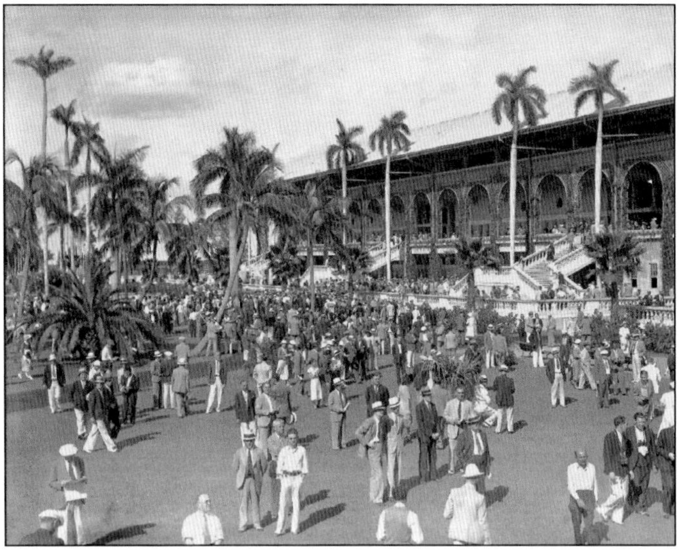

Beautiful Hialeah. After Joseph Widener and his financial partner Col. E.R. Bradley resurrected Hialeah Park near Miami during the midst of the Great Depression, it became the winter capital for East Coast racing. Lester Giesler, the architect of the rebuilt track, received an award at the 1936 Paris Exposition for its utility and beauty of design. This 1935 photograph is a part of the 20,000 images in the C.C. Cook Collection at the Keeneland Library.

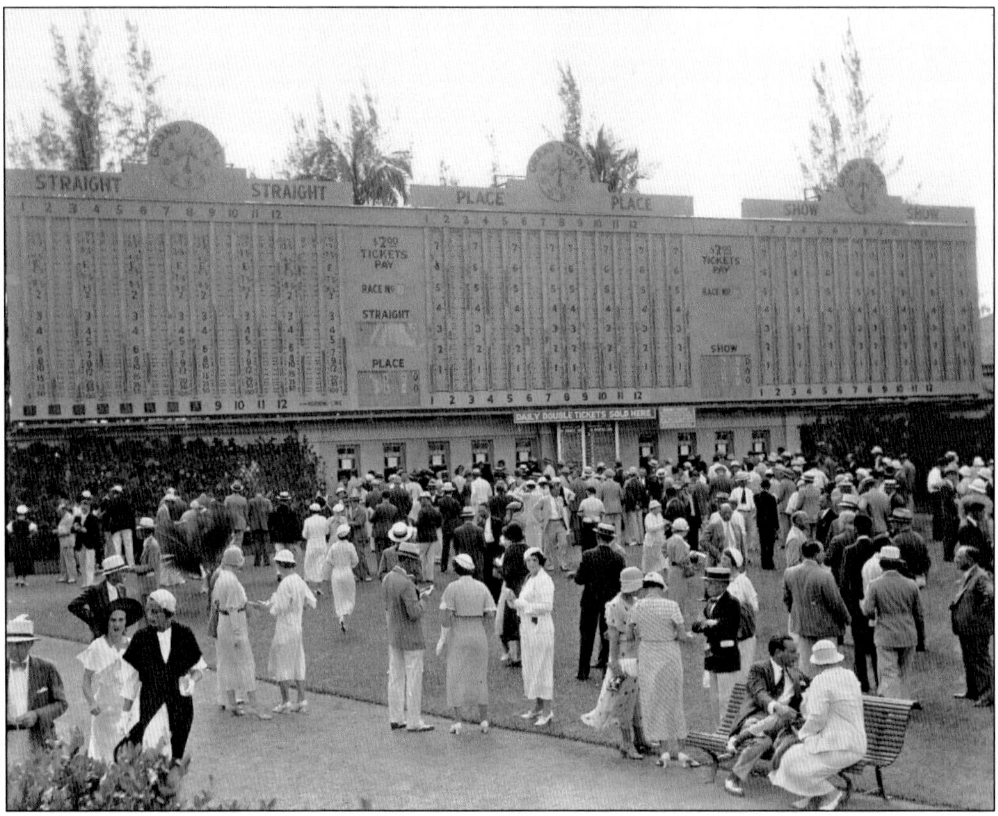

Hialeah Tote Board. This 1936 photograph shows Hialeah's totalizator display board—the first of its kind in the United States—which was installed in 1932. Originating in New Zealand, the electronic system ran the pari-mutuel betting system for the track, calculating payoff odds, displaying them, and producing tickets based on incoming bets. It reportedly cost $300,000, but it did away with individual bookmakers and made Hialeah profitable. Keeneland opened with one in 1936.

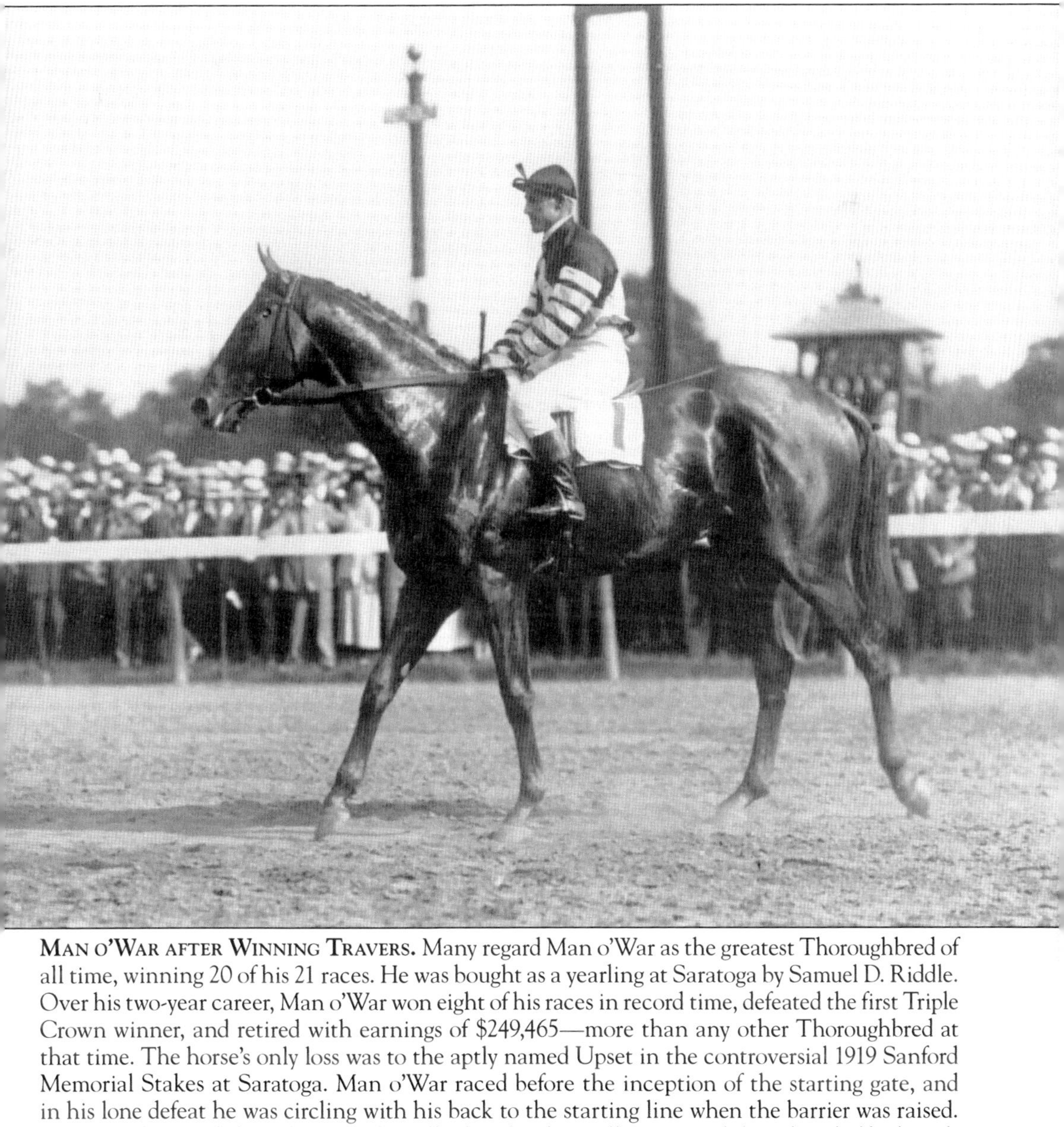

Man o'War after Winning Travers. Many regard Man o'War as the greatest Thoroughbred of all time, winning 20 of his 21 races. He was bought as a yearling at Saratoga by Samuel D. Riddle. Over his two-year career, Man o'War won eight of his races in record time, defeated the first Triple Crown winner, and retired with earnings of $249,465—more than any other Thoroughbred at that time. The horse's only loss was to the aptly named Upset in the controversial 1919 Sanford Memorial Stakes at Saratoga. Man o'War raced before the inception of the starting gate, and in his lone defeat he was circling with his back to the starting line when the barrier was raised. Although he was left at the start, he rallied to finish a gallant second, less than half a length behind Upset. In this photograph from the Cook Collection, Man o'War, with A. Schuttinger up, had just won Saratoga's 1920 Travers, setting a track record that stood for 42 years, and beating his old nemesis Upset.

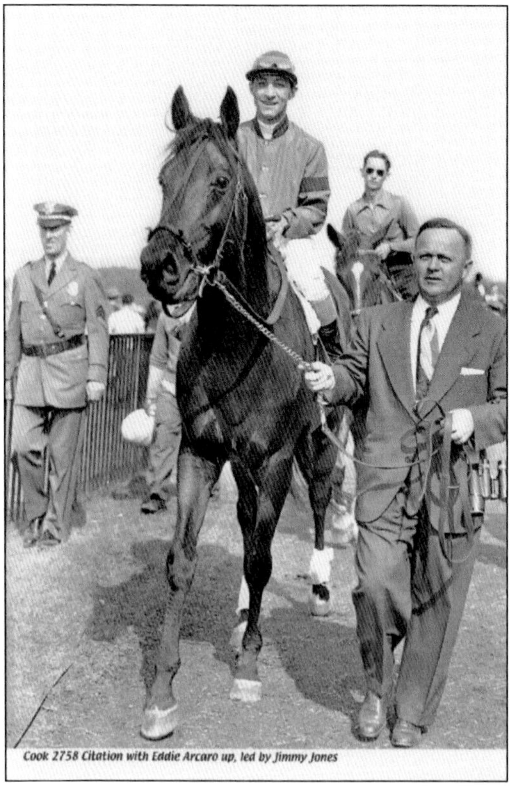

First Millionaire. Citation, a 1945 son of Bull Lea, was bred and raced by Calumet Farm and was the first Thoroughbred to earn more than $1 million in his racing career. He won the Triple Crown and was named Horse of the Year in 1948. He was named champion two-year-old, three-year-old, and finally champion older horse in 1951. He is pictured here with Eddie Arcaro, his most frequent rider, and is being led by trainer Jimmy Jones.

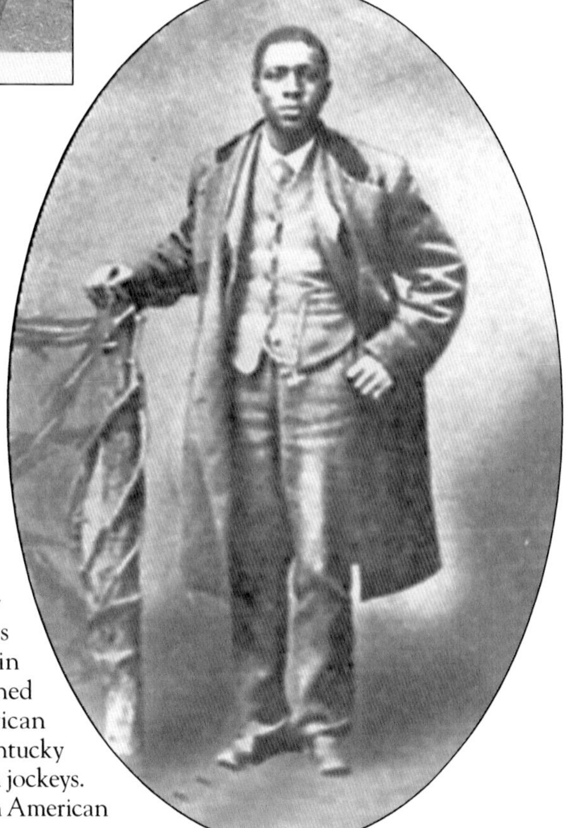

Oliver Lewis, Aristides' Jockey. The first Kentucky Derby in 1875 was won by Aristides, ridden by Oliver Lewis. Lewis is seen here in a rare 1878 photograph found in Keeneland's collection. Aristides was trained by Hall of Famer Ansel Williams, an African American. Of the 15 starters in the first Kentucky Derby, 13 were ridden by African American jockeys. Out of the first 28 Kentucky Derbys, African American jockeys won 15.

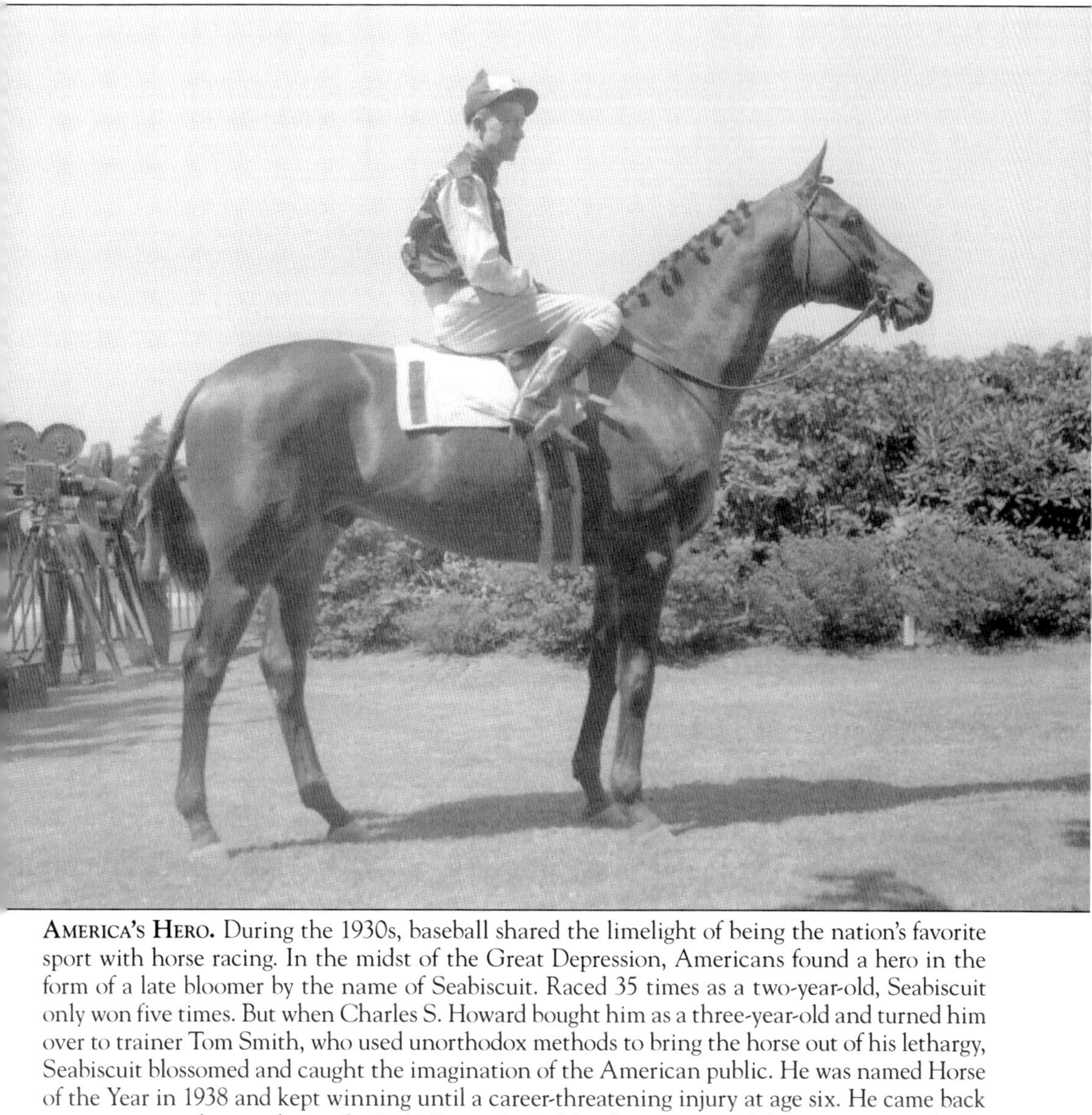

America's Hero. During the 1930s, baseball shared the limelight of being the nation's favorite sport with horse racing. In the midst of the Great Depression, Americans found a hero in the form of a late bloomer by the name of Seabiscuit. Raced 35 times as a two-year-old, Seabiscuit only won five times. But when Charles S. Howard bought him as a three-year-old and turned him over to trainer Tom Smith, who used unorthodox methods to bring the horse out of his lethargy, Seabiscuit blossomed and caught the imagination of the American public. He was named Horse of the Year in 1938 and kept winning until a career-threatening injury at age six. He came back at seven years of age and won the 1940 Santa Anita Handicap in one of the greatest comebacks in sporting lore. In 2001, author Laura Hillenbrand wrote the best-selling *Seabiscuit: An American Legend*, doing much of her research at the Keeneland Library. In 2003, Universal Studios released *Seabiscuit*, which was nominated for seven Academy Awards and filmed extensively at Keeneland. This photograph from the C.C. Cook Collection shows Seabiscuit with John "Red" Pollard in the saddle at Belmont Park in 1938.

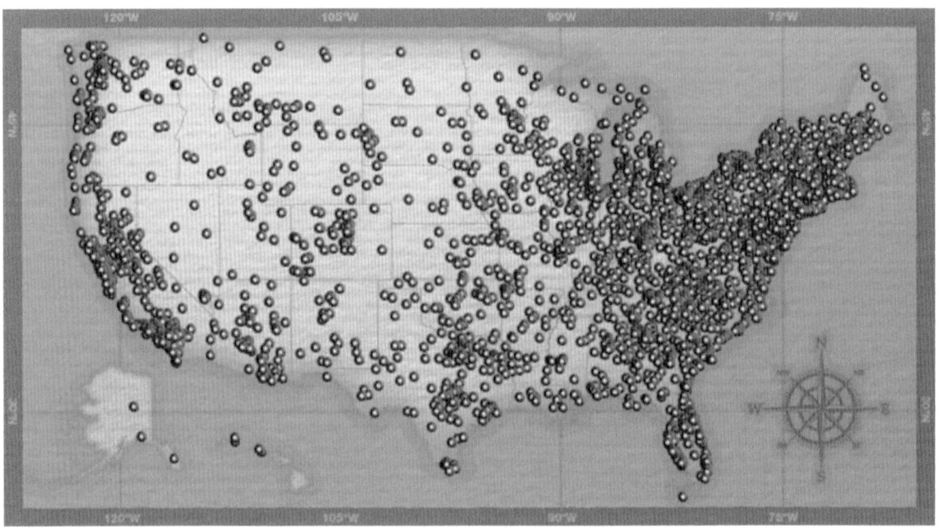